From Classroom to
White House

ALSO BY JAMES MCMURTRY LONGO

*Isabel Orleans-Bragança: The Brazilian Princess
Who Freed the Slaves* (McFarland, 2008)

From Classroom to White House

The Presidents and First Ladies as Students and Teachers

JAMES MCMURTRY LONGO

McFarland & Company, Inc., Publishers

Jefferson, North Carolina, and London

LIBRARY OF CONGRESS CATALOGUING-IN-PUBLICATION DATA

Longo, James McMurtry.
    From classroom to White House : the presidents and first
ladies as students and teachers / James McMurtry Longo.
        p.   cm.
    Includes bibliographical references and index.

    ISBN 978-0-7864-6486-9
    softcover : 50# alkaline paper ∞

    1. Presidents— United States— Biography.   2. Presidents—
Education — United States.   3. Presidents' spouses— United
States— Biography.   4. Presidents' spouses— Education — United
States.   I. Title
    E176.1L86 2012
    973.009'9 — dc23
    [B]   2011040865

BRITISH LIBRARY CATALOGUING DATA ARE AVAILABLE

On the cover: White House drawing by Robin Bauguess;
background images © Shutterstock 2012

Manufactured in the United States of America

McFarland & Company, Inc., Publishers
    Box 611, Jefferson, North Carolina 28640
    www.mcfarlandpub.com

To Patrick L. Right,
teacher, friend, president.

Acknowledgments

I am very grateful for the many named and unnamed people who generously helped to make this book a reality. A special thank you is due to my friends and colleagues at Washington and Jefferson College, especially Diane Day Brzustowicz whose hard work, intelligence, input and insights nurtured and sustained this manuscript from beginning to end. Rosalie Carpenter, Richard and Patti Easton, Heather Painter, and the staff of the W&J Technology Center have all provided time and help when needed. Amy Holscher read many early drafts of the book and her suggestions, comments, and questions proved to be invaluable. Thanks to Will, Ben, Jackson, and Charlie for loaning Amy to the project. My mentors at Harvard University, Donald Oliver, Vito Perrone, Martha Savery, and Harold Howe II, inspired, nurtured, and focused my initial research.

Docents, volunteers, rangers, and librarians at the Adams National Historic Park, the Andrew Johnson Historic Site, the Calvin Coolidge State Historic Site, the Clarke Schools for Hearing and Speech, the Dixon Disciples of Christ Church, the Edward Devotion School, the Eleanor Roosevelt National Historic Site, the Franklin Pierce Homestead, the Groton School, James Buchanan's Wheatland, the James Garfield National Historic Site, the Jimmy Carter National Historic Site, the John F. Kennedy National Historic Site, Monticello's Thomas Jefferson Visitor's Center, the Ohio Historical Society Grant School House, the Ohio Historical Society Harding Home, the Poland Ohio School District, the Rutherford B. Hayes Presidential Center, the William Howard Taft National Historic Site, and the National First Ladies Library have been consistently kind, generous, and helpful in sharing their time, stories, and knowledge about the student and teaching days of the presidents and first ladies. The professionalism and expertise of the presidential libraries and museums staffs, especially the photo archival staffs of the George H. W. Bush, William J. Clinton, Gerald Ford, Herbert Hoover, Lyndon B Johnson, John F. Kennedy, Richard Nixon, Ronald Reagan, Franklin D. Roosevelt, and Harry S Truman libraries and museums have made this research experience a pleasant and enjoyable one. A special photo thank you goes to Scott Goldsmith. One final nod of appreciation to Helen

Thomas for her insights and recollections of the presidents and first ladies from JFK to Michelle and Barack Obama. Thank you Helen.

Lastly, I would like to thank my wife Mary Jo Harwood, my mother Mary McMurtry Longo and my brother Dennis Michael Longo for their spirited assistance, and Patrick Right, Jeanne Norberg, and Noel, Patti, Nicholas and Alyssa Haydon for sharing my journey.

Table of Contents

Part Three. The Twentieth Century

Preface

Half the presidents and first ladies of the United States have been teachers at some point in their careers; but all have been students. This book focuses primarily on their days spent in the classroom, the ups and downs of education during their White House years, and lastly, who was educated and who was not getting educated at their time in history. It tries to answer two simple questions. What kind of students and teachers were our presidents and first ladies? And how have students, teachers, and schools changed over the years?

The original idea for this book grew out of conversations I had in graduate school with Harold Howe II, United States commissioner of education in the Kennedy-Johnson administration. "Doc" Howe shared many wonderful stories with me of how Lyndon Johnson the teacher influenced Lyndon Johnson the president. These conversations made me wonder if other presidents or first ladies once taught. To my surprise, I discovered dozens of former teachers occupied the White House and that they taught a variety of subjects, at all grade levels, and in nearly every type of school.

I decided to take the opportunity to be taught by a president myself. Whenever possible, I traveled to Plains, Georgia, to attend the Sunday school class former president Jimmy Carter taught there. I was impressed with his skills as a teacher and enjoyed the stories he sometimes shared about his own days as a student. His stories and a quote I came across from President John F. Kennedy's mother convinced me to also look into the student experiences of White House couples. Rose Kennedy wrote, "I suppose it is part of the mystique surrounding the presidency that anyone who occupies the office is endowed with qualities that are extraordinary and he must have passed through childhood in a glow of virtue. I can state that was not the case with Jack." She was right. I discovered few White House occupants "passed through childhood in a glow of virtue."

One of President Kennedy's high school reports read, "Studies at the last minute, keeps appointments late, has little sense of material value, and can seldom locate his possessions." An instructor of future president George H. W. Bush wrote, "An upstanding lad with great self confidence. It appears, however, that he may be somewhat eccentric." In high school, classmates of one future presidential candidate used kazoos to play "Hail to the Chief" when he entered the room. His name was John Kerry. Asked about the best and worst grades he earned in school, another presidential candidate answered, "I never got good grades." His name was John McCain. And in 1895, a Missouri teacher surprised her students on graduation day by kissing one graduate, and only one, on the forehead. Her explanation was that she always wanted to kiss a future president. She was close. The recipient of her confidence, Charlie Ross, became the presidential press secretary to the unkissed boy sitting next to him. It was his classmate and best friend, Harry Truman, who became the thirty-third president of the United States.

In 1755 a young Massachusetts teacher wondered what many teachers have wondered over the years: "Which of my pupils will turn out ... a hero, and which a rake, which a young philosopher, and which a parasite?" The teacher was John Adams, the first of many teachers and future presidents who would journey from the classroom to the White House. It is difficult for even the most insightful teacher to predict which student will end up a hero. More than a few future White House residents seemed destined to be consigned to John Adams' "rake" or "parasite" category. One teacher told her "motormouth" sixth-grader his nonstop talking would either get him into a lifetime of trouble or send him to the governor's mansion. That student, Bill Clinton, later wrote she was right on both counts. Clinton was elected governor of Arkansas four times before serving two terms as president. If by some miracle of time travel all the boys and girls who grew up to be presidents or first ladies could be students in the same classroom, at the same time, it might be a teacher's worst nightmare.

President Dwight Eisenhower, who was not always the best student, wrote, "One cannot always read a man's future in the record of his younger days." Warren G. Harding, who many historians consider one of the nation's worst presidents, received excellent grades in school. And Jacqueline Kennedy admitted only late in her school career, "I learned not to be ashamed of a real hunger for knowledge, something I always tried to hide."

These stories also provide glimpses into American schooling over the years, some of the educational issues addressed during various presidencies, and whenever possible the thoughts, policies, and attitudes of presidents and first ladies on schools, teachers, and education. Homeschooling and the rural one-room schoolhouses of nineteenth-century America, urban and suburban schools, and colleges and universities of today are all represented. Also included are some of the educational roadblocks women and minorities faced over the years in their struggle to be educated. On the one-hundredth anniversary of the NAACP, President Barack Obama declared, "The story of the civil rights movement was written in our schools." Many of these stories seem to confirm that statement.

Each of the vignettes offers insights into the nature of students, teachers, schools, and human character. A few future presidents and first ladies had brilliant teachers, but most did not. Some were brilliant scholars, but most were not. Only a few found school a welcoming place where their talents, gifts, and potential were recognized. The most successful students did not always make the best national leaders. And some of the least successful scholars proved to be very successful in later life. Many had their first experiences being leaders in a classroom, but their leadership styles sometimes proved problematic for themselves, or for the students they tried to teach. Still, somewhere along the line, each of these future presidents and first ladies had one or more parents or teachers who believed in them despite their rough edges. I hope these stories serve to remind all of us that the talents and skills of children, students, and teachers are sometimes hidden before our very eyes.

PART ONE

Founding Fathers, Mothers, and Son

Martha Dandridge Custis and George Washington
"Illiterate, Unlearned and Unread"

George Washington's educational odyssey was not an easy one. Like other sons of Virginia planters, he found himself at the mercy of whatever traveling tutors or nearby schools might be available. An early biographer wrote, "George, like most people thereabouts at that time, had no education [other] than reading, writing and accounts which was taught by a convict servant his father bought for a schoolmaster." Virginia planters sometimes hired educated indentured servants to tutor their children until the debt or legal penalties of the "teacher" were paid. According to Virginia legends, George Washington's first teacher was a convict, an indentured servant, or both. Washington's "crude drawings of birds, faces, and other typical school-boy attempts" to ignore, deface or improve the academic content he was "mastering" can be found in his surviving schoolbooks. The president who supposedly could not tell a lie described his formal education in one word: "defective."

Washington's father and his two older brothers traveled from Virginia across the Atlantic Ocean as young boys to attend England's Appleby School. But when George was eleven, his father died. His mother's reluctance to have him travel so far from home ended any possibility for an overseas education.

Washington never attended college or high school and had less formal schooling than any of the other presidents except perhaps Andrew Jackson, Abraham Lincoln, or Andrew Johnson. As a youth, he was known more for his hair-trigger temper than his scholarship. Uneven studies of arithmetic, composition, geography, dancing, and deportment never took him beyond the elementary school level. One biographer gently addressed his writing skills by stating, "His whole life Washington was a nonconformist as regarded the King's English ... the instinct of correct spelling was absent." He concluded, "The end of Washington's school days left him, if a good 'cipherer,' a bad speller, and a still worse grammarian." John Adams noted in private that "Washington was not a scholar is certain. That he was too illiterate, unlearned, and unread for his station and reputation is equally past dispute."

If Washington had been required to pass a high stakes standardized test to serve as commander in chief, we might still be British subjects. Even as a youth Washington was aware that his education was lacking. He read and reread a popular book entitled *Young Man's Companion*, which promised to provide him essential educational fundamentals "without a tutor." When he was fourteen, he carefully copied by hand the *Rules of Civility and Decent Behavior in Company and Conversation,* originally compiled by the Jesuit teaching order in 1595. Washington carried these 110 handwritten rules with him for the rest of his life. Our nation's first president was never a great student, but he learned to temper his anger and act like a gentleman.

Washington's lack of education troubled him, and he frequently included apologies in his personal letters for misspelled words and grammatical lapses. Ever conscious of the importance of proper writing, he took time as president to critique one of his granddaughter's letters to him. He wrote her,

> Your letter ... is written correctly, and in fair characters.... Your ideas are lively, and your descriptions agreeable. Your sentences are pretty well pointed; but you do not as is proper begin a new paragraph when you change the subject.... Attend to these hints and you will deserve more credit from a few lines well adjusted and written in a fair hand, than for a whole sheet scribbled over.

Shortly before his death he spent hours going over his youthful letter books and correspondence scratching out words and correcting spelling and grammar errors. Perhaps because of his sensitivity about his writing or due to her own sense of privacy, his wife Martha Dandridge Custis Washington burned all their private correspondence. Only three of their letters survive. George Washington's lack of confidence in his "defective" education may have deprived history of ever really knowing America's first president.

The formal education of his wife has been described as "better than some planter's daughters, [but] inferior to ... her brothers." She received instruction in the most important educational tools a young girl of her social class needed. She was taught the domestic arts and how to ride a horse like a lady. Martha's only outside tutor may have been a traveling music teacher who provided her the necessary dance steps to assure "social success" and avoid "public humiliation."

George Washington valued education so much that he personally paid for the schooling of many "young relatives and others to go to college." He was especially diligent in providing Martha's children from her previous marriage the educational opportunities he missed. He hired a highly educated Scotsman to move to their home at Mount Vernon to tutor his stepchildren Jackie and Patsy Custis. During seven years of residence, the tutor was joined a few days a month by a traveling "music professor" who taught them to sing and play musical instruments, and a dance teacher to teach them their all-important dance lessons.

Patsy Custis was homeschooled, but her brother Jackie was sent to boarding school when he was twelve. A clue to the challenge faced by Jackie's teachers was hinted at by one biographer who described him as "uneducable." Although Jackie was bright and personable, he had problems focusing on schoolwork. Washington paid Jackie's teacher an additional sum above and beyond his regular salary asking for "special attention" in curbing "the boy's wild temperament." He explained, "His mind is a good deal relaxed from his studies and more than ever turned to Dogs, Horses, and Guns."

Jackie's teacher later wrote in discouragement, "I must confess to you that I never did in my life know a youth so exceedingly indolent or so surprisingly voluptuous; one would suppose nature had intended him for some Asiatic prince." He sadly predicted,

> He will soon lose all relish for mental excellence. He will unwillingly apply to any improvements either in Arts or Sciences. Sunk in unmanly sloth, his estate will [be] left to the management of some worthless overseer; and he will soon be entangled in some matrimonial adventure.... As passion will have much to say, it is not very likely reason will be listened to.

Washington decided to send the boy north to New York's King's College which later became Columbia University. The nearby William and Mary College was rumored to be in a state of "mismanagement" with "little attention [being] paid either to learning or the morals of the boys." Jackie soon dropped out to marry. As his teacher feared, "passion" not "reason" ruled Washington's stepson.

Patsy died unmarried when she was seventeen. Jackie too died young, but not before he and his wife had four children. George and Martha Washington then raised Jackie's two youngest children, Martha's grandson Parke Custis and her granddaughter Nelly. Their efforts to give them an education provide a window into the differing educational expectations for girls and boys in the last years of eighteenth-century America.

Despite the fact that she was more academically gifted than her brother, Nelly was primarily homeschooled in the domestic arts and social graces. Nevertheless, she showed a genuine talent in the arts, music, and languages, studying French, Italian, and Spanish. Her love for Italian was so strong she willingly rose before dawn to take her Italian lessons, but less happily practiced her music four to five hours daily. She was her grandfather's favorite perhaps because of her thirst and enthusiasm for knowledge. Martha Washington favored Nelly's brother who seemed to have inherited his father's learning problems, lack of intellectual focus, and lethargic work ethic.

In 1789, when Nelly was ten and her brother Parke Custis eight, Washington was elected the country's first president. They moved as a family to the nation's capital which was then New York City. Unlike rural Virginia, New York had many schools the children might attend. Nelly quickly thrived in her first formal school. Parke Custis continued having difficulties. A graduate of Dublin's

Trinity College was hired as a tutor to strengthen the boy's academic skills before he was sent off to school, but he made little progress.

Martha blamed teachers who "ignored" students and seemed unable to engage or motivate them. She wrote, "As constant as the day comes ... he does not learn as much as he might if the master took proper care to make the children attentive to their books."

A small school was found for Parke Custis with only seven other boys his own age in attendance. Nelly had developed into a ferocious reader, but her brother had grown to hate anything academic. He would run outside the moment his teachers or grandparents turned their backs. Martha blamed the schools, writing, "In this city everyone complains of the difficulty to get their children educated — my dear little Washington is not doing half as well as I could wish ... and we are mortified that we cannot do better for him."

As Nelly enjoyed her studies and Parke Custis failed his, Martha was shocked in 1796 when her favorite slave, her personal maid, fled to New Hampshire seeking her freedom. Human slavery was still legal throughout most of America at that time, and the president and first lady had always "owned" slaves. A friend of the president's recognized Ona in New Hampshire and asked what she was doing there. Ona admitted she had run away. When pressed why she would leave the Washington family who had provided her "every indulgence," Ona replied, "I wanted to be free, missus, wanted to learn to read and write."

There is no evidence Martha Washington considered that Ona or other slaves might have the abilities or the desire for an education. Martha's thinking about slaves and education never changed. She continued urging her husband to return Ona to her servitude. Ona Judge however remained free. She eventually married a man of her own choosing, had children that were not taken away from her, and pursued an education, none of which she could have done as a slave "owned" by the wife of the president of the United States.

George Washington was the fourth generation of his family to be a slaveholder. But over time he slowly rethought his attitudes about slavery and education for blacks. For many years the Marquis de Lafayette and other friends urged him to end American slavery. Shortly before becoming president, Washington wrote Lafayette that abolition "by degrees" could and should be accomplished. Twice during his presidency he secretly worked on emancipation plans, but found few supporters within his government or his family.

To further complicate his thinking, emancipation of his slaves would separate them from their own families since many had intermarried with those held by his wife and his stepchildren. All the Custis clan, including Martha, firmly opposed emancipating or educating slaves. As one biographer noted, "George and Martha Washington were not even speaking to each other about slavery by the end of their lives together. He had to appeal to his wife's humanity from the grave."

In his last will and testament, Washington wrote,

> Upon the decease of my wife, it is my will and desire that all the Slaves which I hold in my *own right,* shall receive their freedom. To emancipate them during my life, would, though earnestly wished by me, be attended with such insuperable difficulties on account of the intermixture by marriages with the dower [Custis] Negros as to excite the most painful sensations, if not disagreeable consequences from the latter ... it not being in my power, under the tenure by which the dower [Custis] Negros are held, to manumit them.

Washington seemed to hope that by freeing his own slaves, he would encourage or at least apply pressure on Martha to follow his lead. The realization that her slaves might hasten their freedom by hastening her own death may have moved Martha toward emancipation. Whatever the reason, within a year of her husband's death in 1799, all her slaves were freed.

George Washington's last will and testament also addressed the question of educating blacks writing that slave children "with no living parents, or if living are unable, or unwilling to provide for them, shall be bound by the Court.... The Negros thus bound, are [by their Masters or Mistress] to be taught to read and write; and to be brought up to some useful occupation, agreeably to the Laws of the Commonwealth of Virginia." His words recognized the importance of education in preparing Virginia for a slaveless future. Of the ten presidents who would "own" slaves, Washington was the only one to free his slaves after he and his wife died and to urge that they be educated.

George and Martha Washington reflected the conflicting beliefs about education, gender, and race commonly held by most Americans in eighteenth-century America. They would not be the last president or first lady to do so. In many ways, such attitudes hardened after their deaths. In 1831, thirty-two years after Washington's last will and testament urged that education be provided for slaves and former slaves, Virginia legally outlawed education for all black children and black adults within its borders.

The laws condemned Virginia's black men and women to remain, in the harsh words of John Adams, "illiterate, unlearned and unread." Only the Civil War, amendments to the U.S. Constitution, years of financial and political pressure, and military occupation allowed Virginia's former slaves to receive an education.

Washington's bright granddaughter Nelly Custis never attended college. His grandson Parke Custis attended three but graduated from none. Martha Washington may have had only one granddaughter who actively pursued an education and became a teacher in the racially segregated Washington, D.C., school system. Her name is lost to history, perhaps because she was thought to be the illegitimate child of Martha Washington's son Jackie Custis and one of Mrs. Washington's slaves.

George Washington in His First Message to Congress...

"Knowledge is in every country the surest basis of public happiness."

...and in His Last Message to Congress

"Promote, then, as an object of primary importance, institutions for the general diffusion of knowledge."

Abigail Smith, John Adams, and the Remarkable Smith Sisters

"We Should Have More Learned Women"

Four hundred and fifty miles north of George and Martha Washington's Virginia plantation could be found the modest home of John and Abigail Adams of Massachusetts. Their experiences and attitudes toward education and who should be educated reflected more than a distance in miles. For eight years John Adams served as George Washington's vice president. In 1797 he became the second president of the United States, and the first teacher to journey from the classroom to the White House.

Adams' own first teachers were his mother and father, who taught him to read before sending him next door to a neighbor who taught the future president the basics needed to prosper in colonial America. John had no trouble with his only textbook, *The New England Primer; or an Easy and Pleasant Guide to the Art of Reading Adorned with [Wood] Cuts to Which Is Added the Catechism*. He was the teacher's pet, but he preferred playing ball or being outside, rather than inside any classroom. His father was determined, however, that his son should attend college. John was soon sent to a Latin school since reading and translating Latin were the prerequisites then needed to be admitted to college.

At his new school Adams' bright mind slammed shut. He felt his "droning and uninspired" teacher paid him little or no attention. He reciprocated by paying little or no attention to his studies. Adams told his father, "I don't like my schoolmaster. He is so negligent and so cross that I can never learn anything under him." In his autobiography he described his teacher as "the most indolent man I ever knew," adding that "his inattention to his scholars ... gave me a disgust to schools, to books, and to study."

John told his father he would rather be a farmer than a scholar, so his father took him to a nearby creek to work from dawn till dusk cutting and bundling thatch reeds. At the close of the exhausting day, his father asked if he enjoyed the backbreaking life of a farmer. John honestly replied, "I like it very well, Sir." His exasperated father told him, "Well, I *don't* like it so well: so you go *back* to school!" Soon a compromise was reached. John went to a new school to be taught by a new teacher. There the patience and interest of Joseph Marsh, his new teacher, harnessed his "fine mind" and "extraordinary capacity for plain hard work." Attitude, efforts, and grades all improved; but John Adams never lost his genuine affection for farming.

When he was fifteen he traveled to Cambridge, Massachusetts, to apply for admittance to Harvard College. John Adams was such a poor test taker the school authorities allowed him to take an untimed college entrance exam. To his surprise, he passed. Adams later wrote, "I was as light when I came home, as I had been heavy when I went." John and the one hundred male scholars attending Harvard in 1755 never took another written test after their entrance exam. Instead they were verbally tested through formal and informal conversations by their seven professors on their readings and thinking skills. It was at college that his favorite professor, John Winthrop, introduced Adams to the study of mathematics, science, and astronomy. Joined with his love of reading they became the intellectual foundations of his life.

John Adams graduated fourteenth in a graduating class of twenty-five. In colonial America a college student's rankings were based on the social, economic, and political status of a student's family rather than academic performance. On the day of his college commencement the nineteen-year-old was offered a teaching position at a one-room schoolhouse in Worcester, Massachusetts. Adams quickly accepted, naively hoping the position would provide time for "study and self-improvement." Mindful of some of his own unpleasant school memories, he promised himself he would provide his students "a taste of the true excitement of learning."

The new Harvard graduate tried to be a good teacher. But to his "amazing shock," he found teaching twelve young girls and boys difficult and exhausting. At the end of the school day, he was too tired to do anything but seek solitary rest. One of his students later remembered that Adams spent most of his time "absorbed in his own thoughts or busily writing." The second year of his teaching, Adams gloomily wrote a friend, "I have no books, no time, no friends."

John Adams liked his students and at times enjoyed teaching, but he had no idea how to teach. He reminded himself, "Human nature is more easily wrought upon and governed by promises, encouragement and praise than by punishment, threatening, and blame." To that end he took pleasure in "bestow[ing] the proper applause upon virtuous and generous actions." But he found himself frequently struggling to balance the need "to blame and punish every vicious and contracted trick, to wear out of the tender mind everything that is mean and little, [while trying to] fire the new born soul with a noble ardor and emulation." Despite "repeated experiments" to engage, motivate, and instruct his students, their constant talking and "mischievous tricks" wore him out.

Adams finally decided he did not have the temperament, patience, stamina, or sense of humor to teach. Still, his teaching career provided him the opportunity to study human nature and observe the various personality types he would meet the rest of his life. He wrote,

> I sometimes, in my sprightly moments consider myself, in my great chair at school, as some dictator at the head of a commonwealth. In this little state I can discover all the great geniuses, all the surprising actions and revolutions of the great world in miniature. I have several renowned generals but three feet high, and several deep-projecting politicians in petticoats. I have others catching and dissecting flies, accumulating remarkable pebbles, cockleshells, etc., with as ardent curiosity as any virtuoso in the Royal Society. Some rattle and thunder out A B C with as much fire and impetuosity as Alexander fought, and very often sit down and cry as heartily, upon being out-spelt, as Caesar did at Alexander's sepulcher when he recollected that the Macedonian hero had conquered the world before his age. At one table sits Mr. Insipid ... fluttering, spinning his whirligig, or playing with his fingers as gaily and wittily as any ... [dandy] brandishing his cane and rattling his snuff box.... In short, my little school, like the great world, is made up of kings, politicians, divines ... fops, buffoons, fiddlers, sycophants, fools, coxcombs, chimney sweepers, and every other character drawn in history or seen in the world.

Adams soon left teaching to become a lawyer and returned to live in Braintree, Massachusetts. There he met Abigail Smith, his future wife, and her two remarkable sisters. Despite their intelligence and fierce desire for learning, none of the sisters attended one day of school. It was generally believed in eighteenth-century America that "church and home" provided enough education for girls and women.

One of the sisters later remembered, "It was not the fashion for females to know more than writing and a little arithmetic. No books on female education were then in vogue, no academies for female instruction then established." The three were homeschooled to read the Bible, write, and do basic arithmetic by their mother Elizabeth Quincy and their Quincy grandparents. Their father, William Smith, encouraged his daughters to continue their education by reading the books in his fine library. With his support, Mary, Abigail, and little Elizabeth became three of the best-read women of Massachusetts. Abigail's quick mind and appetite for reading mirrored Adam's own intellectual pursuits. Their home would be filled with five children — and thousands of books.

Mary, the oldest Smith daughter, married Richard Cranch, who encouraged his wife and her sisters to read the works of Shakespeare, Milton, Pope and other great authors. The youngest sister, Elizabeth, became a teacher and outlived two husbands who also taught. In 1787 Elizabeth cofounded the Atkinson Academy in New Hampshire with her second husband. It became only the second school in America to open its classrooms to females. She was thrilled to be able to teach female students in a school setting and wrote, "For this purpose came I into the world."

Abigail Adams found time to homeschool not only her own children, but other youngsters willing to put in the time and effort. One such student was a young black boy named James. After mastering his basic academic skills, he asked if she would help him enroll in the local school. She promptly did so, but a neighbor complained that other students objected to having a black child in their class. Abigail told her, "I have not thought it any disgrace myself to take him into my parlor and teach him to read and write." She then peppered her neighbor with several blunt questions: "Why did the other boys not refuse to go to church ... where ... blacks attended the same services? ... Merely because his face is black, is he to be denied instruction? How is he to be qualified to procure a livelihood?"

In a letter to her absent husband, Abigail wrote that she asked all the boys with complaints to be sent directly to her, assuring her neighbor she was confident she "could convince them of their error." ... After all, she explained, "We shall all go to heaven together." No boys or parents came to see her, and James continued attending the local school.

In another letter to her husband, the future first lady wrote, "If we mean

In 1787, Abigail Adams' sister Elizabeth co-founded the Atkinson Academy in New Hampshire, one of the first schools in America to open its classrooms to females (The Atkinson Academy, Atkinson, New Hampshire — author collection).

to have Heroes, Statesmen and Philosophers, we should have learned women.... If much depends ... upon the early education of youth and the first principles which are instilled take the deepest root, great benefit must arise from literary accomplishments in women."

Abigail and John Adams encouraged their sons, daughters, nieces and nephews to pursue education. Abigail wrote, "Knowledge will teach candor and she who aims at the attainment of it will find her countenance improves as her mind is informed and her looks ennobled as her heart is elevated, and thus she shall become a pleasing companion to the man of science and of sensibility, enabled to form the minds of her children to virtue and knowledge."

In 1778 John wrote his oldest daughter, "In your letter to your brother, which is a very pretty one, you express a wish that you understood French. At your age, it is not difficult to learn that language; patience and perseverance is all that is wanting." In another letter he wrote her, "You have reason to wish for a taste for history, which is as entertaining and instructive to the female as to the male sex." And in the midst of the Revolution, Adams wrote his wife, "I have seen the utility of Geometry, Geography, and the Art of drawing so much of late, that I must entreat you, my dear, to teach the elements of those Sciences to my little Girl and Boys."

Near the end of her life in 1818, Abigail Adams wrote to a niece that she was pleased that educational opportunities were beginning to improve for women, but added, "Much yet remains to be done." To John and Abigail Adams, education was as necessary to life as air, water, and food. It connected them to the world of ideas and to each other. Despite years of travel and government responsibilities keeping them apart, their letter writing and shared hunger for knowledge kept them together through fifty-four years of marriage. They believed that education was as essential to the growth of both men and women as to the nation they helped create.

John Adams on Education

"Laws for the liberal education of youth, especially of the lower class of people, are so extremely wise and useful, that to a humane and generous mind, no expense for that purpose would be thought extravagant."

"The preservation of the means of knowledge among the lowest ranks is of more importance to the public than all the property of all the rich men in the country."

"Education makes a greater difference between man and man, than nature has made between man and brute."

Abigail Adams on Education

"Education and example may do almost anything."

"It is a maxim here, that he who dies with studying dies in a good cause, and may go to another world much better calculated to improve his talents, than if he had died a blockhead. Well, knowledge is a fine thing, and mother Eve thought so; but she smarted so severely for hers, that most of her daughters have been afraid of it since."

"When a mind is raised, and animated by scenes that engage the Heart, then those qualities which would other ways lay dormant, wake into Life, and form the character of the Hero and the Statesman."

"If you have made some small attainment in knowledge, yet when you look forward to the immense sum; of which you are still ignorant, you will find you own, but as a grain of sand, a drop, to the ocean."

"Learning is not attained by chance, it must be sought for with ardour and attended to with diligence."

"Teach ... how to think, and they will learn how to act."

Thomas Jefferson
"The Destinies of My Life"

Thomas Jefferson followed John and Abigail Adams to the White House in 1801. Like his fellow Virginian George Washington and his sometime friend–sometime rival John Adams, Jefferson's early student days were uneven and frustrating. He was five when he and his sisters joined their cousins in a one-room schoolhouse on a neighboring plantation. One biographer wrote of Jefferson the schoolboy, "Thomas tried to pay attention to his studies, but the classes were so boring they nearly drove him to tears." His first teacher required memorization, drills, and more memorization. Thinking was not expected or required. When he was nine, Jefferson, without his sisters, was sent to a boarding school to be taught Latin, Greek, and other classical subjects needed for college. He later described his clergyman teacher as being a "superficial Latinist" and an even worse teacher of Greek.

At seventeen, Jefferson enrolled in Virginia's William and Mary College, which was going through a period of chaotic turmoil. The unhappy student found only one faculty member there with whom he connected. Dr. William Small was a Scotsman trying to reform the curriculum and improve the quality of teaching. He was also the only member of the faculty who was not an ordained minister. In his autobiography, Jefferson wrote, "It was my good fortune, and what probably fixed the destinies of my life that Dr. William Small ... was then the Professor of Mathematics, a man profound in most of the useful branches of science, with a happy talent of communication, correct and gentlemanly manners, and an enlarged and liberal mind."

Dr. Small gave Jefferson the most precious commodity in a teacher's life — his time. Years later the seventy-seven-year-old retired president still fondly remembered his former instructor: "He most happily became attached to me and made me his daily companion when not engaged in school; and from his conversation I got my first views of the expansion of science and of the system of things in which we are placed."

Small taught through his keen intellect and forceful personality. He refused to subscribe to the common belief of the time that a teacher's job was to "break the spirit of the student." To him learning was a cognitive dialogue, a verbal and mental conversation connecting student and teacher to life. He taught Jefferson that learning was about relationships and connections.

Following Jefferson's graduation, Dr. Small returned to Scotland to pursue his own studies, but remained Jefferson's friend and mentor. At the outbreak of the American Revolution, Jefferson wrote his former teacher, "Within this week we have received the unhappy news of an action of considerable magnitude between the King's troops and our brethren in Boston.... This ... has cut off our last hope of reconciliation.... I still hope that amidst public dissention private friendship may be preserved inviolate and among the warmest you can ever possess in your humble servant." Small did not respond. He had been taken ill with malaria earlier that month and died at the age of forty-one. Small's influence remained with Jefferson long after his teacher's death.

When he was president, Jefferson wrote his favorite grandson about the need and importance of having role models in a person's life. He fondly recalled becoming "acquainted very early with some characters of very high standing, and to feel the incessant wish that I could ever become what they were." Nearly fifty years after leaving his classroom, Jefferson wrote that he continued to ask himself throughout his life, "What would Dr. Small do in this situation?"

Thomas Jefferson described the rest of his college career as "miserable." He also never forgot his frustration with his earlier schooling. Fifteen years before becoming president, he urged his native state of Virginia to create a statewide system of "common schools, free and open to all." Jefferson hoped institutions of higher learning would draw their scholars from these common schools. Later while serving in the White House, he became the first president of the Washington D.C., school board. Upon reflection, if he had to choose between creating local public schools or a university, Jefferson said he would rather create public schools, reasoning, "It is safer to have a whole people respectably enlightened, than a few in a state of [knowledge], and the many in ignorance."

Jefferson's support for public education seemed well ahead of his time, but it was highly selective. Years later he admitted, "A plan of *female* education had never been a subject of systematic contemplation with me. It has occupied my attention so far only as the education of my own daughters occasionally required."

Following the death of his young wife, Jefferson raised and educated his daughters according to his ideas of what constituted the best education for girls in the eighteenth century. In a 1783 letter to his eleven-year-old daughter Patsy, he revealed his thoughts:

With respect to the distribution of your time the following is what I should approve:

From 8 to 10 o'clock practice music
From 10 to 1 dance one day and draw another
From 1 to 2 draw on the day you dance, and write a letter the next day
From 3 to 4 read French
From 4 to 5 exercise yourself in music
From 5 to bedtime read English, write etc.

When Jefferson traveled as a diplomat to Europe in 1784, he took Patsy with him. There she was tutored in the domestic arts by Abigail Adams who had also accompanied her own diplomat husband. Patsy was then placed in the most prestigious convent boarding school in Paris. Abigail Adams was dumbfounded that Jefferson would place his daughter under the educational influence of Catholic nuns. Later when Jefferson's younger daughter joined him, she was accompanied by a slave girl named Sally Hemings. His younger daughter soon joined her sister in the convent school, but the slave girl did not.

Despite the stirrings of educational opportunities for a select number of females in the new American nation, Jefferson's thoughts on female education remained focused on the social and domestic curriculum his own wife and Martha Washington had experienced. The nuns in Paris did not deviate from those principles. Jefferson's vision of "common schools, free and open to all" did not include girls, women, or free or enslaved male or female blacks.

A wing of Monticello, Jefferson's home, includes a one-room schoolhouse where young men studied law under his guidance and instruction. One of his students was James Monroe who would become the fifth president of the United States. As president, Jefferson also taught Meriwether Lewis in celestial navigation and other scientific areas of exploration needed for the Lewis and Clark expedition. A number of students were educated at Monticello, but Jefferson's slaves were not.

Jefferson, like George Washington, was the fourth generation of his family claiming ownership of human slaves. The slave girl who accompanied his younger daughter to Paris was his wife's own half-sister. Sally Wayles Hemings and her two half brothers were slaves Jefferson "inherited" at his wife's death. Sally's brothers had been taught to read and write before they came to live with Jefferson, but their younger sister Sally, who grew up in the Jefferson household, was not. Jefferson educated none of his slaves, but one of Sally's children claimed

Thomas Jefferson's home, Monticello, included a one-room schoolhouse in one of its wings. Jefferson the teacher tutored James Monroe in the law and Meriwether Lewis in celestial navigation. But none of Jefferson's slaves were ever taught to read or write (the schoolhouse wing of Monticello in Charlottesville, Virginia — author collection).

that a Jefferson grandchild taught him to read and write. The rest of the slaves "owned" by the writer of the Declaration of Independence were not provided any formal education.

Thomas Jefferson, however, did believe in vocational education. At nine years of age, slave boys undertook a seven-year apprenticeship at Jefferson's nail factory learning to make nails for area builders and contractors. James Monroe's nearby home was built with nails manufactured by Jefferson's slaves. For some years, the only regular income Jefferson "earned" was from his nail factory. When boys reached the age of sixteen, Jefferson personally tested their nail-making skills. If the sixteen-year-olds passed, they would spend the rest of their lives manufacturing nails. If they failed, they worked in the fields until death or infirmities ended their lives. Jefferson might be considered a founding father of high stakes testing.

In 1789 the Polish patriot Thaddeus Kosciuszko gave monies to his friend Thomas Jefferson for the purpose of freeing and educating Negros. He also created the Kosciuszko Fund in his will to continue to provide funding for "an education in trade or otherwise, and having them instructed for their new condition in the duties of morality, which may make them good neighbors, good fathers or mothers, husbands or wives, in their duty as citizens teaching them to be defenders of their liberty and country, and of the good order of society, and whatsoever may make them happy and useful." Kosciuszko asked Thomas Jefferson to be the executor of his will, but Jefferson refused. The money Kosciuszko left in his will was never used to purchase the freedom of any slaves, or to educate any present or former slaves.

As a young boy Jefferson learned that a teacher could not only make a difference in a student's life, but that a great teacher could make all the difference. Thomas Jefferson sincerely believed in the power of education, but he was unable or unwilling to extend that intellectual vision beyond his own race and gender.

Thomas Jefferson on Education

"Educate and inform the whole mass of people."

"Knowledge is power, Knowledge is safety, and Knowledge is happiness."

"Enlighten the people generally and tyranny and oppressions of body and mind will vanish."

"Preach, my dear sir, a crusade against ignorance; establish and improve law for educating the common people."

"It is highly interesting to our country, and it is the duty of its functionaries, to provide that every citizen in it should receive an education proportioned to the condition and pursuits of his life."

"There are two subjects, indeed, which I shall claim a right to further as long as I breathe, the public education and the subdivision of the counties into [school districts]. I consider the continuance of republican government as absolutely hanging on these two hooks."

Thomas Jefferson to John Adams

"I hope our successors will turn their attention to the advantages of education ... on the broad scale ... where every branch of science, useful at this day, may be taught in its highest degree.... Above all I hope the education of the common people will be attended to; convinced that in their good sense we may rely on the most security for the preservation of a due degree of liberty."

"Bigotry is the disease of ignorance, of morbid minds; enthusiasm of the free and buoyant. Education and free discussion antidotes of both."

"If we do not force instruction, let us at least strengthen the motive to receive it."

Dolley Payne Todd and
James Madison

"Three Hours Out of Twenty-Four for Sleep?"

In the early years of American education, schools and religion were nearly synonymous. America's first colleges were church affiliated. Many schoolteachers were ordained ministers who earned additional money by teaching. Some clergymen were better teachers than others; but good teachers, clergy or not, were hard to find.

Of the first five presidents, four grew up in rural Virginia, but only one claimed to have a great teacher during his early school years. James Madison wrote in old age, "All that I have been in my life I owe to that great man." Madison was referring to Donald Robertson, a non-clergyman who taught Madison from the time he was eleven until he was fifteen. Robertson's name has largely been forgotten, but the thirst for knowledge he instilled in his pupil ignited Madison's curiosity and inflamed his intelligence.

The first nine years of his life, Madison was homeschooled by his grandmother. By the age of eleven he had read all eighty-five books owned by his father. At that point he was sent to a neighboring county where he boarded with a family and attended a nearby one-room schoolhouse taught by Donald Robertson, a Scottish immigrant schoolmaster.

Madison found in Robertson "a man of extensive learning, and a distinguished teacher" who encouraged natural curiosity. Mr. Robertson taught Madison the logic and beauty of mathematics, the power of the correctly chosen word, and the connections of Greek and Latin to the English, French, and Spanish languages. He had him learn the names of the planets, but also demanded that Madison make a case for whether there was intelligent life on those planets. He also introduced him to the ideas and ideals of the Enlightenment, which served as the foundation for Madison's public and political life. Under his teacher's influence, the future president learned to question and to think.

When he was fifteen, Madison returned home to be taught for two years by the Reverend Thomas Martin, tutor to Madison's younger brothers and sisters. The Madisons were member of the Anglican Church of England, but James was not sent to the Anglican-affiliated William and Mary College. After turning seventeen, Madison traveled north to New Jersey to attend Princeton College, aligned at that time with the Presbyterian church. The decision may have been influenced by Princeton-educated Thomas Martin or because William and

Mary's reputation for "drinking and partying" outweighed its academic and religious foundations.

James Madison was accompanied on the 300-mile journey to school by the Reverend Martin and Sawney, a family slave. Martin and Sawney soon returned to Virginia with textbooks for the younger Madison children while their older brother pursued studies in Latin, Greek, mathematics, natural philosophy, history, government, and religion. Madison never found a Princeton professor more influential than his early schoolmaster. His college experience however did encourage the future president to develop a tolerance for religious dissent and a strong skepticism about the "corrupting coalition" between government and religion.

Madison was an intense student. At college his health broke when he and a friend tried to complete the four-year course of study in two. To expand his study time, Madison allowed only "three hours out of twenty-four for sleep." Madison's friend died shortly before graduation. Madison himself was too ill to attend the ceremonies and was forced to recuperate for several months in Princeton before returning home. It took years for him to regain his health, but he used some of his recovery time to explore an interest in Hebrew and study the conflicts between religion and government.

The unexpected death of his siblings' tutor, Thomas Martin, thrust James Madison into the role of teacher. His father decided that Madison, physically weak but fresh from college, should take Martin's place teaching seventeen-year-old Ambrose, twelve-year-old Nellie, ten-year-old William, and eight-year-old Sarah. A careful balance of teaching, physical exercise, reading, and quiet study slowly helped the future president restore his health.

William Bradford, a close friend from Princeton, wrote Madison seeking advice on whether he should pursue a law career or a divinity degree. Madison responded that if Bradford's goal was "to adhere to truth and probity," he doubted it possible in the practice of law. On the other hand a divinity degree did not necessarily guarantee adherence to "truth and probity" either. He pointed to the example of their mutual older friend Thaddeus Dod, who had only married the mother of his recently born son after Dod was ordained a minister. Madison wrote Bradford, "The world needs to be peopled, but I should be sorry it should be peopled with bastards.... Who would have thought the old monk had been so lecherous?" The hypocrisy of some clerics and their pervasive political influence in colonial America troubled Madison. He asked Bradford, "Is the Ecclesiastical Establishment absolutely necessary to support civil society in a supreme government? How far is it hurtful to a dependent State?"

Madison had become deeply troubled by the political alliance Virginia's legislators had formed with the Anglican Church of England. At the behest of the church establishment, the colony's civil authorities arrested and persecuted Baptist and Presbyterian dissenters for practicing their religion. He wrote Bradford, Virginia's legislators were "too much devoted to the ecclesiastical establishment to hear of the toleration of dissentients" and denounced the "pride, ignorance and knavery among the priesthood." He concluded, "Diabolical Hell conceived persecution rages among some and to their eternal infamy the clergy can furnish their quota of imps for such business."

It was not surprising that when Madison decided to marry late in his life he chose a woman willing to go against the prevailing religious and social orthodoxy of the time. Dolley Payne Todd was born in North Carolina and raised as a member of the Society of Friends, better known as the Quakers. Her first teacher was a family "spinster" who taught her to read, write, and "do sums." Dolley, however, preferred fishing and running outside with her boisterous older brothers to reading, studying, or being inside with her more sedate younger sisters. At the age of eleven she and her brothers were sent to a nearby Quaker school. There they received the same instruction, but at home her brothers were also taught Latin, mathematics, theology and other courses to prepare them for college. Dolley's home instruction was limited to the domestic arts.

Most of her early life Dolley lived in rural Virginia, but when she was fifteen her father freed his slaves and moved his family north. There she attended a Quaker school in Philadelphia. She enjoyed the social part of school, but not its rigorous curriculum. Despite struggling academically, her likable personality attracted girls and boys of all ages to her side. Some female students jealously resented her popularity and complained it was unseemly "for a girl active in the Society of Friends to flirt, encourage the attentions of males, and make a public spectacle of her self." Dolley was just being herself, but Quaker law allowed girls to quit school at sixteen, and she happily complied.

At nineteen she married a fellow Quaker named John Todd, but she found herself a widow and single mother by the time she was twenty-five. The charismatic Dolley Payne Todd was befriended by George and Martha Washington, John and Abigail Adams, Thomas Jefferson, Aaron Burr and other prominent Americans then staying in Philadelphia. Even Virginia congressman, confirmed bachelor, and bookworm James Madison, seventeen years her senior found her attractive. His passions had always been limited to words, books, and ideas. Dolley's passion had always been people. They made an odd pair, but he vigorously courted her. With the help of Washington, Jefferson, and other matchmakers, he finally persuaded her to marry him. Dolley was promptly expelled from her Quaker meetinghouse for marrying a non–Quaker.

With the popular and gregarious Dolley Madison at his side, the shy, socially inept Madison managed in 1809 to follow Thomas Jefferson into the presidency. Dolley did not have any more academic success with her son than the Washington's had trying to educate Martha's son and grandson.

When Madison served as Thomas Jefferson's secretary of state he took over responsibility of his stepson's education and began personally tutoring the ten-year-old boy, but Madison failed miserably as a teacher. Despite his skepticism regarding religion, Madison, with Dolley's approval, eventually sent the boy to a Catholic boarding school in Baltimore. There the boy remained for eight seemingly wasted years. Madison's stepson never found the teacher, or the school, or the books, that could save him from himself. When he died a broken, penniless, alcoholic, he said on his deathbed, "I have been my own worst enemy."

Madison himself found education a comfort at the end of his life. He and James Monroe, his successor in the White House, worked with their friend Thomas Jefferson to help found the University of Virginia.

James Madison on Education

"A well instructed people alone can be permanently free."

"What spectacle can be more edifying or more reasonable than that of liberty and learning, each leaning on the other for their mutual surest support?"

"Knowledge will forever govern ignorance: and a people who mean to be their own governors must arm themselves with the power which knowledge gives."

Dolley Madison

"There is but one secret, and that is the power we have in forming our own destiny."

Elizabeth Kortright and James Monroe

"My Plan of Life Is Now Fixed"

In 1817 James Monroe and his wife Elizabeth Kortright Monroe followed Dolley and James Madison into the White House. Elizabeth was from New York and had received the traditional non-academic domestic arts education expected of wealthy young ladies, but with the addition of the study of French. Years before he became president, much to the delight of his wife, Monroe was appointed minister to the new republican French government. Elizabeth embraced the language, the culture, the cuisine and all things French. Many people who came to dislike her for her cool public demeanor claimed that after living in Paris for a little more than a year, Mrs. Monroe became more French than the French.

Their daughter Eliza attended one of the finest schools in post-revolutionary France. It offered an expanded curriculum that her mother would never have been offered as a young female student in America. Eliza was enrolled in the National Institution for the Education of Young Women. In addition to teaching the traditional domestic arts, courses were offered in mathematics, literature, history, and even physical education. The school was founded by a former lady-in-waiting to Marie Antoinette. An enormous portrait of the late queen hung on one of the school's walls, and on its back could be found written the French Republic's political credo, *The Rights of Man*. This allowed the picture to be easily flipped back and forth depending on the political winds sweeping across France. Politics has never been completely absent from schools. During the French Revolution many of the Parisian nuns who had once taught Thomas Jefferson's daughters were beheaded as enemies of the state.

Eliza's classmates were the daughters of royalists, republicans, and future royals, including Napoleon's stepdaughter Hortense who later became Queen of Holland and the mother of Emperor Napoleon III. After moving into the White House, the Monroe's replaced much of the furniture destroyed during the War of 1812 with exquisite furnishings from France. They also frequently spoke French to each other in order to have privacy, much to the disgust and annoyance of snoops.

James Monroe was born in the same large county in Virginia where Washington and Jefferson had been born. His father inherited a nearly five-hundred-acre plantation compared to the 6,000 acres inherited by George Washington's father. But like Washington, Jefferson, and the Madisons, the Monroes also owned slaves.

Despite being in America for three generations, none of the Monroes had ever attended college, or offered their slaves any schooling of any kind. James's parents hoped he would be the first Monroe to have a college education, and possibly even study abroad. But like many young men of his generation, the political and economic turmoil of revolutions in America and France ended those dreams. James's sister would never attend any school outside of the family home, but Monroe encouraged both his brothers to acquire an education.

Monroe's mother was said to be better educated than his father, but neither parent seems to have had more than a bare minimum of schooling. The future president was a shy, bright, tall, athletic child who was homeschooled by his mother until the age of eleven. He was then sent to live with the Reverend Archibald Campbell who headed the Campbelltown Academy, the finest private boarding school in Virginia. Each year Campbell handpicked twenty-five promising scholars from across Virginia to personally prepare for college. He was a strict disciplinarian who specialized in drilling his pupils in mathematics and Latin. One of Monroe's closest friends there became John Marshall, the future chief justice of the United States.

In 1774 the sixteen-year-old Monroe enrolled in William and Mary College where he was placed in advanced classes due to his training and the reputation of the Campbelltown Academy. Monroe was academically and emotionally overwhelmed. Within the year, both of his parents died, but his maternal uncle and guardian urged him to finish his education. He later wrote, "I had been examined ... and found well qualified ... [but] I was altogether unqualified [and] made a ridiculous figure."

After a terrible first term, he used the two months of his winter break to study intensely, but it was a difficult time for the grieving Monroe to concentrate on school. He found no professor who took an interest in him or his studies and felt alienated from the conservative faculty who were loyal supporters of the British crown. His late father and the rest of his family were strong supporters of American independence, but his uncle wanted him to avoid colonial politics and get an education. Monroe was torn, but he tried to focus on his academics. By the second semester he was able to write, "I had made such good use of my time that I obtained the approbation and praise of my professors." His grades improved, but the tense political atmosphere on the divided campus did not.

If Monroe felt hesitant to join the acrimonious independence debates taking place off campus, he could at least join in campus politics. In the spring of 1775, he and seven other students signed a petition protesting the quality of school food and other problems they had with the college. The students were called to explain themselves before the faculty. When Monroe was asked to provide evidence regarding his complaints, he remained silent. He then sheepishly admitted he had not bothered to read the petition he signed.

Undeterred, Monroe and his roommate became active supporters of a younger faculty member recruiting students to join the American cause. Against school rules, Monroe hid a gun in his dorm room and began participating in demonstrations against the royal government. In 1776 he finally quit school to join the newly formed American army. For three years he fought alongside General Washington before being seriously wounded at the Battle of Trenton. He later reflected that the war introduced him to a wide range of people and ideas he would have never been exposed to at college.

Following his military service he was befriended by Thomas Jefferson who urged him to continue his education. Jefferson taught Monroe the study of the law and became his academic advisor, mentor, and teacher. Jefferson's large library was opened to the twenty-year-old war veteran, and Jefferson personally selected the "great books of western civilization, both ancient and modern" for Monroe to read. Monroe later wrote Jefferson,

> Your kindness and attention to me ... has really put me under such obligations to you that I fear I shall hardly have it in my power to repay them.... You became acquainted with me and undertook the direction of my studies.... I feel that whatever I am at present ... or whatever I am in the future has greatly arisen from your friendship. My plan of life is now fixed.

The political and personal friendship between Monroe and Jefferson continued throughout their public and private lives. When Monroe later served as governor of Virginia, he regularly consulted with Jefferson regarding the best way to deal with the ongoing problems of Virginia's slave insurrections. Through a series of letters they explored ways of dealing with the issue including sending rebellious slaves to the western frontier, the West Indies, South America, or even Sierra Leone in Africa. Providing an education for slaves or preparing them in any way to survive economically or independently was never considered in their correspondence.

As president, James Monroe embraced Jefferson's and Madison's philosophical belief that Congress should encourage "seminaries of learning" for "fellow citizens." He also endorsed proposals that education should be extended to the country's Native American population once Indians settled on individual farms and abandoned their claims to the land. In his first presidential message to Congress, Monroe declared that the "preservation, improvement, and civilization of the native inhabitants" is the duty of the federal government. Two years later Congress appropriated $10,000 out of the federal budget of $32,475,303.93 "to subsidize existing educational institutions [for] Indian education."

James Monroe, like Washington, Adams, Jefferson, and Madison, also favored the creation of a new national public university founded on the highest ideals of the Enlightenment. Each hoped it would educate and unite their new nation. Thomas Jefferson became the moving force to actually make it happen. Jefferson wanted to create a different kind of university, a genuine community of learners where teachers and students would learn together.

Sixteen years after leaving the White House and shortly before his death, the university he helped physically and philosophically to design opened its doors as the University of Virginia. Jefferson became the school's first chancellor; James Madison and James Monroe served on its board of trustees. Unlike the country's twenty or so existing colleges, the University of Virginia was not affiliated with any religious denomination. It was not sponsored by a church, did not have compulsory chapel for all students, and did not have a professor of theology on the faculty.

The University of Virginia became the first school in America to provide an alternative to church-sponsored colleges and the first to separate education from religion. In many ways, it was a product of the Enlightenment, the educational age in which the founding fathers lived. But the new university did not break with all traditions, superstitions, or prejudices of the past. It did not admit women or Native Americans, and it would be one hundred and thirty-three years before a black male or female was permitted to enter the school founded by three American presidents.

James Monroe's First Annual Message to Congress Addresses the Importance of Education ...

"I think it proper to suggest ... that it be recommended to the States ... a right in Congress to institute likewise seminaries of learning, for the all important purpose of diffusing knowledge among our fellow citizens through-out the United States."

... and the Cost of Education for Native Americans

"The care of the Indian tribes within our limits has long been an essential part of our system, but ... their sovereignty over vast territories should cease, in lieu of which the right of soil should be secured to each individual ... and for the territory thus ceded some reasonable equivalent should be granted, to be vested in permanent funds for the support of civil government over them and for the education of their children."

Louisa Johnson and John Quincy Adams
"I Hope I Grow a Better Boy"

In the public square of Quincy, Massachusetts, stands a statue of the youthful John Quincy Adams with one of his most influential teachers. He walks proudly ahead of her holding a book. She rests a hand on his shoulder, grasps a quill pen in her other hand, and stares straight ahead. The teacher is his mother, the indomitable Abigail Adams who supervised his homeschool-ing for the first decade of his life and kept a heavy hand on his life and career for the next forty years. James Thaxter, a cousin, and Nathan Rice, his father's law clerk, also tutored him; but it was his mother who held him accountable for his studies. When he was seven, he wrote his father, "I hope I grow a better boy and that you will have no occasion to be ashamed of me.... Mr. Thaxter says I learn my books well — he is a very good master. I read my books to Mamma."

Great things were expected of John Quincy Adams. As the oldest male child in his family, he was told from an early age he would be the third gener-ation of his family to attend Harvard College. His older sister Abigail, known as Nabby, was also expected to develop her mind, but without the benefit of a Harvard education. Harvard would not admit women for another two centuries. Nabby's daughter, however, did attend the school her Aunt Elizabeth helped found in New Hampshire.

"Scholarship," Johnny was told by his father, should be his "preeminent entertainment." But the serious ten-year-old wrote, "I make but a poor figure at composition, my head is much too fickle, my thoughts are running after bird eggs, play, and trifles, till I get vexed with myself. Mamma has a troublesome task to keep me steady, and I own I am ashamed of myself." Quincy Adams eventually did develop a love for reading and studying the arts, science, and literature, but his parents wanted the shy, socially awkward boy to follow his father into a life of public service. He dutifully followed their wishes, but as an adult he accurately described himself as "a very introverted, self critical individual of enormous pride and low personal esteem." Privately he recognized himself as a "gloomy misanthropist ... a social savage ... without the pliability to reform it." Many people he alienated throughout his long public life would agree.

During the American Revolution, eleven-year-old Quincy Adams traveled to Europe on a diplomatic mission with his father. The 3,000-mile crossing took six weeks at the height of the Atlantic Ocean's storm season. Their destination was Paris, where he was enrolled in a private school while his father worked with Benjamin Franklin to persuade France to support American independence.

One of John Quincy Adams' first teachers was his mother, the "indomitable" but heavy-handed Abigail Adams (Adams statue, Quincy, Massachusetts — author collection).

John Quincy Adams received the overseas education George Washington and other founding fathers had dreamed of but never achieved. He studied "French, Latin, and mathematics, along with fencing, dancing, and drawing." His school day began at 6 A.M. and ended at 7:30 P.M., with occasional breaks for meals and play. Within a year he returned to Boston with his father, accompanied by France's first envoy to America and the diplomat's secretary. On the voyage, the twelve-year-old boy taught both men English, displaying a genuine gift and talent for teaching which he put to good use later in life. John Adams proudly wrote, "They are in raptures with my son…. The Ambassador said he was astonished at my son's knowledge; that he was a master of his own language, like a professor."

Four months later Quincy Adams returned to Europe with his father. For the next two years he continued his education, first in Paris, then at Amsterdam's Latin School, and briefly at the University of Leyden. He soon traveled to Russia to serve as a private secretary and interpreter at the court of Catherine the Great. In Russia, he took the opportunity to travel to Copenhagen and Stockholm before returning to The Hague to continue his studies.

Europe's vaulted classical education was not all he or his father hoped it would be. When the young Adams attended Amsterdam's world-famous Latin School, the teenager spoke no Dutch and was embarrassed by being placed in a classroom with much younger children. He withdrew socially and academically, causing Dutch schoolmasters to decide that the best remedy would be a good thrashing. John Adams immediately pulled his son from the school. That same night he wrote Abigail, "The masters are mean-spirited wretches, punching, kicking, and boxing the children upon every turn." Adams found an American student at the University of Leyden who not only became his son's teacher, but arranged for him to attend lectures at the university.

After several years in Europe, the seventeen-year-old John Quincy Adams returned to America to complete his education, but not before his father tutored him in "geometry, trigonometry, conic sections, and the differential calculus." At home he stayed with his Aunt Elizabeth and her husband who helped prepare him for the Harvard entrance exam his father once feared. The exam went well. He was admitted as a junior, but he found it difficult to focus on his studies and regularly missed classes. He thought his professors arrogant and conceited, writing his father, "If anything in the world can teach me humility, it will be to see myself subjected to the commands of a person that I must despise." Despite his critical attitude, he managed to graduate from Harvard with academic honors.

Within a few years, George Washington appointed John Quincy Adams as minister to the Netherlands—perhaps giving his former teachers there a moment's pause. It was during his diplomatic sojourn in Europe that he met and married Louisa Catherine Johnson whose father served as American consul in England. During the American Revolution, Louisa's American father and British mother had moved the family to France. Louisa's excellent ear for language and music allowed her to receive a superb French education. Her natural curiosity, fine mind, and continental education matched her husband's, but he used his own considerable gifts to ignore or dismiss those of his wife. In time, her intelligence endeared her to Abigail Adams, her remarkable mother-in-law, but not her own husband.

When John Quincy Adams and Catherine returned to the United States, he became "industriously employed" in academia when he was appointed professor of rhetoric and oratory at Harvard College. To his surprise he enjoyed teaching as much as his somber temperament allowed, yet he still managed to find much to criticize. Conveniently forgetting his own irregular attendance as a Harvard student, he regularly grumbled about his students' attendance. He also complained of the constant interruptions caused by special events sponsored by the college. But his greatest frustration was the amount of time it took to prepare lessons and lectures. He wrote, "These lectures are indeed precisely the labor of Sisyphus."

Most teachers struggle with time management, but Adams was quite good at it. He served as a United States senator during most of the time he taught at Harvard. Adams took great care to prepare his lessons, and his hard work paid off. His classes soon filled to overflowing. Students arriving late discovered they could not get into his packed lecture hall. The efforts of his students soon matched his own. At their urging, his lectures were compiled and published. Adams continued to teach at Harvard for five years until President James Madison appointed him ambassador to Russia.

The appointment caused him to reluctantly leave the classroom. His final lecture was moved to the college chapel, the largest meeting place on campus, to accommodate the crowds wishing to attend. He surprised many by taking the opportunity to graciously salute his students as friends and colleagues.

In 1824 John Quincy Adams was elected president with Catherine Louisa Adams at his side. A national magazine saluted her as "the most scholarly woman who has presided at the White House," but their White House years were not happy ones. It had been a disputed, bitterly partisan, and highly controversial election. After one four-year term, Adams was defeated for reelection by Andrew Jackson.

Jackson's hardscrabble existence stood in sharp contrast to the social, cosmopolitan, and impressive educational foundations of John Quincy Adams' life. Andrew Jackson was born and bred on the American frontier. He had been orphaned by the age of fourteen, massacred Indian men, women, and children, become a military hero fighting the British, scandalously married a woman not yet divorced from her first husband, and fought and killed men in duels. Perhaps his youthful experiences of teaching in a one-room schoolhouse prepared him for the ups and downs of life. One of the few things the two men had in common was a hatred of preparing lessons. Jackson claimed it was the principal reason he left teaching.

The election of 1828 provided an example of one of the great success stories in the arc of American history. Andrew Jackson the former teacher from a one-room schoolhouse defeated John Quincy Adams the former Harvard College professor. The irony that Adams' father also began his career teaching in a one-room schoolhouse did nothing to remove the sting of his defeat. But worse was to come for the illustrious Adams.

Harvard College, the oldest and most prestigious academic institution in the nation, announced it would award Andrew Jackson an honorary degree. John Quincy Adams was livid. He refused to attend the ceremony, declaring he would not legitimatize the "disgrace" of his beloved college conferring its highest honor on a barbarian hardly able to write his name. The college president explained, "As the people ... decided that this man knows law enough to be their ruler it is not for Harvard to maintain they are mistaken." In spite of having a brilliant mind, brilliant parents, and an equally brilliant wife, extensive schooling in Europe and a Harvard education, John Quincy Adams had never learned to be a good loser.

John Adams to John Quincy Adams

"Have you kept a regular journal? If you have not you will be likely to forget most of the observations you have made.... We think and improve our judgments, by committing our thoughts to paper."

"Has it ever been recommended to read poetry? You will never be alone, with a poet in your pocket. You will never have an idle hour."

Abigail Adams to John Quincy Adams

"Youth is the proper season for observation and attention."

"Great learning and superior abilities, should you ever possess them, will be of little value and small estimation, unless Virtue, Honor, Truth and Integrity are added to them."

John Quincy Adams' Diary Notation on His First Day of Teaching at Harvard

"I this day commenced my course of lectures on rhetoric and oratory, — an undertaking of magnitude and importance, for the proper accomplishment of which I pray for patience and perseverance, and the favor from above, without which no human industry can avail, but without persevering industry, it is presumption to ask."

John Quincy Adams on Education for Men ... and Women

"Among the first, perhaps the very first, instrument for the improvement of the condition of men is knowledge."

"There is something in the very nature of mental abilities which seems unbecoming in a female."

Louisa Adams to Her Son

"When I see such women as your grandmother [Abigail Adams] go through years of exertion, of suffering, and of privation, with all the activity, judgment, skill and fortitude, which any man could display; I cannot believe there is any inferiority in the sexes, as far as the mind and intellect are concerned."

Louisa Adams to John Adams

"I have dipped into other [philosophers] and thrown them aside, but I have never seen anything that would satisfy my mind, or that would compare with the chaste and exquisitely simple doctrines of Christianity."

PART TWO

The Golden Age
of Education — For Some

Rachel Donelson Robards
and Andrew Jackson

"He Never Stayed Throwed"

Some people think of the nineteenth century's one-room schoolhouse as the birthplace of the Golden Age of Education. Within its four walls was preached the gospel that any man could be successful with a little education and a lot of hard work. Andrew Jackson seemed to epitomize that belief to the majority of American voters, much to the disgust of John Quincy Adams. Adams and Jackson were both hardworking men, but voters preferred the simpler plainspoken Jackson to the highly educated articulate Adams. Jackson was the first genuinely poor boy to grow up to be the president. The age of the elite founding fathers (and son) seemed over. The men that followed Adams to the White House presented themselves as having the common touch. It would be nearly fifty years before another Harvard man became president.

In the early nineteenth century no one seemed to represent the rise of the common man better than Andrew Jackson. Yet, like the country of his birth, he was full of contradictions. Jackson was an Indian fighter who adopted and raised an Indian child as a member of his own family. He was infamously quick-tempered yet could be patiently kind and gentle with a wounded soldier, a mother in need, or a crying infant. He claimed to have read only one book his entire life, *The Vicar of Wakefield*. Yet he could easily quote from the Bible and other great works of literature. Perhaps because of such contradictions, he aroused passions and deep emotions in friends and foes alike. He seemed to represent many people's highest hopes, and their darkest fears and prejudices. Jackson once said, "I know human nature"—and he did. He was a politician smart enough to know when to appeal to the best or the worst in people. And he was enough of an actor and a survivor to know when to take the high road and when to take the low.

One early biographer wrote of Jackson, "He learned to read, to write, and cast accounts—little more." As always, the truth with Jackson was more complicated. He was better educated than most of his contemporaries, and more intelligent than his enemies ever imagined. He once got into an argument with an uncle over "what makes a gentleman." His uncle said "good principles," but Jackson insisted it was education.

His Scotch-Irish immigrant father worked himself to death on their Carolina farm before Andrew was born. His mother worked as a servant for room and board for herself and his two older brothers in the home of an invalid relative. Jackson's seventeen-year-old brother died fighting in the American Revolution. He and his fifteen-year-old brother were then betrayed by loyalist neighbors and captured by British soldiers. That brother died shortly afterward from wounds and illness acquired during captivity. Andrew also became deathly ill. His mother nursed him back to life but then died caring for other sick relatives. No one could tell him where she was buried. At fourteen, Jackson was an orphan. When he spoke of his childhood, he recalled, "Men hunted each other like beasts of prey and the savages were outdone in cruelties to the living and indignities to the dead." His knowledge of the darkness of the human heart took root when he was very young.

As a small boy, Jackson joined his brothers at their school. He proved to be so bright his mother arranged for him to attend a nearby academy to prepare him to become a minister or for further education. His brothers remained at the local one-room schoolhouse. By five years of age Jackson could read from books and maps and wrote in "a neat legible hand." He soon became one of the community's "town readers."

Since few people on the frontier were literate, representatives were selected to read newspapers and other important notices aloud at public meetings. Despite his high-pitched girlish voice, Jackson became a popular reader because he "could read a paper clear through without getting hoarse or stopping to spell out words." It was the nine-year-old Jackson who was picked to read aloud the Declaration of Independence to his neighbors when it arrived in the backcountry.

The smart, red-headed, freckled-faced, fatherless boy in the Carolina backwoods soon learned to be a fighter. Jackson did not always win fights, but he never gave up. One schoolmate remembered, "I could throw him three times out of four, but he never stayed throwed." His bright red hair and uncontrollable drooling from the side of his mouth caused teasing, but his hair-trigger temper and reputation as a fighter quickly stopped any tormentors. By the time he was a teenager, Jackson learned to control his slobbering and to intimidate other boys. Once when some friends gave him a larger than usual musket to fire, the recoil knocked him down. He quickly jumped up yelling, "By God, if any of you laugh, I'll kill him!" No one laughed.

When he was older, his mother sent him to a boarding school run by a well-educated Presbyterian minister where he would learn the required Latin and Greek needed for college, but the approaching American Revolution soon closed the school. Within nineteen months, both of his brothers and his mother were dead. Perhaps because of his hot-tempered reputation, the orphaned Jackson was unable to find relatives willing to take or keep him.

Jackson briefly went to Charlotte to attend school, but in 1783 the sixteen-year-old wandered back to the borderlands to become a teacher himself in a one-room schoolhouse. Any male with some education and the ability to maintain discipline could usually get a teaching job. Jackson was younger and smaller than some of his students, but he had no problems maintaining discipline. It was the self-discipline of planning and preparing lessons that ended his teaching career. He decided to study law and within a few years was admitted to the bar in North Carolina, before traveling to Tennessee and becoming a lawyer there.

In Tennessee he met and married Rachel Donelson Robards, who it later turned out had not been legally divorced from her first husband. The accompanying gossip and scandal provoked Jackson's infamous temper, adding to his reputation as a fighter. Rachel had less schooling than her husband but loved to read, especially the Bible which she read daily. She also kept up a regular correspondence with family and friends. As Jackson's political star rose, Rachel provided him the stability and security of home with her extended family. During the first decade of their marriage, Jackson was elected to the U.S. Congress, the U.S. Senate, and then to the state supreme court.

The Jacksons had no children of their own, but they adopted one of Rachel's nephews three days after his birth. He was christened Andrew Jackson Jr. and raised and educated as their son. A few years later, during the War of 1812, Jackson was called on to lead a group of volunteer militiamen against the growing threat of an Indian war with the Creek Nation. After he and his men destroyed a Creek village, an infant boy named Lyncoya was found with the dead women. Jackson overheard an argument about whether to kill the boy since "his whole race and family" were dead. Jackson decided to take the child home to be raised with their adopted son. In a letter to Rachel he wrote,

> Keep Lyncoya in the house. He is a savage but one that fortune has thrown into my hands.... I therefore want him well taken care of, he may have been given me for some valuable purpose. In fact, when I reflect that he as to his relations is so much like myself — I feel an unusual sympathy for him.

Lyncoya was raised and educated by the Jacksons as if he were another adopted son. In one of the many contradictions in Jackson's life, he decided to send Andrew Jackson Jr. to Davidson College and Lyncoya to West Point, but Lyncoya became ill and died of tuberculosis at sixteen. A few months later, Rachel died of a heart attack shortly before the Jacksons were to move into the White House.

Andrew Jackson's genuine interest in Lyncoya is a part of his mystery. There is no record he offered any of his slaves the opportunity to be educated or that he viewed female education as a necessary or important thing. Yet American education was changing. During his presidency, Ohio's Oberlin College became the first college in America to open its doors to men and women, whites and blacks.

Shortly after his inauguration, Jackson wrote the Creek peoples, the same tribe of his late adopted son Lyncoya, a letter. Its message was soon extended to all Native Americans living west of the Mississippi River and south of the Ohio River.

> Friends and brothers, listen: Where you live now, you and my white children are too near to each other to live in harmony and peace.... Beyond the great Mississippi, where a part of your nation had gone, your father has provided a country large enough for all of you, and he advises you to remove to it.... There your white brothers will not trouble you; they will have no claim to the land, and you can live upon it, you and all your children, as long as the grass grows or the water runs, in peace and plenty. It will be yours forever.

Whether Jackson's Indian removal policy was a response to the political realities of the time, or because he sincerely believed the only way of saving the Native Americans was to remove them from the path of the land-hungry settlers, the result was the same. Every American president since George Washington had urged that Native Americans become "civilized" by the federal government. Jefferson even said that with "time" and "literacy." "The American Indians might even produce an individual comparable to Isaac Newton." But with the election of Andrew Jackson, the federal government's time and patience in trying to "civilize" their Indian neighbors in their midst had run its course. Presidents Monroe and Adams had drafted Indian removal plans, but never acted on them. Jackson intended to act.

Impatient southern governors and other state and federal officeholders from Jackson's own part of the country threatened to take Indian lands by force if the federal government did not act first. The agricultural techniques favored by southern planters regularly wore out the soil of their plantations and farms. To southerners the solution to the problem was to acquire the ancestral lands of their Cherokee neighbors and repeat the process all over again.

Jackson had a long and friendly relationship with the Cherokee. They had been his loyal allies in his wars against the Creeks. For generations they had been the traditional allies, trading partners, and friends of their advancing American neighbors.

Cherokee women had cultivated the soil for centuries. Of all the First Nations, the Cherokee had been most willing to learn English, convert to Christianity, embrace the idea of owning property, send their children to schools, and educate them in the ways of their European-descended neighbors. In some ways, they were more advanced and civilized. In the year Jackson was elected president, a visitor noted that most of the Cherokee Indian children could read and write and had a centralized democratic government that accepted women's property rights—a claim that could not be made in Jackson's American republic.

Nevertheless, Jackson believed that despite Cherokee accomplishments, the advancing settlers who wanted their land would never accept them as equals. His knowledge of human nature and what land-hungry interlopers were capable of doing was darker than those of his old Cherokee allies. Jackson felt that the declining number of Indians and increasing numbers and demands of settlers would inevitably erupt in terrible violence.

The Cherokee, led by John Ross and his "National Party," rejected any and all proposals to buy or force them off their lands, away from their homes, farms, and schools. Ross gathered a petition signed by 16,000 of the 17,000 Cherokees supporting his position. Federal agents however got several of Ross's political opponents to sign a removal treaty that subsequently passed the United States Senate by one vote. The Cherokee took their case to the Supreme Court, which ruled in their favor, but which Jackson ignored.

John Quincy Adams and others denounced the Indian removal policy as a political payoff to "southern politicians and land grabbers," but Jackson declared the Indians' removal to the west necessary because "there the benevolent may endeavor to teach them the arts of civilization." Privately he may have believed that destroying the Indian way of life in the east, was the only way of preserving it somewhere else.

The expulsion of the Cherokee took place after Jackson left the presidency. It was brutal and deadly. Nearly one out of every four men, women, and children who began the march, died on it. In history it became known as the Trail of Tears. A career soldier who witnessed it later wrote, "I fought through the Civil War and have seen men shot to pieces and slaughtered by thousands, but the Cherokee removal was the cruelest work I ever knew."

Andrew Jackson on the Treatment of Native Americans in His Inaugural Address

"It is my sincere and constant desire to observe toward the Indian Tribes within our limits a just and liberal policy, and to give that humane and considerate attention to their rights and their wants which is consistent with the habits of our Government and the feelings of our people."

Andrew Jackson on Regrets

"It is to be regretted that the rich and powerful too often bend the acts of government to their selfish purposes. Distinctions in society will always exist under every just government. Equality of talents, of education, or of wealth cannot be produced by human institutions."

Andrew Jackson on Being Good Children

"Oh do not cry. Be good children, and we shall all meet in heaven.... I want to meet you all, white and black in Heaven."

Hannah Hoes and Martin Van Buren

"The Village Academy"

Martin Van Buren succeeded his close friend Andrew Jackson to the White House in 1837 and loyally continued his policies. Like Jackson, Van Buren was a widower who portrayed himself as rising to the presidency from humble roots. He wrote in his autobiography, "My father was an unassuming amiable man who was never known to have an enemy. Utterly devoid of any spirit of accumulation, his property, originally moderate, was gradually reduced until he could ill afford to bestow the necessary means upon the education of his children. My advantages, in that respect, were limited to those offered by the Village Academy." Like many "self-made" men, Martin Van Buren was perhaps too modest regarding his economic roots, if not his educational foundations. His father "inherited the family farm, the family's inn and tavern, and an unknown number of slaves." Martin was born in the story-and-a-half home his family shared with his father's tavern on their one-hundred-acre farm. By the time he began school his father owned six slaves.

Van Buren was the first president of the United States born in the United States. All the previous presidents were born British citizens when the original states were English colonies. In some ways, the Van Burens were a typical blended American family of the time. His mother had been married before and brought three children into her marriage with Martin's father. George Washington had four half siblings from his father's first marriage. Van Buren's parents were from immigrant stock. They were second-generation Americans from the Netherlands. Along with many of their neighbors, family, and friends in their New York village of Kinderhook, Dutch was their first language and the language they spoke at home. Martin learned to speak and write English at school, but he always spoke with a Dutch accent.

The year Van Buren was born, the Yale-educated Noah Webster began teaching school in the Hudson River Valley near Martin's hometown. Webster was distressed when he found people speaking "Dutch, French, German, Swedish, Gaelic, and varieties of English [he] had never heard before." The experience convinced the twenty-four-year-old teacher to compile a spelling book and dictionary to transform "the nation from a Babel of conflicting tongues" into "a great nation with a universal language without dialects." Webster's dictionary can still be found in most American classrooms.

Martin Van Buren's teacher was better spoken and better educated than many of the traveling teachers that passed through the Kinderhook Academy.

He told Van Buren's mother her son was the smartest boy in the class, better able to speak and write English than any of his Dutch-speaking classmates—including his classmate and cousin Hannah Hoes whom the future president later married. Hannah was described by a contemporary as "a woman of sweet nature, but few intellectual gifts." Martin, however, preferred the "Babel of conflicting tongues" talking politics in his father's tavern to his school lessons or the allure of his sweet cousin. The tavern stood on the busy post road between the state capital of Albany and New York City, then serving as the nation's first capital. Alexander Hamilton, Aaron Burr, and John Jay were among its many customers.

Martin, Hannah, his three step-siblings and four full siblings all went to the Kinderhook school, but his father's six slaves did not. There is no record the Van Buren slaves received any formal education.

Aside from the Bible and a few of Shakespeare's works, the Kinderhook school had few books. The curriculum consisted of a smattering of Latin and the traditional Rs taught in early nineteenth-century American schools—reading, 'riting, 'rithmatic, religion, and rhetoric. To the disappointment of his teacher, Van Buren left school at fourteen and never returned. As an adult, he admitted having a "secondary intellect ... preferred light reading to heavy" and could only write with an "atrocious scrawl." Outside of politics, he had no intellectual curiosity.

In Van Buren's 800-page autobiography, he dismissed his own school days with one short sentence and never once mentioned his wife and former classmate, who was mother to his four sons. The school dropout later wrote about the pressures he felt due to his lack of education: "How often have I felt the necessity of a regular course of reading to enable me to maintain the reputation I had acquired and to sustain me in my conflicts with able and better educated men."

Despite his lack of additional schooling, Van Buren successfully navigated the political landscape of early nineteenth-century America. He became a New York state senator and attorney general, a United States senator, governor of New York, secretary of state, vice president and then president of the United States. He also insisted his sons acquire the education he lacked; one of them graduated from Yale University and another from West Point.

After becoming successful, Van Buren purchased Lindenwald, one of the largest homes in the village of his youth. Halfway between his mansion and his hometown stood Martin Van Buren's old one-room schoolhouse. The school he left behind and the teacher who never taught him there provided Van Buren's strongest connection to American education.

Years earlier, the author Washington Irving stopped at Lindenwald when visiting Jesse Merwin, a childhood friend then teaching at the Kinderhook Academy. In 1851, Irving reminisced in a letter to the retired teacher, "I should have liked to see the old schoolhouse where after my morning's literary task was over, I used to come and wait for you occasionally until school was dismissed; and you used to promise to keep back the punishment of some little tough broad-bottomed Dutch boy until I should come, for my amusement, but [you] never kept your promise."

It was Washington Irving's teacher friend, Jesse Merwin, whom he mockingly recreated as his fictitious character Ichabod Crane in his story *The Legend of Sleepy Hollow*. In the famed tale, Irving provided a legendary literary description of the sights and sounds of Martin Van Buren's former school.

> His school-house was a low building of one large room, rudely construed of logs; the windows partly glazed, and partly patched with leaves of old copy books.... The schoolhouse stood in a rather lonely, but pleasant situation just at the foot of a woody hill, with a brook running close by, and a formidable birch tree growing at one end of it. From the low murmur of his pupils' voices, conning over their lessons, might be heard in a drowsy summer's day, like the hum of a bee-hive; interrupted now and then by the authoritative voice of the master, in the tone of menace to command; or, peradventure, by the appalling sound of the birch, as he urged some tardy loiterer along the flowery path of knowledge.

Irving also provided a painfully memorable caricature of the early American teacher.

> He was tall, but exceededly lank, with narrow shoulders, long arms and legs, hands that dangled a mile out of his sleeves, feet that might have served as shovels, and his whole frame most loosely hung together. His nose, so that it looked like a weathercock, perched upon his spindle neck, to tell which way the wind blew. To see him striding along the profile of a hill on a windy day, with his clothes bagging and fluttering about him one might have mistaken him for the genius of famine descending upon the earth, or some scarecrow eloped from a cornfield.

Martin Van Buren later befriended the apparently good-natured, good-humored, and very forgiving prototype of "Ichabod Crane," Jesse Merwin, although he never had him as a teacher. Merwin's mother-in-law lived with the retired teacher and spoke the same Dutch dialect of the former president's childhood. Van Buren regularly visited them to converse with the old woman in the first language of his youth.

In 1846, Jesse Merwin traveled to New York to collect money for the Kinderhook Methodist Episcopal Church Temperance Fund. He took with him a letter of introduction from former president Martin Van Buren that read, "This is to certify that I have known Jesse Merwin Esq. of Kinderhook for about a third of a century, and believe him to be a man of honor and integrity; and that he is the same person celebrated in the writings of Washington Irving under the character of Ichabod Crane in his famous *Legend of Sleepy Hollow*." Apparently Merwin was willing to associate himself with the buffoonish image that haunted the teaching profession for years to come, an image that outlived the author, the teacher, and the president from Old Kinderhook.

The eighth president of the United States, like several of his predecessors, reflected the commonly held racial and educational attitudes of early nineteenth-century America. Education in moderation and the institution of slavery were tolerated, but the two did not go together. Education for slaves, even free blacks, was not acceptable. Like many of his contemporaries, Martin Van Buren seemed to believe the best education for slaves was no education, and the way to begin to "civilize" Native Americans was to move them away from American civilization. It was a myopic but genuinely accepted view at that time and place in history.

Martin Van Buren's Presidential Message on the Cultivation of the Indian Mind

"The decrease in the number of the tribes within the limit of the States and territories has been most rapid. If they can be removed, they can be protected, from those associations and evil practices which exert so pernicious and destructive influence over their destinies. They can be induced to labor and to acquire property, and its acquisition will inspire them with a feeling of independence. Their minds can be cultivated, and they can be taught the value of salutary and uniform laws and be made sensible of the blessings of free government."

Anna Symmes and William Henry Harrison
"He Can Neither Breed, Plead, Nor Preach"

In 1841, William Henry Harrison followed Martin Van Buren to the White House. In many ways he and his wife represented three competing visions of early nineteenth century America. They were well-educated gentry from the east, established southern aristocrats, and rough-and-tumble pioneers of the western frontier. It was the last image that helped him get elected president.

Harrison never attended a day of school outside his Virginia plantation home until leaving for college when he was fourteen. The youngest of seven, he was homeschooled and drilled in the classics by private tutors. His father was a political contemporary and sometime adversary of Jefferson, Madison, and Monroe. But like them, he had concerns about the turmoil and Loyalist conservatism of William and Mary College during the Revolution. Harrison's father decided to send his son to Hampden-Sydney College, a small liberal arts college with fewer ties to England.

Like most colleges of the time, Hampden-Sydney College offered a classical curriculum consisting of Latin and Greek and other coursework most Americans would never need, read, or use during their lifetimes. Harrison proved to be an excellent student but did not stay there long. Thomas Jefferson noted that many students were driven away from the school when it was swept by a Methodist frenzy of evangelism. William Henry Harrison was among them. Family tradition reports that his father's Episcopalian sensibilities were offended causing him to withdraw his son. William's father however continued to be heavily involved in his son's studies, a practice the future president later continued with his own sons.

In 1790, the seventeen-year-old William Henry Harrison traveled to Richmond, Virginia, to study medicine. The following year his father sent him to the University of Pennsylvania for further study with the renowned Dr. Benjamin Rush. William's academic motivation and career ended with his father's unexpected death. He quit school to become a soldier on the western frontier. It was there he met his future wife.

Anna Symmes was born in the comfortable New Jersey farmhouse of her parents in 1775. Shortly after her birth, her mother died and her father was commissioned as a colonel in the American Revolutionary army. During the war years Anna was raised and homeschooled in the Long Island home of her maternal grandparents. When she was old enough to begin her formal schooling, they took full advantage of the growing educational opportunities available for wealthy females. She was sent to the Clinton Academy for Young Girls which gave her a firm foundation in academics and the domestic arts. She was then sent to the Isabella Marshall Graham Boarding and Finishing School in New York City. There one of her classmates was Nelly Custis, Martha Washington's talented granddaughter.

At nineteen, Anna followed her father and her new stepmother to North Bend, Indiana, the Northwest Territory of the American frontier. It was during a stay with an older sister in Kentucky that she met William Henry Harrison who soon began courting her. Anne's father was less than happy that his highly educated daughter was involved with a mere soldier. He acknowledged that Harrison had "understanding, prudence, education, and resources in conversation, and ... property, but what is to be lamented is, that he has no profession but that of arms."

The couple married against her father's wishes, causing him to write in resignation, "He can neither breed, plead, nor preach, and if he could plow I would be satisfied. His best prospect is in the army, he has talents, and if he can dodge [bullets for] a few years, it is probable he may become conspicuous."

Following their wedding Anna embraced the role of an army officer's wife, regularly uprooting herself to follow her husband's latest posting. Their married life began in a log cabin built by Harrison a short distance from Cincinnati. They briefly moved east but soon returned to the edge of the western frontier.

Their final house in Vincennes, Indiana, was built as both a home and a fort, with heavy shutters, eighteen-inch thick walls and sharpshooter holes in attic windows for protection from Indian attacks. It was a difficult rugged existence.

Horace Mann, the father of American public education, once visited their simple home and wrote, "The furniture of the parlor could not have drawn very largely upon anyone's resources. The walls were ornamented with a few portraits, some in frames, some disembodied from a frame. The drawing room was fitted up in more modern styles; but the whole furniture and ornaments in these rooms might have cost $200 or $250."

Anna's sense of isolation was captured in a letter she wrote to a cousin also living on the frontier: "I should like to know whether your father is still living, and how many brothers and sisters you have, indeed anything and everything that relates to any of my relations, friends or relatives, will be truly grateful to me, in this far off country."

Over the years the Harrison family grew to include ten children. William entrusted the early education of their young daughters and sons entirely to his wife. Only when the boys grew older did he dictate to them the educational and career choices he expected each to follow.

In the isolation and loneliness of frontier life, Anna used her eastern education to good advantage. Whenever she could hire a traveling teacher, she housed and fed them in the Harrison home. When no teachers were available, she taught her own children and the children of far-flung neighbors who traveled to her home to benefit from her teaching. Anna Symmes Harrison is credited with founding one of the first schools in the west when Indiana was still considered an uncharted wilderness of unfriendly Indians and wild game.

William Henry Harrison devoted much of his military career, public service, and private activities to removing the Indians from the lands of their ancestors and turning the land over to settlers and slaveholders. Berkeley, the large home of Harrison's youth, was one of the most historic plantations in Virginia. In 1622 it was the site of an Indian massacre that eventually claimed the lives of nearly one-third of the entire white population of the colony. By the time William was born, the Indians were gone. But the stories of the massacres were the stories of his childhood. His playmates were the children of the slaves serving his family. But all the children at Berkeley, white and black, were brought up hearing frightening tales about the Indians. The stories shaped his attitudes toward the way he viewed the land and the native people who claimed it. From before he could walk he learned that Indians were bad, slavery was good, and the white man was the master.

Harrison considered himself a child of the American Revolution. He believed he understood America and its needs, wants, and dreams better than most men. His father was a delegate to the first and second Continental Congress where his roommate was his close friend George Washington. Harrison's father was also a signer of the Declaration of Independence who became governor of

Virginia by defeating fellow patriot Thomas Jefferson for the position As a young soldier on the American frontier, Harrison felt it his duty to clear the Indians off the western lands and turn that land over to white settlers and their slaves. It was a policy he actively pursued for the rest of his life.

Anna accepted the views of her father and her husband who both became western land speculators. There is no evidence she provided any education to the seven slaves William inherited from his father or the indentured servants who worked on the 2,800 acres of land they eventually purchased and farmed.

In 1798 Harrison left the army to become the secretary and sometimes acting governor of the Northwest Territory. He later became a nonvoting delegate to Congress representing the vast Territory. While there, he refused to pursue an investigation into why the law was not being enforced to set aside land in the region to support public education. It was not that Harrison opposed education. But he was aware an investigation would reveal that powerful land speculators, like he and his father-in-law, were refusing to divert profits from their land deals into paying for public schools. Anne Symmes' father had received 1,000,000 acres of government land and wanted to keep his profits in the family.

In 1800, President John Adams appointed Harrison territorial governor of the Indiana territory, an area that at that time included all of what was to become Indiana, Illinois, Wisconsin and large tracks of Minnesota and Michigan. Harrison worked to remove the existing Native Americans from the land, and if possible expand slavery into the Northwest Territory. His Indian removal policies proved popular and successful with pioneers, but his proslavery positions were not.

Nevertheless, Harrison was later returned to Congress. He had been a self-educated soldier, reading Cicero's *Orations* and every book he was able to find on ancient warfare when he was a raw recruit. His childhood and his years on the frontier had taught him the need to be ever vigilant and prepared. When he became a congressman, Harrison proposed that every public school in America incorporate military training into its curriculum, but his proposal was never brought out of committee for a vote.

In 1840, the sixty-eight-year-old Harrison came out of retirement to run for president. His successful election campaign presented him as a rugged frontiersman and Indian fighter, rather than the educated, slaveholding son of a Virginia governor. He died after serving only one month in office and before his wife even moved to the White House. Anna Symmes Harrison, however, had the distinction of being the first first lady to have received a formal education. She remained in her home in Indiana and helped educate her grandson Benjamin Harrison who later became the twenty-third president of the United States. Anna died in 1864 just as the Civil War was settling the slavery question that had occupied much of her husband's career.

William Henry Harrison to His Son

"If you have not the Perfect Education which I design for you — you shall in your future life blame yourself for the misfortune."

Anna Symmes Harrison to Her Son

"I hope my dear, you will always bear upon your mind that you are born to die and we know not how soon death may overtake us, it will be of little consequence if we are rightly prepared for the event." Anna Harrison outlived her husband and nine of her ten children.

Letitia Christian, Julia Gardiner, and John Tyler
"The Rebellious Former Student, Lived and Died a Rebel"

John Tyler, the aristocratic vice president who became president after Harrison's death, grew up on a thousand-acre Virginia plantation near Harrison's childhood home. Tyler's privileged way of life was made possible by forty unschooled slaves who served his family. When he was seven, his mother died, and John's previously docile school days became noted for occasional outbursts. His angry outbursts caused problems for all but the most skilled teacher. Such teachers were hard to find and difficult to keep.

The age of preacher-teachers was dying out. In the first decades of the nineteenth century, most teachers were young unmarried men traveling from one schoolhouse to another to teach whenever and wherever they could keep a job. They taught children of all ages, lived with the families of their students, and were only paid if they could control their scholars. Teaching a few basic skills was expected; but classroom control and discipline was always the first order of business and the first testing point for students. There were always students who enjoyed outsmarting their teachers, and some who delighted in driving them out of the schoolhouse. Washington Irving's fictional Ichabod Crane was not the only teacher to suddenly vanish before the end of the school term. Life in nineteenth-century classrooms often witnessed a battle of wits, a battle of wills, and at times a physical battle of strength. By the time he was eleven, John Tyler was more than up to the challenge.

John McMurdo was Tyler's Scottish schoolmaster who ruled his classroom with a birch switch and iron hand. Tyler's classmates were all the sons of Virginia slaveholders, more used to giving orders than receiving them. Most felt their teacher's switch at one time or the other. Tyler later recalled, "It was a wonder that he did not whip all the senses out of his scholars." As one of the quietest and smallest boys in class, Tyler was usually adept at avoiding harsh punishments; but that did not mean his sense of justice or entitlement could not reach a breaking point. It was Tyler who led a revolt against McMurdo, knocking him down, thrashing him thoroughly, binding him hand and foot, throwing him in the closet, and leaving him there at the end of the school day. Some hours later a neighbor heard screaming coming from the schoolhouse and found the unhappy schoolmaster tied up in the closet.

McMurdo marched to the Tyler plantation and told John's father of the class rebellion and his son's role in it. His harsh teaching methods were well known, tolerated by parents only because they seemed to be working. But since his actions triggered a successful mutiny, Mr. Tyler blamed McMurdo. He dismissed the teacher with the Latin motto of Virginia: "Sic Semper Tyrannis"— "Ever thus to Tyrants." John Tyler's father believed a nineteenth-century teacher unable to control his students was like an overseer unable to control his slaves. Neither deserved his job or his wages. Teaching in the Golden Age of Education was not for the faint of heart.

In 1807 fourteen-year-old John Tyler entered William and Mary College. He graduated four years later listening to a commencement address on female education. No predictions were made at the time of when a woman or anyone besides white males might someday attend the college, but it was a long wait. It took one hundred and eleven years before a white woman was admitted to the school, and one hundred and thirty years for a student of Asian descent to be accepted there. But it was one hundred and fifty three years later, ten years after the United States Supreme Court outlawed public school segregation, that an African American woman became the college's first black student in residence.

John Tyler loved William and Mary College. Later in his life he served on its board and eventually became its chancellor, a position originally created for George Washington. He involved himself in hiring faculty, stabilizing its finances, upgrading its campus, and regularly speaking at graduation ceremonies. One of his sons later even served as president of the school. Tyler was a strong believer in education. Early in his career he served as governor of Virginia. Like Thomas Jefferson, he proposed "a system of public schools for all classes of people." And like Jefferson, Tyler meant schools for white males. Nothing came of his proposal.

He married twice. His first wife, Letitia Christian, received a traditional domestic arts education not very different from Tyler's distant cousin Martha Washington. Letitia never attended school but was an avid reader with a fine head for business. She was able to successfully run a plantation in the absence of her husband and supervise the education of their eight children. Her daughters and sons were tutored at home, but the sons were later sent to boarding school to prepare for William and Mary College. Letitia Christian Tyler's interest in education did not extend to slaves—a position supported by her husband.

In regards to his own children, John Tyler believed in education. One biographer noted, "Evidence of sloppy penmanship, academic malingering and superficial thought brought instant paternal condemnation." Tyler wrote his fifteen-year-old daughter,

> Your resolution to attend to your studies and not to be led away by the vanities of the world affords me sincere pleasure. Without intellectual improvements, the most beautiful of the sex is but a figure of wax work. The world is but a sealed book to such a one; and to eat, to drink, to dance, to sleep, to gaze upon objects without seeing them, and to move in creation with scarcely a sense of anything, is a poor existence.... The mind has been compared to the marble in the quarry, ere the light of science has shed its rays upon it; but when instructed and informed, like that same marble formed into a beautiful statue and polished by the hand of the artist.

Tyler married his second wife Julia Gardiner twenty-one months after Letitia died in the White House. Julia was thirty years younger than President Tyler, and they would have seven children together. She grew up on a large estate on Long Island. Until four years before her birth, the estate was serviced by unschooled black and Indian slaves. Her family reluctantly freed their slaves after New York State abolished slavery in 1816.

Gardiner's two brothers attended Princeton where her older brother Alexander delivered a school address that captured the growing American belief in education. In it he proclaimed,

> Be not deceived on the importance of knowledge. Who are they that govern the land? Who are they that direct enterprise? Who are they that accumulate wealth? Behold the triumph of the educated!

The Gardiners clearly believed in education—for people like the Gardiners. In the same speech Alexander denounced the nation's growing number of abolitionists who advocated legally abolishing slavery and emancipating the country's slaves. He called such troublemakers "cunning ... demagogues" who "violated the rights of property and person, and trampled on the laws of this country."

Julia Gardiner and her sister attended the finest private high school for girls then available in New York City. The school epitomized the sanitized direction American female education was taking. Its strict curriculum was carefully constructed to avoid encouraging any critical thinking and was taught in a manner that never addressed "life itself." Girls studied "music, French literature, ancient history, arithmetic, and composition—nothing controversial, nothing transcending the superficially literate polish the young ladies were sent there to acquire."

John and Julia Tyler lived together in the White House for less than a year.

Lacking the common touch many had come to expect of the nation's first family, Tyler was not nominated for reelection in 1844. He and Julia left Washington but not the public stage. In 1853 Julia wrote an article in the Southern Literary Messenger defending slavery as a civilizing institution. Mrs. James K. Polk and other prominent slaveholders sent her their warm "congratulations." But Harriet Jacobs, a former slave, offered a different response. She questioned how slavery could be a "civilizing institution" when blacks were denied an education and any opportunity to learn to read and write. The former first lady did not reply. When the Civil War broke out in 1861, Julia Tyler followed her husband's lead and actively supported the "Great Rebellion." True to his childhood self, John Tyler the rebellious former student, lived and died a rebel.

John Tyler to His College-Age Sons

"I would have you go into genteel company when you can do so without neglecting your studies."

"I regard you as lying under the strongest obligations of honor to abide rigidly by the college laws.... Be affable and polite to all the students, without cultivating extreme intimacy with any. Do not be too captious or prone to take offense.... A suavity of manners—a constant respect for the feelings of others is indispensably necessary for success in life."

John Tyler to His Oldest Daughter

He reminded her that an educated woman must "exhibit no temper.... Remember the maxim of Mr. Jefferson, in which he bids you, 'if you are angry count ten, if you are very angry count an hundred,' before you speak."

Julia Gardiner Tyler's Response in the Richmond Enquirer

To the Duchess of Sutherland who publicly asked that southern women condemn slavery, she replied, "Spare from the well-fed Negros ... one drop of your super abounding sympathy to pour into that bitter cup [of Ireland] which is overrunning with sorrow ... relieve many a poor female of England, who is now cold and shivering.... We are content to leave England in the enjoyment of her peculiar institutions; and we must insist on the right to regulate ours without her aid. I pray you bear in mind that the golden rule of life is for each to attend to his own business, and let his neighbor's alone!"

Sarah Childress and James K. Polk

"Her Occupation as a School Teacher
Barred Her from Social Equality"

James K. Polk, America's next president, was homeschooled by his parents on his family's Carolina farm for the first ten years of his life. Later his family, accompanied by their unschooled slaves, moved to Tennessee. Polk's poor health kept him close to home and he received no formal education until he was eighteen. At that point he could barely read or write, yet he was sent to a school run by a Presbyterian preacher-teacher to study Greek and Latin.

Polk proved to be a good student and progressed so quickly that within a year he transferred to the Murfreesboro Academy to study mathematics, philosophy, and the sciences. He was then admitted to the University of North Carolina as a twenty-four-year-old incoming student. Within two years Polk graduated with honors in mathematics, but he severely damaged his health in the process. His final oral exams in "algebra, geometry, and English grammar" placed him at the top of his class, and he was allowed to present his class's commencement address in Latin. Following an extended period of rest, he returned home and apprenticed himself to a local attorney to study law. Polk met his future wife Sarah Childress in 1819 shortly after she completed her own education.

Sarah's intelligence and love of politics immediately attracted Polk's attention. Her father, one of the wealthiest men in Tennessee, wanted all his children to have the best education money could buy. After his daughters graduated from the local public school, Mr. Childress arranged for them to be instructed by the principal of the Murfreesboro Academy where her brothers and her future husband were enrolled.

She and her sister were then sent to Mr. Abercrombie's Finishing School for Young Ladies in Nashville. While there she began a friendship with Rachel and Andrew Jackson — a friendship that shaped the rest of her life.

When her brother Anderson went to the University of North Carolina at Chapel Hill in 1817, Sarah, her older sister, and a family slave traveled with him to attend a nearby school in the town of Salem. The 500-mile journey on horseback took them one month to complete. Once there, the sisters enrolled in the widely respected Moravian Female Academy. The academy was one of the few schools in America that offered girls the opportunity to study serious academic subjects such as Greek and Roman literature, history, English, and geography as well as the more traditional courses in the Bible, drawing, music, and needlework. Many considered it "the most superior girl's school in America."

Her father's death caused Sarah and her sister to return to Tennessee where Andrew Jackson acted as a matchmaker. He supposedly told Polk to marry Sarah, "who will never give you any trouble. Her wealthy family, education, health and appearance are all superior." But he cautioned the young lawyer to not marry until he was financially able to provide for her future. Four years later they wed, and in time became not only lifelong partners but a powerful political team. One friend later wrote, "Their character gradually expanded, unfolded, and rose under the mutually stimulating, helpful, and elevating power of thoroughly congenial daily intercourse, in which one was exactly complemented by the other."

Twenty years later they moved into the White House. A snobbishly proud Sarah Childress Polk gloried where her education, her marriage, her hard work, and her social position had taken her. One of her first acts as first lady was to remove all the longtime servants in the White House. She replaced them with freshly bought slaves or slaves brought from her husband's plantation. Mrs. Polk wanted no confusion regarding who was the absolute mistress of her new home.

When a schoolteacher on a White House tour cheerfully informed the new first lady it was her first visit to the mansion, Mrs. Polk said she was not surprised. Although she said she was sure the "lady was a woman of culture and of high character her occupation of school teacher barred her from social equality." Sarah Polk could not have imagined that in a few short years the new president and first lady would both be former teachers.

The Polks never had any children, but as the oldest of ten, James and Sarah filled the White House with nieces and nephews. James also tried to provide an education for his younger brothers and nephews, but without success. His brother Marshall was expelled from both Georgetown and West Point, and his youngest brother Sam was expelled from Yale University. Sam came to live with the future president who personally supervised his studies hoping this favorite younger brother might return to school. But Sam died within a year and Marshall died in prison. Although women were beginning to be admitted for the first time into some colleges, none of James or Sarah's nieces were provided an opportunity to receive a higher education.

Despite Polk's admission that slaves were "rational ... human beings," the Polks also never felt the need to provide an education for the two slaves he inherited from his father, the ten slaves Sarah brought into their marriage, the several slaves they brought to the White House, or the more than fifty slaves they claimed as "property" during their lifetime.

Polk requested in his last will and testament that after his wife's death his slaves should be freed. He died shortly after leaving the presidency, but Sarah lived another forty-two years. None of the Polk slaves were freed until she was forced to emancipate them during the Civil War. No female relatives or slave was ever offered or provided an education that might have helped them establish the kind of secure economic life President and Mrs. Polk enjoyed.

James K. Polk Diary Entry for July 16, 1846

On providing financial support for education, he wrote, "I am applied to almost daily and sometimes half a dozen times a day for money.... They call on me to contribute to build Academies, to aid colleges.... I am compelled to decline.... The idea seems to be prevalent that the President is from a position compelled to contribute to every loafer who applies, provided he represents that the sum he wants is to build ... an academy, or a college.... They may censure and slander me, but better this than to be rendered bankrupt without contributing to the public good."

Sarah Childress Polk on Why Education Was Not for Everyone.

"The writers of the Declaration of Independence were mistaken when they affirmed that all men are created equal. There are ... men toiling in the heat of the sun while ... I am sitting here fanning myself. Those men did not chose such a lot in life, neither did we ask for ours. We were created for these places."

Margaret Smith and Zachary Taylor

"Of Very Ordinary Capacity"

Zachary and Margaret Taylor became the next White House residents. Sarah Polk, as she did on most matters, had a strong opinion regarding the new president. "He is uneducated, exceedingly ignorant of public affairs, and, I should judge, of very ordinary capacity."

According to family legends Taylor was born in the Virginia of 1784 as his family was making their way to their new home in Kentucky. His educated parents were from well-established Virginia families, but the depleted soil of the family farm and the promise of better, cheaper, and more plentiful land out west caused them to move their family and slaves. It was the beginning of a lifetime of moving from place to place for Zachary Taylor.

Taylor and his two older brothers were taught to read and write by their mother, who had been educated by European-trained tutors. She then shared that experience with all six of her children, but none of the family slaves.

Except for his own family and their slaves, Zachary's childhood years in the Kentucky wilderness were spent in isolation. A visitor recalled, "Here we were saluted every night with the howling of wolves." By the time Taylor was six, a dirt-floored one-room log cabin schoolhouse had been built a far distance from his home. He briefly attended school there whenever a teacher could be found to teach, but his education was inconsistent and incomplete.

With the help of his slaves, his father's farm grew to one thousand acres, allowing Zachary to roam and explore in all directions. As a boy he loved being in nature and could read and understand the natural world better than he could read and appreciate books. Learning the skills and particulars of hunting and fishing was his curriculum of choice, and he took more pride in swimming the Ohio River back and forth from Kentucky to Indiana than in literary pursuits.

His first teacher reported that he was "quick in learning and still patient in study," but traditional schooling did not stick with him. Taylor was briefly taught by three different itinerant teachers. One tried to give him a foundation in the classics, but it seemed wasted on him. Although bright and alert, his handwriting, grammar, and spelling remained nearly impossible to read.

During the American Revolution, Taylor's father served under Patrick Henry as a lieutenant in the First Virginia Regiment. By the end of the war he was a lieutenant general. Zachary Taylor knew from his earliest memories that he too wanted to be a soldier. In 1808 he joined the army, traveled to New Orleans, and quickly became ill with dysentery. He was sent home to recover in Kentucky where he met and later married Margaret Mackall Smith.

Smith had been born, raised, and homeschooled on her father's Maryland plantation. Like Anna Symmes Harrison, she was a childhood friend of Martha Washington's granddaughter Nelly Custis, but was not provided similar educational opportunities. Instead she was trained in the traditional domestic arts expected of a well-bred Southern girl. In addition to music, embroidery, reading, writing, dancing, and riding, she learned the basic arithmetic and management skills that might someday be needed to manage a plantation.

Margaret followed her husband's military career for nearly forty years. Since Taylor was not a graduate of West Point and lacked the educational credentials of many other officers, his promotions through army ranks were slow. General Winfield Scott, a fellow officer and college graduate wrote, "General Taylor's mind had not been enlarged and refreshed by reading, or much converse with the world.... He was quite ignorant for his rank, and quite bigoted in his ignorance." The Taylors were frequently assigned to obscure military outposts from Florida to Minnesota to Missouri, where better educated and better connected officers did not want to serve. At times Margaret lived in tents, forts, log cabins, or poorly constructed barracks, the only woman on an army base completely surrounded by men. Taylor once told Jefferson Davis, "You know my wife was as much of a soldier as I was."

The Taylors did not mind their restless military life but were determined that their children not be handicapped by the lack of education that had haunted their own rootless existence. When they were young, the children were homeschooled or the Taylors hired tutors to educate them. But as soon as possible, they were sent east to boarding schools. In 1837, Taylor asked for a leave of absence to, "visit my children who are in schools in Philadelphia and Kentucky, and who have been absent for ... several years." Each child received a superior education, but their parents' fierce commitment to their schooling caused years of separation and loneliness. At times the Taylor children must have felt like hostages to their parents' educational dreams.

Their youngest child and only son, Richard, whom they described as "warm and affectionate," was sent away to a Kentucky boarding school when he was ten. He did not see his parents again until he was nineteen. From Kentucky, he was sent to a prep school in Boston, then overseas to study in Edinburgh and Paris, and finally to Yale. At Yale, he did not hear from his parents for a full year and a half. By the time he graduated, he was "fluent in French ... a student of Spanish, a tireless reader, fond of history, and master of a ready wit," but a stranger to his mother and father. A breach opened between them that was never repaired. Asked at one point how his son was doing in school, Zachary Taylor honestly admitted, "In consequence of having been separated from him, I am not sufficiently acquainted with the progress he has made."

Despite their hopes that their children would escape lives spent on lonely military bases, their son became a soldier and their three daughters all married military men. At one point, Taylor exploded, "I will be damned if another daughter of mine shall marry into the Army. I scarcely know my own children or they me." Later in his life Taylor ruefully concluded it was, "better to make no very great calculations as regards the prominent positions our children are to occupy ... they are rarely realized."

During Taylor's military career, he and Margaret worked to improve the quality of schools on or near army bases. At one remote posting on an upper branch of the Wisconsin and Mississippi Rivers, Taylor supported the construction of a "voluntarily" school for the children of the Winnebago tribe. A stone schoolhouse was built on the Yellow River in Iowa that offered "reading, writing, arithmetic, gardening, agriculture, carding, spinning, weaving, sewing ... and such other branches of useful knowledge as the President of the United States may prescribe."

Margaret helped supervise the instruction of the Winnebago children. She also served as their protector against the powerful agents of the American Fur Company who did not want Indians to be educated or quit trading animal pelts. Taylor quickly became frustrated by the well-connected political machinations of the fur trappers and the indifference of the federal government in maintaining the school. When he was posted to St. Louis, he happily left the school behind him.

Margaret Taylor's interest in schools, the education of her own children, and the children of Native Americans never extended to the one hundred and eighteen slaves working on her husband's two plantations or the sixty-four additional slaves he bought during his sixteen months as president. She had not wanted him to become president and had no desire to serve as first lady.

After moving into the executive mansion, Margaret became a near recluse. Following her husband's death, she retired to her home in Louisiana and reportedly devoted her last years to quietly teaching Sunday school at her local church. Vice President Millard and his wife, both former schoolteachers, moved into the White House in 1850.

Zachary Taylor on Education

"Education will be of little service ... unless practice be blended with theory."

"There is nothing more important to ensure a young man a high standing either in the army or navy than literary attainments."

"The rearing up our children and establishing them in life so that they can sustain themselves is in my opinion the most important of our duties."

Abigail Powers and Millard Fillmore
"A Very Rough and Uncultivated Place"

Millard Fillmore was taught to read by his mother using the only three books she owned: a Bible, an almanac, and a hymnal. His only other opportunity for formal schooling was during the winter months when harsh weather allowed him a brief respite from boyhood chores. He explained in his autobiography, "I could not be spared from the farm during the summer, and therefore, only attended school for two or three months in the winter. Consequently I forgot nearly as much as I learned."

Fillmore later described his first school:

> [It was] an old deserted log house, which had been furnished with a few benches without backs, and a board for writing upon. In this school I learned my alphabet, at the age of six or seven. Of course, nothing was taught but the most simple lessons in spelling and reading.... When I was about ten years old, a man ... gave some instruction in writing and arithmetic, and drilled us most thoroughly in Webster's spelling books. I think I went through that book without missing the spelling of a word; but I did not learn the definition of a single one. In fact, there was no such thing as a dictionary in school.... I acquired some knowledge of arithmetic and read Dwight's old geography.... [But without] a map or atlas in school ... I never saw either till I was nineteen years of age.

The future president began regularly visiting a local library but was frustrated because he could not understand what he read. He saved his money and purchased his own dictionary, but he still found reading and grammar a challenge. Despite his own lack of education, he got a job teaching in a one-room schoolhouse. Little had changed since Andrew Jackson taught, except a few intrepid women with a little education had also begun to teach. Fillmore's salary was ten dollars a month, more money than he had ever had his entire life, but he had to deal with difficult students and their equally difficult parents. He later wrote about being a teacher in 1818 rural America:

> The winter I was eighteen years of age, I was employed to teach ... at ... a very rough and uncultivated place, where the boys, the winter before, had driven the teacher out and broken up the school. It was not long before I saw that the question of who was master had got to be decided. One of the boys set my authority at defiance, — evidently with the intention of bringing on a fight. I ordered him up for chastisement. Immediately, the larger boys sprang to their feet, and one attempted to seize the wooden poker, but I told him to sit down — and they obeyed. I punished the guilty one without further interference; but it raised a breeze in the neighborhood. A school meeting was called, which I was invited to attend, and did. I then found it to be represented, that I punished scholars with the poker. I stated the facts, and told them that I was ready to quit the school if they desired it, but that while I remained, I should be the master, even if I used the poker in self-defense. After some discussion they concluded that the school should go on, and I had no further trouble.

Teaching frustrated Fillmore because it continually reminded him of how little he knew. When the term ended, he decided to return to school as a student. The nineteen-year-old traveled to a nearby town to enroll in a school taught by an experienced twenty-two-year-old teacher named Abigail Powers. Powers had been teaching since she was sixteen years old. Fillmore discovered he was the oldest student in her class, yet he didn't mind. He quickly fell in love with her but was too poor and too shy to do anything about it. At the end of the school term, Abigail moved away and successfully started her own school for girls. But they remained in contact and she encouraged him to continue his education.

Within a year Fillmore returned to teaching, and his father and family friends arranged for him to apprentice with a judge to study law. Years later he wrote of the moment he discovered he would be able to further his education:

> Some persons, without my knowledge, had suggested to my father that it was possible for me to be something more ... and he was induced to apply to Judge Wood to know if he would receive me into his office.... I knew nothing of this, until at the dinner table, my mother informed me of it; and the news was so sudden and unexpected that, in spite of myself, I burst out crying, and had to leave the table, much to my mortification.

As he studied the law, he and Abigail continued teaching at different schools. Seven years after he became her student, she became his wife. Almost all female teachers in early nineteenth-century America remained unmarried. If they wed, they were expected to resign immediately. But Abigail did not quit teaching and remained in the classroom until she had their first child. The young couple needed the money, and she enjoyed being a teacher. When she entered the White House she was the first wife of a president to have had a career.

The Fillmores both loved to read, and their favorite form of relaxation was reading aloud to one another. Abigail founded her town's first public circulation library and continued buying her own books until she eventually accumulated over 4,000 volumes. In 1850 the former teachers brought their love of reading to the White House but found no books there. Abigail devoted her time and energy to creating a White House library for future residents.

During his term as president, Fillmore became a quiet supporter of the social reformer Dorothea Dix. Dix, like Fillmore and his wife, was a former teacher. She was one of the first national advocates to encourage education and hospitalization for the mentally handicapped rather than imprisonment and harsh punishments. The Dix-Fillmore correspondence continued for nearly twenty years. In September 1850, Fillmore wrote Dix, "If I can do anything in your work of mercy, command me and I am at your service." In October of that year he wrote again, "In looking over the pamphlets which you sent me I was struck with the large number of insane in some of our penitentiaries, and horrified at some of the statements that they were insane when convicted and sent to prison."

Many politicians, educators, and clergymen vehemently opposed Dix's controversial efforts, but Fillmore urged her on. In 1851, Dix wrote Fillmore of the intolerance that confronted her as she tried to educate an uninterested country about the need to help the mentally handicapped. "Of all the fanaticism, the fanaticism of ignorance is the most hopeless." President Fillmore sympathized with Dix. He believed, as she did, in the need for humane treatment of the mentally ill, but he left the presidency before he was able to use his office to support her efforts. It would be over a century before an American president embraced education as a mental health issue.

Abigail Fillmore's health declined during her years as first lady. Her daughter Mary, who was also a teacher, stepped in to serve as hostess of the White House. Shortly after Fillmore left the presidency, his wife and daughter both died. The grief-stricken Fillmore traveled to England where Queen Victoria exclaimed he was the "handsomest man she had ever met." During his visit he turned down an honorary degree from Oxford University because it was written in Latin. Fillmore humbly explained, "No man should, in my judgment, accept a degree he cannot read."

Fillmore ran for the presidency again in 1856 on the American Party ticket. The new party was born as a backlash to the growing numbers of immigrants entering the country. It was anti-immigrant, anti–Catholic, and anti–Irish and had the unique distinction of being the first major political party in the nation's history to dedicate two planks in its party platform to education. The first urged that all public school teachers be of the Protestant faith and would bar all Catholics from teaching in public schools. The second mandated daily readings from the King James or Protestant Bible in any tax-supported schools. Fillmore and the American Party carried only one state and received only 24 percent of the national vote.

Much of the rest of Fillmore's life was devoted to education. He was an "enthusiastic" supporter of the racially segregated Buffalo public school system, strongly favored the teaching of science in schools, and was one of the founders of the University of Buffalo Medical College. Fillmore served as the college's first chancellor, helped hire its faculty, presided over commencements, and passed out degrees. He continued in the post before, during, and after his White House years.

Millard Fillmore was a poor boy who believed in education, become a teacher, and served as president of the United States. Like Andrew Jackson before him, he was a man of many contradictions. Fillmore favored educating and humanely treating the mentally handicapped, and strongly supported public education, if students were segregated by race and not taught by Catholic teachers. He was also an early advocate of having science classes join daily Bible readings as part of the school curriculum. Fillmore seemed confident and comfortable that the racial and religious attitudes of nineteenth-century students would not be threatened by modern science or the Christian Bible.

Millard Fillmore on Education

"There are two educations—scholastic and practical. Books are of value, but in all professions practice was the great teacher."

Abigail Powers Fillmore

As a teacher and mother, she wrote in a letter to her ten-year-old son at boarding school, "Take pains my dear little boy that every letter we receive from you is written better than the last one."

In a letter to her absent husband, she wrote, "I wish you could read to me as you frequently have done after I sit down to sewing."

Jane Appleton and Franklin Pierce

"There Are Scores of Men in the Country That Seem Brighter than He Is"

In 1852 Franklin Pierce followed Millard Fillmore into the White House. A biographer of Pierce noted that as a student, "the boy was not particularly fond of school." Pierce found the social part of school to his liking, but not the academics. He followed a family tradition. His oldest brother was expelled from Dartmouth College. His next brother never even considered college and the brother closest to him in age flunked out of West Point. Nothing but the most basic education was ever considered for any female in the family; but Pierce's father was determined Franklin, his fourth son, would be a college graduate.

Pierce attended a public one-room schoolhouse two miles from his New Hampshire home until the age of twelve when he was sent to boarding school. He quickly decided he had enough education. Pierce walked fifteen miles home rehearsing all the reasons he should be allowed to quit school. His surprised father did not reprimand Franklin, had him join the family for dinner, then hitched up the family carriage and drove him half-way back to school. He asked him to get out, turned the carriage around, and told him, "Now remember not to come home again until you're asked." Pierce's father then drove away. On the long walk back to school, a thunderstorm broke out and soaked him to the skin. By the time he arrived there, he had a deeper appreciation of how serious his father was about him pursuing his education.

Shortly after turning fifteen, Pierce left his first boarding school to study Latin and Greek at the Francestown Academy. There he became known for his hunting, fishing, and social skills. Pierce also earned a reputation for getting by with as little academic effort as possible, yet he seldom got in trouble for it. His charm, good looks, and endearing personality allowed him a great deal of leeway with school authorities. Like most of the boys at school he often broke rules, but unlike them, he never flaunted or felt the need to advertise his misconduct. The future president hated unpleasant confrontations. At Francestown the athletic outdoorsman often stayed inside to tutor a struggling classmate in lessons he himself had ignored. Such kindness endeared him to students and teachers alike.

Pierce traveled to Maine to take the college entrance exam for Bowdoin College. He was tested on his Latin grammar, geography, arithmetic, Cicero's select orations, and "other classical texts." Pierce did well in everything but mathematics and was admitted. His youthful approach to academic excellence was captured in his statement, "My spirits were exuberant. I was far from my home without restraint."

Pierce enjoyed college and made friends there quicker than he made good grades. One biographer recorded his ability to charm his way through school. "At Bowdoin, he was equally popular with the most demanding professors and with the most mischievous students." In algebra class he had to work algebra problems out on a slate and then review his answers one on one with the professor. His professor later recalled being surprised to find Pierce's slate had the correct answer to a particularly difficult problem. He asked him how he had solved the problem. Pierce quickly smiled and confessed, "I got it from Stowe's slate!"

Calvin Ellis Stowe was a classmate who later married the author Harriet

Beecher. Another classmate was the future poet Henry Wadsworth Longfellow, and a third was Nathaniel Hawthorne who became his lifelong friend. Hawthorne later wrote of their school days together, "Lads together at a country college, gathering blueberries in study hours ... shooting pigeons or gray squirrels in the woods ... catching trout in that shadow little stream ... idle lads ... doing a hundred things that the Faculty never heard of, or it would have been worse for us."

Pierce was busy at college with his friends, hunting, fishing and making mischief. Occasionally he found time to attend to his studies, but not much time. By the beginning of his junior year, he ranked academically at the bottom of his class. One classmate explained, "He trailed along, getting his work from others." Faculty members had long ceased investing in him as a scholar. A Bowdoin professor recalled, "The first half of his college career was idled or played away."

The realization that every other student in his class outranked him, coupled with the thought of confronting his disappointed father called for desperate measures. Pierce made an "iron resolution" to turn things around. His first step was to select a new roommate. He asked to room with someone he knew as a "serious ... dedicated" student. He also put himself on a strict study schedule, waking at 4:00 A.M. every morning to study and then religiously returning to his studies at every opportunity day and night.

During his winter break he stayed in Maine to teach at a district school. The role reversal from being a student to being a teacher helped Franklin Pierce grow up. The teenage Pierce was paid twelve dollars a month to teach fifty students in a "one story, low posted building, [with] two huge chimneys and big fireplaces ... with the 'master's' desk between them." One of his students later wrote, "It was true that two or three of the older boys thought they would try the mettle of the young New Hampshire collegian, but it took only one or two old-fashioned floggings to cure them of all delusive ideas."

The unhappy father of one of his bullying students soon visited the school. A former student recalled how the young teacher disarmed the angry parent.

> Pierce met him with one of his blandest smiles, shook him heartily by the hand, invited him into the schoolroom, gave him his own chair, told him how pleased he was to see him, and so mesmerized him with special attention and kind words that the old fellow forgot what he was there for, and soon quietly retired and ever after was one of Pierce's best friends ... [Pierce] earned the goodwill of the entire school. The scholars not only feared but loved and respected him. His whole term was one of the most pleasant and profitable of any ever held in the old No. 6 schoolhouse.

Franklin Pierce was able to write home, "To think ... I am by my own exertions obtaining a little cash and at the same time gaining some useful lessons of instruction is to me no small source of satisfaction." Teaching school became a turning point in Franklin Pierce's life. His own grades steadily improved. By the time he graduated from Bowdoin College in 1824, he had gone from the last in his class to third from the top.

Ten years later he married Jane Appleton. Jane's father, the Reverend Jesse Appleton, was a preacher-teacher and former president of Bowdoin College who had raised her in a highly educated household. She displayed a genuine talent for music which she did not pursue, and a love for literature which she restricted by only reading the Bible. In addition to homeschooling from her parents, Jane attended public schools in Amherst, New Hampshire, and later boarded at a ladies seminary in Keene studying an advanced pre-college academic curriculum then available to few females. Mrs. Robert E. Lee later commented that Mrs. Pierce was the best educated first lady to ever occupy the White House.

When Jane was thirteen, the health of her forty-two-year-old father broke and he soon died. To present himself as a role model to his students and in order to have more time to study and pray, Appleton had strictly limited his food intake and slept only a few hours each night. Such exemplary self-discipline was wasted on his students who concluded his death was a warning on the dangers of studying oneself to death.

Jane was a proper New England woman who hated politics, the chosen occupation of her husband, and slavery which Franklin Pierce refused to publicly repudiate. Pierce's domestic tensions over slavery were also reflected in his public split with a Bowdoin classmate and fellow New Hampshire politician named John Hale. Their bitter conflict mirrored the growing abolitionist debate dividing family, friends, political parties, religious denominations, and the nation. No amount of Franklin Pierce's charisma, good looks or pleasing personality seemed able to reconcile the growing number of abolitionists wanting to end slavery and vehement states' rights opponents who supported it. Pierce tried to appeal for compromise, reconciliation and a peaceful resolution to the nation's divisions, but his gentlemanly leadership failed him and his country. He wanted to avoid conflict and be a peacemaker, but there would be no peace.

The death of three sons, their last-surviving child just weeks before the Pierces moved to the White House, and his efforts to support his grief-stricken wife sapped his spirit and darkened his presidency. Despite being from New England where opposition to slavery was growing, he refused to support the emancipation or education of slaves, or forcefully confront the escalating demands of states' rights secessionists. Unlike his days as a student, President Pierce could not find the "iron resolution" to dramatically turn things around. And unlike his time as a teacher, he failed to confront the nation's political bullies with firmness. It was a weakness he shared with his successor, James Buchanan, who would be the last president of the United States before civil war nearly destroyed the country.

Pierce's schoolmate and old friend Nathaniel Hawthorne confidently wrote of him, "There are scores of men in the country that seem brighter than he is; but Frank has the directing mind, and will move them about like pawns on a chess board, and turn all their abilities to better purpose than they themselves could.... Nothing could ruin him." Hawthorne's prediction proved wrong. Pierce left the presidency a thoroughly defeated, ruined man.

Franklin Pierce Educational Advice to a Niece Twenty Years before Becoming President:

"You should study the graces—what ever you do, let it be done gracefully and with ease. Observe this course at all times and in all situations." Pierce discovered during the constitutional crisis leading to the Civil War that "doing things gracefully and with ease" was sometimes not enough.

James Buchanan
"Misconduct, Arrogant Attitude, and Disrespect for Teachers"

James Buchanan seemed like the perfect man to serve as president when he was elected in 1856. He had been a successful Pennsylvania lawyer elected to the state's General Assembly followed by eight years as a U.S. congressman. He then served as minister to Russia for Andrew Jackson, was elected to the United States Senate, and was then appointed secretary of state by James Polk. Franklin Pierce appointed him minister to Great Britain where he quickly became a favorite of Queen Victoria and the royal family. A long resume, years of preparation and experience, and expertise in the areas of national statesmanship and international diplomacy however did not add up to a successful presidency. It was an ironic fate for a man with such a fine, analytical, logical mind who had been trained as an accountant.

Few children seemed smarter, more intelligent, or more promising than James Buchanan as a child. His taskmaster father trained James, the oldest surviving of his eleven children, to be the bookkeeper of his extensive business interests. Even as a young boy James was expected to squeeze a profit from his father's ventures by crunching and balancing ledgers in order to feed and clothe their large family. He succeeded admirably in a job that would have challenged even the most expert accountant.

Still Buchanan was never able to please his skeptical father who trusted no one, including his own son. Yet to his mother, and most of his ten brothers and sisters, James could do no wrong. He later admirably wrote of his mother who was his first teacher,

What she read once, she could remember forever. She had a fondness for poetry, and could repeat with ease all the passages of her favorite authors ... she was a delightful and instructive companion.... It was chiefly to her influence that all her sons were indebted for a liberal education.

Buchanan made no mention of any educational opportunities provided for his sisters because there were none.

As one of his community's most prosperous men, Buchanan's father decided James should grow up to become a lawyer to better protect his business affairs. He sent him as a six-year-old to the Old Stone Academy near their home in Mercersburg, Pennsylvania, to begin his formal schooling. Memorization and learning came easily to the boy. James was the smartest, wealthiest, and tallest student in his class. He quickly decided he knew more than all his teachers and gained a reputation as a know-it-all and a bully with his classmates. Academically he mastered the required subjects of mathematics, Latin, and Greek and received what he called "a tolerably good English education."

At sixteen years of age he confidently traveled the forty miles from his home to attend Dickinson College. He later wrote,

There was no efficient discipline, and the young men pretty much did as they pleased. To be a sober, plodding industrious youth was to incur the ridicule of the mass of students.... Chiefly from the example of others, and in order to be considered a clever and spirited youth, I engaged in every sort of extravagance and mischief.... Unlike the rest of this class, however, I was always a tolerably hard student, and never was deficient in my college exercises.

With the mind of an accountant and the confident immaturity of an adolescent, he calculated that his strong academic performance would more than balance out any outlandish behavior on his part. Breaking school rules, treating his teachers and studies with contempt, and filling his hours with drinking, smoking, dancing and carousing soon earned him the popularity of his peers, and the contempt of the faculty. Buchanan was smart enough to keep his grades up, but arrogant enough to believe his conduct would not catch up with him.

Years later, Buchanan vividly recalled his father's reaction to receiving a letter during his summer recess dismissing him from school.

I observed that his countenance fell. He then handed it to me and left the room ... it was from Dr. Davidson, the principal of Dickinson College. He stated that, but for the respect the faculty entertained for my father, I would have been expelled from the college on account of my disorderly conduct. That they had borne with me as best they could until that period; but that they could not receive me again, and that the letter was written to save him the mortification of sending me back and having me rejected.

"Misconduct, arrogant attitude, and disrespect for teachers" were the stated reasons for his dismissal from school. But the particular incident that sealed his fate was being discovered drunk dancing boisterously on a tabletop. It took a family friend to salvage Buchanan's college career. He got James to promise to play by the school rules and persuaded Dickinson College to give him another chance. Buchanan returned and completed his coursework, but made no attempt to conceal his scorn for the faculty or his inflated opinion of his own intelligence. Of his final oral examinations he boastfully noted, "I answered every question without difficulty."

Based on the numbers, his grades allowed him to be nominated to be class valedictorian. But the faculty firmly rejected rewarding such a distinction to "a troublesome and disrespectful" student. He never forgot the sting of their refusal "to confer an honor of the college upon a student who had shown such little respect as I had done for the rules of the college and for the professors." Buchanan complained bitterly, and many of his college friends loyally rallied to support him. He later wrote, "I held out for some time, but at last yielded.... I left college, however, feeling but little attachment towards the Alma Mater."

The bitter experience taught Buchanan a renewed respect for the law. It also provided him with a nearly blind loyalty toward friends who stood with him during tough times. He recorded at the time, "I have scarcely ever been so much mortified at any occurrence of my life as this disappointment, nor has friendship ever been manifested towards me in a more striking manner."

A wiser more somber Buchanan traveled to Lancaster, Pennsylvania, to study law — a subject which he quickly came to revere. He later wrote,

> I can say, with truth, that I have never known a harder student than I was at that period of my life. I studied law and nothing but law.... I took pains to understand thoroughly, as far as I was capable, everything which I read; and in order to fix it upon my memory and give myself the habit of extempore speaking, I almost every evening took a lonely walk, and embodied the ideas which I had acquired during the day into my own language.

James Buchanan became the lawyer his father wanted him to be and eventually the patriarch of his large extended family. He never married, but after the death of several of his brothers and sisters, he adopted and raised a niece, became the guardian of other nieces and nephews, and provided an education — a strict education — for twenty-two assorted relatives and their children.

The reformed school troublemaker never tired of urging his nieces and nephews to be nice, to respect authority, and to follow the rules. It was a lesson he had learned the hard way — and one which guided him the rest of his life. When a nephew he was raising at his home in Lancaster refused to eat his vegetables, Buchanan left his position in Washington D.C. as the nation's secretary of state to personally deal with the matter. He wrote at the time, "I intend to commence with him tomorrow and make him eat vegetables or he shall have no meat." The rules of the house triumphed and his nephew eventually ate his vegetables, grew up to be a respectful law-abiding young man, and had his college tuition at Princeton paid for by his Uncle James.

James Buchanan's public career mirrored his private convictions. He became a strict interpreter of the Constitution, unwilling and unable to understand anything but the letter of the law. Moral questions and emotional angst surrounding such issues as slavery were irrelevant to Buchanan. The law of the land legally sanctioned and protected slavery. In his mind, such legal dictates fit as dispassionately into law books as simple numbers filled a bookkeeper's ledgers. Growing moral outrage arousing the nation's psyche confounded Buchanan. His rigid legal interpretation of slave laws and willingness to support states' rights advocates gained him many Southern friends. And since his college days, Buchanan always treasured friendship.

Personally, he thought slavery wrong; but the law was clear and unambiguous on the subject. He publicly supported the controversial Dred Scott decision of 1857 when the Supreme Court declared slaves were legal property, and therefore, unable to be citizens of the United States. Buchanan even advocated a constitutional amendment that would strengthen and legally protect slavery in the future, hoping such a legal action could put to rest the slavery controversy.

James Buchanan as president retained the singular mind of a small town country lawyer with the heart of an accountant. To him all the emotional issues surrounding slavery could be reduced to a simple equation. Regardless of whether slavery was right or wrong, existing law must be obeyed. As his reputation and the nation he led were being devoured by the impending Civil War, he believed he did not have the legal authority to stop slavery or prevent states from leaving the union. In 1860 he was succeeded by Abraham Lincoln, another country lawyer who viewed things differently.

James Buchanan on the Place of Education in a Woman's Life

"After your education shall have been completed and your conduct approved by me ... I shall be most happy to aid in introducing you to the world in the best manner."

"I would give almost anything in the world for a niece that everyone could love for her amiability, and all respect for her intelligence."

"She is very industrious. If not smart, she is very good, and that is better."

Mary Todd and Abraham Lincoln
"The Most Important Subject"

It has been said a good education begins or ends with a good teacher. Few men who became president spent fewer days in school or had a better teacher than Abraham Lincoln. He was almost completely self-taught. No other president had the advantage of having Abraham Lincoln as a teacher.

Lincoln was not the nicest looking boy or the handsomest man to become president. That might have been Franklin Pierce or Millard Fillmore. He did not have the large vocabulary of John Quincy Adams or the mathematical mind of James K. Polk. Lincoln never traveled to Europe like John Adams or James Buchanan. Abraham Lincoln had little formal schooling, and almost all other presidents surpassed him in traditional academic achievement. He did not have the best-educated parents. His father thought education a waste of time. His mother and stepmother could read, but barely write. Lincoln wasn't even the smartest child in his family. That would have been his older sister Sally who died young. In another time and place, Sally might have been the Lincoln everyone remembered. But only Thomas Jefferson may have matched Lincoln's curiosity and passion for learning.

As a young child, Lincoln

Abraham Lincoln believed education "the most important subject we as a people can be engaged in." Few men who became president spent fewer days in school or had a better teacher than Lincoln. He was almost completely self-taught (Lincoln statue, Vandalia, Illinois — author collection).

and his sister Sally walked nine miles to and from the one-room school they infrequently attended. All the time the future president spent in school added up to less than one full school year. During the single term he served in Congress, he described his education in the biographical congressional directory with the same word George Washington used to describe his own education, "defective." Twenty years later, his presidential campaign biography wrote, "He regrets his lack of education, and does what he can to supply the want."

Abraham Lincoln recognized his educational shortcomings and became his own teacher. His curriculum came from any book that would teach him something new. He loved reading from the time he was a small boy. Lincoln studied grammar and math and practiced penmanship. He read everything he could and took every opportunity to read. Most people who knew him as a child described him as "lazy" because he was reading when he was supposed to be working. Looking back on his childhood, friends remembered, "He read sitting, lying down, and walking the streets. He was always reading." One of Lincoln's classmates remembered he was "clearly exceptional." More than one biographer wrote, "He carried away from his brief schooling the self-confidence of a man who has never met his intellectual equal."

Many parts of Abraham Lincoln's life caused controversy, including his marriage to Mary Todd who was born into a wealthy family of southern slaveholders. Even friends who knew the couple were surprised they married, but they shared a love for reading, writing, and learning.

Mary Todd received as fine a formal education as Lincoln had not. Her father Robert Smith Todd strongly believed in educating all his children, but not his slaves. Mary began school shortly after her ninth birthday, her mother's death, and her father's quick remarriage. School became a refuge and sanctuary for Mary after her new stepmother denounced her as "a limb of Satan" and "the Devil's spawn."

Robert Smith Todd believed female education needed to "go beyond the training in etiquette, conversation, and the decorative arts" that served as the traditional core curriculum in female academies of the time. Todd found two schools near his home sharing his unorthodox views. Still, female education, even at the more modern academies, did not encourage independent thinking. But Mary did not need school to teach her that skill. As a child she had quickly figured out that the "mysterious late-night rapping on the back door" was a signal from runaway slaves seeking help from Mary's beloved Mammy Sally as they escaped north. Mary kept their secret.

For most of the next ten years, Mary attended one or the other of the schools her father selected. She did not receive the same classical Greek and Latin education her brothers, and later her stepbrothers, received at their all-male schools. But she was exposed to a richer more academically challenging curriculum than most "educated" women. Mary's schools provided textbooks geared to instructing the female mind such as *The Young Ladies' Geography, Miss Swift's Natural History, The Young Ladies' Class Book,* and *A Mirror for the Female Sex.*

Still neither school allowed original compositions to be written. Writing was taught and evaluated based on "retraced homilies specially designed for females," such as, "Evil communications corrupt good manners." Like most nineteenth-century schools, teaching consisted of rote memorization and oral regurgitation. But Mary loved school, perhaps because it allowed her time away from the home where her stepmother ruled, and her father was frequently away on business. When she was older, Mary boarded at her school five nights a week, even though she was within a short walk from her father's house where her six brothers and sisters were eventually joined by nine step-siblings.

A classmate remembered, "She had a retentive memory and mind that enabled her to grasp and understand thoroughly." Mary especially enjoyed studying French and acted in a number of plays, usually in leading roles wearing elaborate costumes. She developed a talent for mimicry and sarcasm that did not endear her to classmates, but did bring her the attention she desired. At school she could lose herself for hours in her books, plays, and daydreams.

School was the only "true" home of her youth, she recalled. Later her marriage provided a final escape from her unhappy childhood. She was briefly courted by former schoolteacher Stephen Douglas but married his friend and political rival Abraham Lincoln. Following her marriage, she embraced the anti-slavery views of her husband, and as first lady raised money for foundations and charities helping freed slaves.

It was Mary who took the most active role in the education of the Lincolns' four sons. When her oldest son Robert was ten, she bragged to friends he was already studying Latin and Greek. It was a sure sign he was college bound. At sixteen Robert took the entrance exam for Harvard, failing fifteen of the sixteen required tests. Following a year of study at the Philips Exeter Academy, he was admitted to Harvard and graduated four years later.

As president, Lincoln signed into law the Morrill Land Grant College Act of 1862, which president Buchanan had previously vetoed. For the first time in the nation's history, college doors became affordable to a large number of people from all social classes. The law allowed public lands in each state to be sold, with the proceeds to be used to build inexpensive public colleges.

Kansas State University soon joined such existing state land-granted schools such as Michigan State, Pennsylvania State, and Iowa State in welcoming students. Their curriculum could include classical studies but could not use the study of Latin and Greek to keep students from being admitted to study there. The goal of the law read in part, "to promote the liberal and practical education of the industrial classes in the several pursuits and professions of life."

Abraham Lincoln began and ended his public career speaking about education. On March 9, 1832, in his first public speech Lincoln declared,

> Upon the subject of education, not presuming to dictate any plan or system respecting it, I can only say that I view it as the most important subject which we, as a people, can be engaged in. That every man may receive at least a moderate education, and thereby be enabled to read histories of his own and other countries, by which he may duly appreciate the value of our free institutions, appears to be an object of vital importance, even on this account alone, to say nothing of the advantages and satisfaction to be derived from being able to read the scriptures and other fine works, both of a religious and moral nature, for ourselves.

From the time he was a boy, Lincoln believed in the power of education and detested the institution of slavery. His love for education and hatred of slavery shaped the private and public man. He addressed both passions in the final public speech of his life on April 11, 1865.

In the closing days of the Civil War he urged full citizenship be granted to "very intelligent" men of color. Lincoln cited, as an example to other states, Louisiana's new constitution that provided "the benefit of public schools equally to black and white." In doing so, he became the first president to publicly advocate education for blacks. One man in the crowd listening to the speech became so enraged by the implications of Lincoln's words he vowed to kill him. The man was John Wilkes Booth. Four days later he murdered Abraham Lincoln.

Abraham Lincoln on Education:

"For my part, I desire to see the time when education — and by its means morality, sobriety, enterprise, and industry — shall become much more general than at present; and should be gratified to have it in my power to contribute something to the advancement of any measure which might have a tendency to accelerate the happy period."

Eliza McCardle and Andrew Johnson

"If He Can Only Educate Himself, He Has a Destiny"

When Abraham Lincoln was assassinated in 1865, Andrew Johnson became president. If possible, Johnson was even poorer as a child than Lincoln. Andrew's father died when the future president was three, and his parents, stepfather and only brother were all illiterate. Johnson never attended school a day in his life. As a young boy in North Carolina he was sold as an apprentice to a tailor who taught him the trade until he would be released from bondage at the age of twenty-one. Andrew was one of many apprentices who sat "crossed-legged on a tailor's bench from sunrise to sunset cutting, stitching, patching, and pressing clothes with no let ups for meals."

To distract their minds from their dull backbreaking work, readers were sometimes hired to read aloud newspapers and books to them. Johnson clearly enjoyed being read to so much that a reader once gave him his book when he was finished reading it. Andrew took the book but was unable to read a word in it. Over time a foreman taught him the alphabet and enough reading to be able to understand simple written instructions.

Despite his long hours at work, he found time at night to get into trouble with the law. Fearful of being arrested and jailed for his boyish pranks, he and his brother ran away from home. Johnson eventually made his way to Tennessee where at eighteen he met and married sixteen-year-old Eliza McCardle. She was as poor as her new husband but had attended the local Rhea Female Academy where she excelled in mathematics. Eliza became not only Andrew's wife, but his teacher. They opened up a tailor shop in Greenville, Tennessee, where he did the tailoring and Eliza handled their finances. While Andrew worked, she read to him from her old schoolbooks, teaching him arithmetic, writing, and spelling.

From interactions with his customers and through Eliza's coaching, Johnson became a powerful speaker. Within a few years he joined the debating club at the nearby Greenville College but never enrolled at the school. His reading and writing steadily improved, but he remained a creative speller his entire life. When Eliza was raising their five children and his business grew to several tailors, he hired students from the local college to read to his workers as he had once been read to as a young apprentice.

Their financial success allowed the Johnson children to attend the best schools available. Andrew continued his own education by reading his children's textbooks with them and reviewing their lessons. With his wife's encouragement, Johnson entered local politics becoming an alderman, a mayor, a state representative, a state senator, and then governor of Tennessee as an emancipationist in a state that overwhelmingly supported slavery. He bought several slaves, some at their own request, in order to free them. It was a tactic used by some anti-slavery advocates to keep families together and away from slaveholders who mistreated them.

Shortly before his death, Lincoln signed into law the Freedman's Bureau Bill which provided educational, vocational, and health care support for freed slaves up to one year following the close of the Civil War. Johnson supported the law and appointed Civil War general Oliver Howard, a strong supporter of education for blacks, as the bureau's first commissioner.

During the year of its authorization, nearly 1,000 public schools, teacher training colleges, and universities were created. Ninety thousand former slaves eagerly enrolled in the Freedman's Bureau schools, with an average daily attendance from seventy-nine to eighty-two percent on any given day.

As governor of Tennessee in the 1850s, Johnson was the first governor in the state's history to persuade the legislature to fund monies for public schools. Prior to the Civil War, none of the Deep Southern states provided tax-funded public schools for any child black or white. As president, Johnson supported Lincoln's policies regarding citizenship, voting rights, and education for blacks, but he was a strict constructionist regarding the Constitution. Once the year of the Freedman's Bureau authorization ended, Johnson believed the voting franchise and responsibility for education legally reverted to the states.

In 1866, Congress attempted to reauthorize the Freedman's Bureau beyond its one-year mandate, but Johnson vetoed the bill. To him the Constitution clearly reserved education as the province of the states, not the federal government. Confiscated land which had previously supplied the bureau's budget was also returned to the southern landowners, drying up funding for the agency. Congress overturned Johnson's veto and appropriated some funding for its programs, but without the president's full support and additional funding, the programs suffered.

Privately and publicly Johnson believed America "a white man's country." Yet he willingly freed the slaves he owned, and as the wartime governor of Tennessee, he legally abolished slavery in the state. In 1867, he donated land near his home to build a public school for freed slaves. As president, he invited a former slave who was a strong proponent of public education for blacks to the White House after an abolitionist senator refused to receive him. Despite his own personal beliefs or the political consequences, he consistently enforced all existing laws.

Johnson's strict interpretation of the Constitution and stubborn nature contributed to articles of impeachment being filed against him. He was acquitted and saved from being thrown out of office by one vote. To the end of his life, he insisted he was a genuine friend of blacks, a champion of education for all, and a fierce supporter of the U.S. Constitution. In spite of his refusal to renew the Freedman's Bureau Bill beyond its original single year of authorization, it was during his presidency that thousands of former slaves first began to receive the education previously denied them.

Johnson Letter to His Wife on the Education of His Grandchildren, March 27, 1863.

"Tell Mary [Johnson's daughter] she must devote much of her time and attention to the instruction and training of her children and say to them that their grandfather thinks of them every day and prays for their future happiness. You must tell Andrew that his father's hopes rest upon him now and that he must make a man of himself. He can learn to do it and I expect it of him. If he can only educate himself, he has a destiny of no ordinary character. When I get to Louisville I shall expect to find that he has made considerable progress in writing as well as in his books."

Julia Dent and Ulysses S. Grant

"I Did Not Take Hold of My Studies with Avidity"

Johnson's presidential successor was Ulysses Grant whose full name, Hiram Ulysses Grant, caused him considerable grief in and out of school. The future president as a child was sickly, gullible, shy, non-athletic, tenderhearted, small for his age and lonely. He did not get along with his father, was not close to his mother, and was subjected to endless teasing by other children. His unusual first name and the fact that his initials spelled "HUG" did not make his life easier. Classmates and teachers frequently referred to him as "Useless Grant." Such childhood mockery was not forgotten. Years after he earned the highest military rank of any officer in the Civil War and was elected the eighteenth President of the United States, he could still sum up his unhappy childhood with seven telling words: "Boys enjoy the misery of their companions."

Grant was never a brilliant student. "Slow" and "dull" were the adjectives usually used to describe him. One childhood friend recalled his "sluggishness of mind and body." Grant described "laziness" as his greatest sin. School in his hometown of Georgetown, Ohio, was not a happy place for him, but there was no escaping it. His first school was just a few steps from his front door. His second could be seen on a nearby hilltop from his bedroom window. One of his teachers lived just two doors away. Grant seldom studied or read a lesson more than once. He was "slovenly in manner," hated to recite in class, and would do whatever it took to keep from answering questions. He was a frustrating student to teach, and he found school a frustrating place to be.

Ulysses S. Grant's two-room schoolhouse where the future savior of the union and two-term president was bullied and tormented by students and teachers alike. Grant was described as "a frustrating student to teach" and found school "a frustrating place to be" (Grant schoolhouse in Georgetown, Ohio — author collection).

In his *Personal Memoirs* Grant remembered,

> The schools, at the time ... were very indifferent. There were no free schools.... They were all supported by subscription. And a single teacher — who was often a man or woman incapable of teaching much, even if they imparted all they knew — would have thirty or forty scholars, male and female, from the infant learning the A B C's up to the young lady and the boy of twenty, studying the highest branches taught — the three R's, Reading, 'Riting, 'Rithmatic.' I never saw a ... mathematical work higher than arithmetic ... until after I was appointed to West Point. I then bought a work on algebra in Cincinnati, but having no teacher, it was Greek to me.

Grant also recalled the way teachers commonly tried to gain and keep the attention of students.

> I have no recollection of having been punished at home, either by scolding or by the rod. But at school the case was different. The rod was freely used there, and I was not exempt from its influence. I can see ... the schoolteacher ... with his long beech switch always in his hand.... Switches were brought in bundles, from the beech wood near the schoolhouse by the boys for whose benefit they were intended. Often a whole bundle would be used up in a single day.

The only subject he did well in was mathematics. That was good enough for his father who wanted him to go to college. After learning what he could in Georgetown, his father sent him to the Maysville Seminary, a boarding school in Kentucky, and then to the Presbyterian Academy, in Ripley, Ohio. It was his father's idea that his son should attend West Point despite the fact that Grant had no interest in a military career. The future Civil War hero hated all things military and later admitted, "I did not take hold of my studies with avidity."

At West Point his favorite class was art, and his favorite readings were novels. Grant earned good grades in math, but his highest grades were in horsemanship. He got along better with horses than his classmates and at graduation ranked twenty-first in a class of thirty-nine.

Grant married a wealthy Missouri country girl raised by doting parents and eighteen unschooled slaves smart enough to dote on the spoiled daughter of their master. Except for her own lack of scholarly effort, Julia's memories of school contrasted with those of her future husband. She fondly reminisced,

> My school days are only pleasant memories.... The old school house was a picture. This temple of ours was built of logs hewn from the adjacent forest ... about twenty-five feet square. We entered its only door from the east. To the right ... sat the teacher, always kind to me. The north of the cabin was occupied by a large fireplace, which was filled by green branches and flowers in summer and a glowing fire in winter. On the west side was a long narrow window: the girls sat on this side; on the south was a high, wide window: the boys sat on that side. The little fellows sat in front of the large boys, or between them and the teacher.... There were no backs on any of the seats [so] Mamma sent a nice little arm chair for my use.
>
> We often changed teachers.... Mr. J. F. Long, my last teacher in this sylvan center ... was so kind to me, too kind. I remember on one occasion he gave to our class some of those dreadful Roman numerals to learn for Monday morning, saying if we

did not know the task set, he would punish us with the rod. Well, I spent all of my Saturday holiday conning this ... most unpleasant task. Mr. Long called up my little sister Ella to recite. She did not know her lesson — and he kept his word. I was the next one called up, and lo! Not a number did I know. I could not tell whether the I's came before or after the V's and X's. I turned pale and trembled, when kind Mr. Long stooped down (he was well over six feet, four inches high in height) and said in a low tone. "You don't know it, do you, little one." I replied: "I thought I did when I came, but I don't know." He said kindly: "Never mind, don't trouble your little head about it any more. You will learn it in good time." I never did though.

Being the favorite daughter of a rich indulgent father had many such benefits. When she was ten, Julia was sent to a boarding school where she remembered,

[I] did just as I pleased, declining to recite ... English grammar and absolutely refusing to look at the multiplication table, spending this most valuable time in reading ... all the books I could lay my hands on.... In every other branch, I was below the standard, and worse still, my indifference was very exasperating.

In spite of their mediocre academic performance as students, Ulysses and Julia Dent Grant were both considered successful during their lifetimes. Still the two greatest intellectual passions of Grant's life were never professionally realized. As the most celebrated horseman at West Point, he wanted to be assigned to the cavalry; but after graduation, he was placed in the infantry where he remained for the rest of his long military career.

Grant's fondest wish, however, was to become a college mathematics professor, sharing his knowledge and love of mathematics in ways none of his teachers ever shared with him. Mathematics was the only academic subject that excited the bored student. He wrote in his memoirs, "The subject was so easy to me as to come almost by intuition." But he was rejected for teaching jobs at the West Point Military Academy, Washington University in St. Louis, and even a tiny college in Ohio. The frustrated math teacher never got a teaching job.

Grant did become known as the general who won the Civil War, the military hero who saved the Union, and as one of the few men who served eight full years as president of the United States. From the time he was elected president in 1868 until his death twenty years later, he was one of the most popular but controversial men of the century. Many of his most bitter political controversies had to do with his ideas and policies regarding education.

When he was still a general, Grant broke politically with President Johnson in part over Grant's support for extending the life of the Freedman's Bureau. As president, he vigorously fought and defeated the Ku Klux Klan, who was trying to restrict the spread of public education for southern blacks. Two years into his first term of office, five-thousand teachers were teaching nearly 150,000 former slaves in newly opened schools throughout the South. One-third of the teachers were black men, but the majority of teachers were white women from liberal arts colleges in the North. Frederick Douglas declared, "We are ... transplanting the whole South with the higher civilization of the North. The New England Schoolhouse is bound to take the place of the Southern whipping post."

In 1873, Grant focused on the status of black Americans in and out of school in his second inaugural address. "Social equality is not a subject to be legislated upon, nor shall I ask that anything be done to address the social status of the colored man, except to give him a fair chance to develop what good there is in him, give him access to the schools, and when he travels let him feel assured that his conduct will regulate the treatment and fare he will receive."

Grant also waded into one of the nation's bitterest educational controversies — the place of religion in public schools. "Protestant hymn singing, praying, and Bible reading" had always been a part of American public education; but growing numbers of Catholic and Jewish immigrants to northern cities found those practices offensive to their own religious traditions and beliefs. Parochial schools were being founded, but their supporters wanted public funding for their schools or relief from paying taxes for public schools their children did not attend.

Grant believed public schools needed to change to become more inclusive of other religions and nationalities. In a widely publicized speech Grant declared,

> Resolve that neither the State nor the education shall support institutions of learning other than those sufficient to afford every child the opportunity of a good common school education, unmixed with sectarian, pagan, or atheistic dogma. Leave the matter of religion to the family altar, the church and the private school supported entirely by private contributions. Keep the church and state forever separated.

In his annual message to Congress, Grant asked that a constitutional amendment be passed making it "the duty of each state to establish and maintain free public schools for the education of all children irrespective of sex, color, birthplace, or religion." But he also added, "Schools should be entirely secular, the teaching of religion should be banned, and public aid to sectarian schools ... forbidden."

Grant then proposed to ensure the complete separation of church and state, that all church property be taxed with the exception of "the last resting place of the dead and possibly, with proper restrictions, church edifices." He explained his rationale by stating, "So vast a sum, receiving all protection and benefits of government without bearing its proportion of the burden and expenses of the same, will not be looked upon acquiescently by those who have to pay taxes." To some Americans, Grant was a prophet, but to others, he was an apostate.

Grant's bold proposals were not legislatively approved, but they did have the effect of making public education more inclusive to children from diverse backgrounds, religions, and nationalities. His advocacy of taxing church property also caused religious activists on all sides to tone down their rhetoric. Yet today, nearly a century and a half after Grant left the White House, the arguments on multicultural education and the role of religion and taxes in schools continue.

Grant on Education

"Free education lay at the root of the nation's liberty."

"The true prosperity and greatness of a nation is to be found in the elevation and education of its laborers."

"A large association of ignorant men cannot for any considerable period oppose a successful resistance to the tyranny of oppression ... hence the education of the masses becomes the first necessity of our institutions. They are worth preserving because they have secured the greatest good to the greatest proportion of the population of any form of government."

Ulysses S. Grant on the establishment the First Bureau of Education in the Federal Government, 1873

"The evidently increasing interest in the cause of education is a most encouraging feature in the general progress and prosperity of the country and the Bureau of Education is earnest in its efforts to give proper direction to the new appliances and increased facilities which are being offered to aid the education of the country in their great work."

Grant's Final Address on Education

"As this will be my last annual message ... I will repeat or encapsulate the questions which I deem of vital importance.... First that the states shall be required to afford the opportunity of a good common-school education to every child within their limits. Second no sectarian tenets shall ever be taught in any school supported in whole or in part by the state, nation, or by the proceeds of any tax levied upon any community."

Lucy Webb and Rutherford B. Hayes

"Elections without Education ... Must Always and Everywhere Be a Farce"

Lucy Webb and Rutherford B. Hayes followed the Grant family to the White House in 1877. Like his predecessor, Hayes had few warm memories of his early schooling, but still became an outspoken champion of public education. His future wife, Lucy Webb, the first first lady to earn a college degree, had only positive memories of her own academic experiences.

Like Andrew Jackson, Hayes' father died before he was born. Like Tyler, Polk, and Grant, he was a sickly child who many feared might not live to adulthood. Like Lincoln, Hayes was close to a sister who died. And following the tradition of William Henry Harrison and James K. Polk, he was homeschooled for many years. But unlike all of them, his overprotective mother never allowed him to play outside until he was seven, and she did not send him to school until he was twelve.

Despite the death of his father, his family was not poor. Still Hayes lived a very sheltered childhood. When his mother had to attend to a sick relative, she sent Rutherford and his sister to live with relatives in Delaware, Ohio. There they sent them to a newly opened public school that terrified them. Hayes wrote in his diary that his teacher transformed into "a demon of ferocity" when his scholars disappointed him. "He flogged great strapping fellows of twice his size, and talked savagely of throwing them through the walls of the schoolhouse. He threw a large jackknife, carefully aimed so as to just miss, at the head of a boy who was whispering near me."

Hayes's relatives found nothing unusual about the experience, but his mother was horrified. She found another nearby school where she placed her children under the care of Mrs. Joan Hills Murray. This small female teacher did what his bullying male teacher failed to do. She created a classroom environment where he and other students felt safe, were well-behaved, and thrived socially and academically. Hayes later saluted Mrs. Murray as the ideal teacher who modeled the transforming power a deeply committed teacher could have on students.

At fourteen, Rud as he was then called, was placed in a Methodist boarding school where he excelled in public speaking and writing. The following year he attended a preparatory school in Connecticut. The school accepted only "twenty boys of good character" each year and intensely drilled them to prepare for college. He thrived in the highly structured, nurturing atmosphere. Rud described his school day in a letter home: "We get up at half past six o'clock, breakfast at seven, [have] prayers, and school begins at nine; dinner at twelve, [return to classes] one till four, then [study] six to nine.... All the scholars like the school very much, and that is more than can be said of most schools."

After a year in Connecticut, Hayes returned to Ohio, easily passed the college entrance exams, and went to Kenyon College. He did well at Kenyon but complained about the ridiculous rules, the indifferent food, and all of his professors. His sister, who was never provided the educational opportunities of her brother, urged him to find something to like about his teachers. Rud told her he liked being physically away from them!

Hayes graduated with highest honors, later attended Harvard Law School, and made a reputation as a lawyer prior to the Civil War defending fugitive slaves. He married Lucy Webb in 1852, fought in the Civil War on the Northern side, was wounded four times, and rose to the rank of major general. Hayes then served three terms as governor of Ohio before being elected president in the bitterly disputed election of 1876.

Lucy Webb took advantage of the growing number of schools for women that had begun offering many of the same courses found in male institutions. As a child, she attended the Chillicothe Female School, where she excelled in all academic subjects but math. When her older brothers were sent to Ohio Wesleyan University she was allowed to earn college credits there despite the fact that no females could formally enroll at the University. Her mother, however, became concerned when Lucy began attracting too much attention from the college men. One of them was Rutherford Hayes, who met the fifteen-year-old Lucy when he visited the campus. Once she turned sixteen, her mother sent her to the Wesleyan Female College in Cincinnati where she studied astronomy, geology, geometry and other courses once reserved for male scholars. During her college years, Lucy became an outspoken proponent of equal pay for women and declared, a "woman's mind is as strong as man's, equal in all things, and in some ways superior." Hayes was waiting when she graduated from college, and they married.

When Rutherford and Lucy Hayes entered the White House eleven years after the Civil War, the nation remained badly divided. Racial and religious differences and growing numbers of immigrants aggravated national divisions.

Hayes agreed to remove the occupying armies from the South that had enforced federal laws, defeated the Ku Klux Klan, and protected the homes, farms, and schools of former slaves. He believed the time had come for education, not bayonets, to bring the country together. All the Southern states had by that time set up tax-supported public school systems. Hayes agreed with President Grant that non-sectarian public education, and good teachers and teaching were the answers to many of the ills besetting America.

Lucy Hayes was held up as a role model of a modern educated woman. When her husband was governor of Ohio, she worked as a teacher of hearing- and speech-impaired orphans. As first lady she regularly visited schools in the North, South, East and West. She made a special effort to include visits to schools dedicated to educating black men and women, Native Americans, and poor whites such as Virginia's Hampton Normal and Agricultural Institute. Lucy supported her husband's commitment to public education and served as president of the Women's Home Missionary Society, dedicated to enlightening the minds and improving the lives of the poor.

Hayes devoted much of his time after leaving the White House to education. He served as a trustee of the Peabody Education Fund and president of the Slater Fund for the Education of the Freedmen, dedicated to training African American teachers.

It was through Hayes' personal intervention that money was provided to the future African American leader W. E. B. DuBois to study abroad. In 1891 Hayes toured six Southern states and visited eighteen different schools devoted to the education of black Americans. He planned a second tour but died shortly before it was to begin.

His death deprived supporters of education for black Americans of perhaps their greatest white champion just as the struggle over the role of the federal government in education reached a climax in the last decades of the nineteenth-century.

Rutherford B. Hayes on Education

"Universal suffrage should rest with universal education. To this end, liberal and permanent provision should be made for the support of free schools by the State governments, and, if need be supplemented by legitimate aid from national authority."

"Give the young wide diversity of education. There are talents buried in every neighborhood."

"We hail with unstinted delight the teacher who hunts up and educates promising boys and girls whose gifts might otherwise be cramped and crushed."

"On what ground do free schools stand? Our government rests on the intelligence and virtue of the people. Without free schools we cannot have intelligence and virtue."

"Education — discussion, general and intelligent, is the conserving force and at the same time the progressive force."

"Aid to Education ... seems to be our best chance to bring up the neglected elements in our population."

"We have no new gospels to offer. The ideas and aims of last year are still the leading ones. Education, education, education are the words."

"Slavery and education could not exist together. It is equally true that ignorance and free government cannot exist together."

"Elections without education — universal suffrage without universal education, must always and everywhere be a farce."

"Universal education is the common interest of the whole people."

"Law without education is a dead letter."

Hayes Quoting Jefferson

"Men cannot be fitted for the duties of citizenship in a republic without free schools."

Lucretia Rudolph and James Garfield
"Outrages of the School House"

Rutherford and Lucy Webb Hayes were succeeded in the White House by a president, vice president, and first lady who had all been teachers. President James A. Garfield and Vice President Chester A. Arthur once taught at different times in the same Vermont school. The new first lady, Lucretia Rudolph Garfield, met the future president when they attended school together in Ohio. Later he became one of her teachers. Following college graduation, Lucretia taught reading, arithmetic, algebra, and French in public schools in Ravenna, then Cleveland, Ohio. When she announced to her students she was leaving teaching to marry Garfield, they cried.

James Garfield was the youngest of five children but had no memory of his father who died eighteen months after his birth. Garfield's mother struggled financially to raise her children and provide them a good education. She sold a small parcel of land she owned to build a new school closer to her home so her children would not have to walk through six miles of winter snow to the nearest school. Lucretia also came from a hardworking family committed to providing their children an education. The only respite afforded Lucretia, her sister and two brothers from their backbreaking chores was attending school and church. School lessons and reading provided James and Lucretia an escape from the difficult world of their childhoods.

They met as teenagers at Geauga Seminary, a co-educational boarding school where each was sent to pursue an education. The conservative religious school allowed no dancing or casual dress, but did permit Lucretia to study the Latin and Greek classics, science and mathematics, public speaking and English courses that only recently had been opened to female scholars.

In order to help pay his tuition, the seventeen-year-old Garfield began teaching school for thirteen dollars a month during winter terms at local schools. His diary captured the daily variety found during his first teaching experience:

NOVEMBER 1849

Week One
> Monday: "Had seven scholars. They behaved very well."
> Tuesday: "Had eleven scholars—rather noisy P.M. I feel rather down."
> Wednesday: "Had sixteen scholars today. Scholars uneasy in the afternoon. Resolved to *separate* some of the boys that they would not play so much."

Week Two

    Monday: "Branches taught are algebra, geography, history, arithmetic, mental and written geometry, reading, writing, grammar, spelling etc."

    Tuesday: "Punished S. Herrington severely for disobeying and being saucy. He endeavors to fight me but finally gives up and is now a good boy."

    Wednesday: "Twenty-five scholars"

Week Three

    Monday: "This morning I am eighteen years old. Rather young to have the care of a school consisting of a company of youths several of whom are older than myself."

Week Four

    Monday: "Large scholars coming in —feel rather dubious."

    Thursday: "School rather *noisy*. I hardly know what to do. I cannot whip a scholar for making a noise and talking will not do any good. Here is a dilemma."

Week Five

    Tuesday: "Thirty-seven scholars. Great many large ones. Busy times."

Week Seven

    Monday: "School as usual — not quite so noisy."

Week Nine

    Friday: "A boy sixteen years old refused to obey me and was very saucy. I flogged him severely and told him to take his seat. He caught a billet of wood and came at me and we had a merry time. He vamoosed."

Week Fourteen

    Tuesday: "Quelled a difficulty."

    Friday: "Good times."

Week Fifteen

    Thursday: "No Wood." (for the classroom stove)

    Friday: "No Wood."

    Saturday: "Helped Southwick get some wood and had school about 3/4 of day."

Week Sixteen

    Friday: "Good Times."

FEBRUARY 1850

Week Seventeen

    Wednesday: "Very busy in preparing declamations [student oral presentations/open house] for the last evening of my school."

    Saturday: "School for the last time in District #2. There were about one hundred persons in the afternoon. School closes. Some regrets and some rejoicing. Feel that I have done my duty."

The following winter Garfield taught at another one-room school with a reputation for having a "hard nature." One day, he had nearly forty students in attendance and the next day seventeen. Garfield had the usual physical conflicts with male scholars, but he also struggled with female scholars who verbally sniped, attacked, and assaulted one another with words. He wrote, "Of all the places I ever was acquainted with, I never saw one that was so given to slander and talking as this ... the young ladies came to an open rupture; and now while I am writing [at twenty minutes past one in school] I see flushed faces and angry looks.... May God deliver me from the tongues of foul mouthed slander."

Garfield was happy to return to being a student. Not far from Geauga, a new college, the Western Reserve Eclectic Institute, was being built by the Disciples of Christ Church. When it was completed, James and Lucretia both enrolled. Garfield helped pay his tuition working as a part-time janitor and part-time teacher. Occasionally, he found himself teaching Lucretia even though she was a year older.

Following graduation, Lucretia began her own teaching career, while James attended Williams College in Massachusetts. There he fell under the influence of its president Mark Hopkins, who he thought was the perfect teacher. Garfield later wrote, "The ideal college is Mark Hopkins on one end of a log and a student on the other." While attending Williams, Garfield taught the winter term at North Pownal's Oak Grove Seminary in nearby Vermont. It was the same school where his future vice president once taught. Another term he taught in Poestenkill, New York.

Garfield returned to Ohio to teach at the Western Reserve Eclectic Institute when he was twenty-five. Within a year he was made president of the school, which changed its name to Hiram College. One of his first acts was to institute teacher-training workshops. Garfield had thought a great deal about teaching, especially after his experience with Mark Hopkins. He hated the drill, repetition, and rote memory work found in most schools, preferring instead the critical thinking and problem-solving methodologies favored by Hopkins. Garfield wrote in his diary the traditional method of teaching "keeps a little child sitting in silence, in a vain attempt to hold its mind to the words of the printed page, for six hours a day. Herod was merciful, for he finished his slaughter of the innocents in a day; but this practice kills by savagery of slow torture." It amazed him "that any child's love of knowledge survives the outrages of the schoolhouse."

As the college president, Garfield continued teaching courses in English grammar, Latin, and Greek, but when needed, he also taught English analysis, English literature, geology, history, mathematics, philosophy, and rhetoric. His reputation as a teacher was so great that the 5:00 A.M. geology class he taught became the talk of the campus. Not only was it intellectually stimulating, it was well attended. Garfield continually asked questions that tried to connect lessons to the students' own lives. He was determined that his scholars think beyond the narrow physical and intellectual confines of a typical classroom.

Garfield was academically strict, but relaxed and approachable outside of class. One student recalled, "A bow of recognition, or a single word from him, was to me an inspiration." Another wrote, "He was more than a teacher and administrator; the students found him a helper and a friend." Garfield cared not

James Garfield, his wife Lucretia Rudolph, and his vice president Chester Arthur had all been teachers. Garfield and Arthur once taught in the same school in Vermont. On the side of his tomb in Ohio, the seventeen-year-old Garfield is pictured teaching in a one-room schoolhouse. It amazed him that "any child's love of knowledge survives the outrages of the schoolhouse" (Photograph courtesy of the Lake View Cemetery, Cleveland, Ohio).

only about his students and teaching, but actively involved everyone in maintaining the campus, planting trees, and developing a sense of school community.

Over time he became recognized as "one of the most powerful orators of his generation," first as a teacher, then as a professor, college president, and finally as a politician. He left Hiram to serve in the Ohio Infantry during the Civil War, but in 1863 was elected to the United States Congress. Seventeen years later he ran for and was elected president.

For the first time in the country's history, federal aid to education became an issue in a presidential election. Campaign songs proclaimed, "We'll pay the debt Rebellion made, we'll guard our public schools" and "Free schools, free speech, free thought, free press. We will have these things and nothing less." The Republican Party platform endorsed "aid to education as a duty of the National government." Both proponents and opponents of federal aid to public schools saw the endorsement as a lifeline for southern educators trying to provide education for blacks.

Shortly following his election, Garfield was visited by Robert B. Elliott and a delegation of African Americans concerned that state funding for already underfunded southern schools was being further cut. Since the Civil War, Elliott had devoted his professional life to fighting for the educational rights of former slaves. He told Garfield southern blacks could only be saved by "a national system of education for the toiling masses." Garfield responded, "Government ought to do everything it could ... but ... government alone could not do the job." Before ending the meeting, he told the dispirited delegation that parents needed to work harder to cultivate every child's "thirst and hunger" for learning. Garfield admitted in his diary later that night that his response was "less than satisfactory."

As he prepared to enter the White House, the new president struggled with the same constitutional challenge that once confronted Andrew Johnson: Was it possible within the limits of the Constitution to elevate "the negro race from slavery to the full rights of citizenship" without federal aid to education?

The new president soon received a fifteen-page letter from Albion Tourgée, a childhood friend and outspoken advocate of universal public education. He urged Garfield to not abandon his party's promise to provide aid to education. The president of Hiram College and other old friends also urged him to embrace the issue — and he did.

A third of Garfield's inaugural address was devoted to three problems facing the nation: the need for civil rights, the need to fight illiteracy, and the necessity of binding the nation together through universal education. Garfield declared,

> The responsibility for the existence of slavery did not rest upon the South alone. The nation itself is responsible for the extension of the suffrage, and is under special obligations to aid in removing the illiteracy which it has added to the voting population. For the North and South alike there is but one remedy. All the constitutional power of the nation and of the States and all the volunteer forces of the people should be surrendered to meet this danger by the savory influence of universal education.

Educational reformers were thrilled, but Garfield never addressed the issue again. Four months after his inaugural address, he was shot by an assassin. The hopes for federal aide to education seemed buried with him.

James Garfield on Education

"Next in importance to freedom and justice is popular education, without which neither freedom nor justice can be permanently maintained" — an excerpt from Garfield's letter accepting his nomination for president.

"I have no doubt that the final cure for the 'Solid South' will be found in the education of its youth."

"It is the high privilege and sacred duty of those now living to educate their successors and fit them, by intelligence and virtue, for the inheritance which awaits them."

"If parents were themselves sufficiently educated, most of this knowledge might be acquired at the mother's knee; but by the strangest perversion and misdirection of the educational forces, these essential elements of education are neglected more than any other."

"The man shall be a benefactor of his race who shall teach us how to manage rightly the first years of a child's education."

Lucretia Rudolph Garfield Letter to James Garfield at the Beginning and End of Her First Year of Teaching

"I am very pleasantly situated with over ninety little fellows in charge. The school [students] will be divided in a few days when I shall have a fine time. I am not going to fail. You needn't have a fear of it." September 1, 1857

"I love my little school very much — never felt better satisfied with my efforts than now. I am continually becoming more and more pleased with the method of teaching and drilling in these Union Schools. I am sure it is far ahead of anything I have known about before. I am getting every day slower and more thorough — I try to teach the children only a few things, but try to make those few thoroughly understood and leave them impressed." May 8, 1857

Garfield and the Department of Education

Following the Civil War in 1866, Congressman James Garfield introduced a bill into Congress to formally establish a United States Department of Education. The department's initial purpose was to provide equal educational opportunities for all children, "without regard to race or color," if states failed to do so. But due to Garfield's fear that the federal government would "dictate textbooks, schoolhouses, teachers and every minutiae of the work of education," the bill was written with no enforcement procedures. It was passed with the help of another one time teacher and future presidential candidate, Congressman James G. Blaine. The department soon became the Bureau of Education. Over a century later, it became a cabinet position in the Jimmy Carter administration.

Chester A. Arthur

"Pupils Are Altogether Separated from the Surroundings of Savage Life"

Chester A. Arthur became president in 1881 after James Garfield was assassinated. Arthur, two of his sisters and his father were all teachers. Arthur's father, William, graduated from Ireland's Belfast University before traveling to Canada to teach. Following his marriage, William then moved to Vermont where he taught for three years, studied law, and became a Baptist minister. The Arthurs eventually had nine children, including the future president, their fifth child and first boy. His large family and the abundance of churches and poverty throughout the area forced William to preach and continue teaching to earn a living. But his fierce abolitionist beliefs and Irish temper often terrorized and alienated students and congregations alike, forcing him to move on. By the time Chester was nine, his family had moved five times. One of the few constants in Chester Arthur's young life was his father as his teacher.

At fifteen, the future president attended the winter term at Schenectady Lyceum to prepare him for college. Arthur entered Union College the next fall as a sophomore taking Latin, Greek and other courses from the classical curriculum favored by his father. Chester was a popular student remembered for his genial personality and easygoing manner, personality traits seemingly inherited from his mother. His father's influence, however, was also evident. In his most serious collegiate literary effort, Arthur wrote an essay on the "political pestilence" of slavery.

Chester was not considered a particularly diligent student, but he graduated three years later in the top third of his class and was elected to Phi Beta Kappa. Aside from regularly leaving campus without permission and throwing the college bell into the Erie Canal, the only other disciplinary marks Arthur earned came from skipping the school's twice-a-day mandatory chapel. Still there is physical evidence he occasionally attended. On one of the chapel windowsills, his name can still be found where he carved C. A. Arthur in the wood.

During two different winter terms, Chester earned money by teaching at the neighboring district school in Schaghticoke, New York. Following graduation, he returned to Schaghticoke to teach, earning fifteen dollars a month. In a letter written home in 1848, the eighteen-year-old teacher shared his personal insights into the joys of teaching in a one-room schoolhouse in mid-nineteenth-century America.

On the Schoolhouse

"On the morrow the hour for commencing the literary instruction came, and with it the scholars. The schoolhouse was an old red fabric, situated at the crossroads.... It was an old building, and had occupied the same position in the community for many years. It has sent forth many enterprising [scholars].... Spelling-schools numberless had taken place within its walls; hearts lost and won."

On the Classroom

"In the plastering above were the remains of the blank leaves of many books—having been reduced to a pulpy state, by a process well known to urchins, and then projected with unerring aim to their destined location. Here the weary pedagogue had spent his energies, and counted the dragging hours in pouring knowledge through youthful heads, wondering why the alphabet was not innate as a matter of convenience."

On His Students

"My school commenced. It was composed of motley races of brats. There were nearly all the goddesses, all the saints, and many of the wise men of antiquity nominally present. There was an African damsel, a score of aspirants for alphabetical mastery, and many a specimen of the Yankee swop-jack-knives ... the oldest boy in school descanting upon the merits of some wooden combs and endeavoring to negotiate a sale with some small boy."

On Parent Teacher Conferences

"The materfamilias had a tongue as glib as a great anteater, and it was used to the particular detriment of her neighbors and to the praise of her own domestic arrangements."

On Discipline

"There was but one battle — a strong farmer's boy endeavored to overthrow your humble servant and his authority at the same time, but thanks to agility and gymnastic practice, there was a triumph for the teacher."

On Class Size, Salary, and Time Constraints

"Beware of trusting to the statistical calculations of the [school] committeemen in respect to the number of scholars, for they are as fallacious as the idea of getting your pay. And, when you have over forty youngsters learning the rudiments of an education, do not delude yourself by complying with the directions to hear them four times a day."

Arthur's next teaching position was at the Oak Grove Seminary in North Pownal, Vermont, where he also served as principal. The school was located in the local Congregational Church. Like most schools of the time, lessons and tests were verbally administered. At the end of the term, examination day arrived when students were expected to stand in front of the teacher, parents, relatives, neighbors, and strangers to recite a verse, poem, or some recitation of what had been learned.

One of Arthur's students, Asa Stillman, an extremely shy eight-year-old, pleaded to be excused from the exercise because of his fear of public speaking. Arthur was well-liked, but a strict teacher who refused to take no from any student. He insisted the boy make the presentation and told Asa to see him after school. The boy feared he was to be punished, but discovered Arthur had printed out a poem by hand about overcoming fear and rehearsed it with the boy until the end of the term. The nervous student successfully made the presentation and never forgot the teacher who made him do it. He saved the handwritten poem the rest of his life, became a respected doctor, and named his first son Chester Arthur Stillman for his favorite teacher.

After leaving North Pownal, Arthur continued teaching in other schools until becoming a lawyer and politician. Three years after his departure, James Garfield taught at the same small school where Chester Arthur was still fondly remembered. The future twentieth president of the United States claimed that one of the reasons he selected Arthur as his running mate in the 1880 election was because of the genuine affection and respect the former students and their parents retained for him.

Arthur was still in mourning over the recent death of his wife when he became president. He asked his sister, Mary Arthur McElroy, to serve as hostess for social events at the White House. She was educated at the Emma Willard School, one of the first college preparatory schools for women in America, and had children near the age of his own nine-year-old daughter Ellen. Arthur's daughter was privately tutored and off limits to the prying press. His older son Alan attended Princeton. When asked about his children, Arthur defiantly declared, "I may be president of the United States, but my private life is nobody's damn business."

The former teacher and abolitionist hoped to resurrect the federal aid to education movement to help those "who had just emerged from a condition of slavery." He also wanted to provide better educational opportunities for Native American children. In his first annual message to Congress, he boldly proposed that literacy rates be used to determine where federal money should be spent: "All that can be done by local legislation and private generosity should be supplemented by such aid as can be constitutionally afforded by the national government. I suggest that if any fund be dedicated to this purpose it may be wisely distributed in the different states according to the rate of illiteracy as by this means those localities which are most in need will reap its special benefits."

Congress flatly rejected funding direct federal aid for education based on illiteracy rates or providing money for those emerging "from a condition of slavery." They did eventually fund Native American boarding schools where the prevailing educational philosophy was, "Kill the Indian and Save the Man." In his annual message to Congress, Arthur explained, "The success of the schools which are in operation at Hampton, Carlisle, and Forest Grove should not only encourage a more generous provision for the support of those institutions, but should prompt the establishment of others of similar character. They are doubtless much more potent for good than the day schools upon reservations as the pupils are altogether separated from the surroundings of savage life and brought into constant contact with civilization."

Congress ignored Arthur's proposal to address the nation's illiteracy rates and achievement gap, as well the need to educate former slaves and their children. They did, however, find in their hearts and wallets education funds to "civilize" Native American children, even if that meant separating them from their parents and families.

*Chester A. Arthur, Third Annual Message
to Congress — Dec. 4, 1883*

"I have previously referred to the alarming rate of illiteracy in certain portions of the country, and again submit for the consideration of congress whether some federal aid should not be extended to public primary education wherever adequate provision has not already been made." Congress again rejected Arthur's request.

Frances Folsom and Grover Cleveland

"As a Student, Grover Did Not Shine"

Immigrant children continued filling the classrooms of America's northern cities in the last half of the nineteenth-century. Big urban schools had become the education centers of the nation rather than the traditional one-room schoolhouses of rural America. For the first time children who were blind, deaf, or physically handicapped could be educated in large schools big enough to accommodate their special needs. In the 1884 presidential election, two former teachers from these schools ran for president. As a young man Grover Cleveland taught at the New York State Institution for the Blind. His opponent James Gillespie Blaine had once been a teacher at the Philadelphia Institute for the Blind and earlier taught Greek, Latin and mathematics at a military academy in Kentucky.

Blaine graduated first in his class from Pennsylvania's Washington & Jefferson College, a school famous for producing teachers, preachers, and college presidents. Cleveland never attended college. His dreams for higher education ended at sixteen when his forty-nine-year-old preacher-teacher father unexpectedly died. Although his father had graduated with high honors from Yale and later attended Princeton, his small salary as a minister kept his large family nearly impoverished. Following his father's sudden death, there was little chance that Grover, the fifth of nine children, could afford college.

Grover Cleveland's desire for an education never waivered, but as one biographer gently wrote, he possessed few "scholarly gifts." Another recorded, "Scholarliness did not emerge as his strong suit." His sister Margaret remembered, "As a student, Grover did not shine." Yet when an older brother traveled to New York City to teach at the state school for the blind, Grover joined him there to be a teacher.

The huge residential school filled an entire city block and was populated by blind students from eight to twenty-five years of age who were wards of the state. Parents had been forced to give up legal custody of their children in exchange for a state-funded education. Cleveland quickly came to hate the school's prison-like atmosphere and the harsh physical punishments meted out to its defenseless students. It did not take him long to clash with the school's superintendent, whom he found to be a cruel bully.

When not bumping heads with the superintendant, Cleveland taught the younger students arithmetic, reading, writing and geography six days a week from nine in the morning until four-thirty in the afternoon. He and his brother also supervised the boy's dormitories where the students were sent when they were not in class. Little if any time was allowed for relaxation, so Cleveland and his brother read nightly to the students, teaching them to recite verse and poetry as a form of recreation.

A former teacher from the school, who was herself blind, always remembered Cleveland's kindness to his students and his attempts to get the teachers to stand up to the school superintendent. Cleveland quit after a particularly severe beating of a small blind boy who was powerless to defend himself. His sense of justice and hatred of anyone who abused power never left him. During his later rise to political power, first as mayor of Buffalo and then as governor of New York, he made many powerful enemies. His supporters proudly claimed, "We love him for the enemies he has made."

Grover Cleveland never forgot his teaching experiences or his students. As governor of New York, he was a strong supporter of public education and returned to the Institution for the Blind where he once taught to make sure harsh discipline was no longer practiced there. As president, Cleveland traveled to Baltimore to meet educators of the blind and their students attending a convention. The visit of the president of the United States to a meeting of teachers and students with special needs was an unusual public event, especially in 1884.

Cleveland entered the White House as a bachelor. For the first year of his presidency, his youngest sister Rose, who was a schoolteacher, served as his official hostess. He then married Frances Folsom, the young daughter of his former business partner who quickly became a popular first lady. Frances had attended the best private and public schools available in Buffalo and was fluent in both French and German. She then graduated from Wells College, one of the first liberal arts colleges for women in America.

As first lady, she became a trustee of her alma mater and an influential advocate of higher education for women. Following her years in the White House, Frances successfully lobbied New Jersey's educational and political leaders to "open up educational opportunities for girls." One result of her efforts was the creation of the New Jersey College for Women, which offered the same college curriculum offered to men. Her love of learning continued throughout her lifetime. The last decade of her life Frances learned Braille and laboriously typed out texts on a Braille typewriter for a blind Native American schoolteacher. The Navajo woman was unable to afford the costly Braille textbooks and too proud to accept charity. She did accept Frances Cleveland's typed texts as a labor of love which she was then able to share with her students.

President Cleveland seldom addressed educational issues, but he vetoed a bill restricting illiterate foreign immigrants from entering the country. He wrote at the time, "The ability to read and write in and of itself ... supplies unsatisfactory evidence of desirable citizenship or a proper application of the benefits of our institutions." Privately, however, he believed assimilation among racial groups "an impossible goal." After signing into law an anti–Chinese immigration bill he declared, "The experiment of blending the social habits and mutual race idiosyncrasies of the Chinese laboring classes with those of the people of the United States has been ... in every sense unwise, impolitic, and injurious to both nations."

Cleveland's racial attitudes extended to America's black citizens. In 1896, the Supreme Court ruled in *Plessy vs. Ferguson* that black and white students could be legally segregated by race in public schools and public transportation. Cleveland agreed with the decision and supported the controversial ruling the rest of his life.

After serving one term as president, Cleveland was defeated for reelection in 1888 by Benjamin Harrison. In 1892 he reclaimed the White House, becoming the only president to serve two non-consecutive terms. When the Clevelands retired from public life they moved to Princeton, New Jersey. In 1897, the former president and unschooled former teacher was awarded an honorary degree by the university. He eventually joined Princeton's Board of Trustees and even taught classes at the university on American politics.

The school was the site of what many considered Cleveland's greatest public speech. During the university's 1896 Sesquicentennial Celebration he expressed his optimistic, some might say naïve, hopes on the role a modern university and its graduates should play in a democracy.

Excerpts from Grover Cleveland's Princeton Address on Education, Democracy, and the American University:

"A government resting upon the will and universal suffrage of the people has no anchorage except in the people's intelligence."

"Who can better caution against passion and bitterness than those who know by thought and study their baneful consequences, and who are themselves within the noble brotherhood of higher education."

"A constant stream of thoughtful, educated men should come from our universities and colleges preaching national honor and integrity."

"When the excitement of party warfare presses dangerously near our national safeguards, I would have the intelligent conservatism of our universities and colleges warn the contestants in impressive tones against the perils of a breach impossible to repair.... When popular discontent and passion are stimulated by the arts of designing partisans to a pitch perilously near to class hatred or sectional anger, I would have our universities and colleges sound the alarm in the name of American brotherhood and fraternal dependence.... I would have our universities and colleges persuade people to a relinquishment of the demand for party spoils and exhort them to a disinterested and patriotic love of government for its own sake, because in its true adjustment and unperverted operation it secures to every citizen his just share of the safety and prosperity it holds in store for all."

Grover Cleveland Address at the 250th Anniversary of Harvard College

"If the fact is recalled that only twelve of my twenty-one predecessors in office had the advantage of a collegiate or university education, a proof is presented of the democratic sense of our people, rather than an argument against the supreme value of the best and most liberal education in high public positions."

Grover Cleveland School Essay Age 9

"If we expect to become great and good men and be respected and esteemed by our friends we must improve our time when we are young. If we wish to become great and useful in the world we must improve our time in school."

Grover Cleveland to the Students of the University of Michigan

"Of all the legends containing words of advice and encouragement which hung upon the walls of the little district schoolhouse where a large share of my education was gained, I remember but one, which was in these words: 'George Washington had but only a common school education.'"

Caroline Scott and Benjamin Harrison
"Abstain from Eating Cucumbers"

Benjamin Harrison was a champion of public education, believing it was the glue that held the nation together. It was an age when large families were needed to work on family farms, and Harrison was the fifth president in a row to be the fifth child from a large family. When he was eight, despite the fact that his father was a U.S. congressman and his grandfather, William Henry Harrison, was president of the United States, Ben still had farm chores to do.

A childhood friend remembered, "He was a farmer's boy, lived in a little farm house, had to hustle out of bed between 4 and 5 o'clock in the morning the year round to feed stock, get ready to drop corn or potatoes, or rake hay by the time the sun was up." Then he and his brothers and sisters, cousins and neighbors went to school in a one-room log schoolhouse built by their father. One of his first teachers was his grandmother Anna Symmes Harrison. She encouraged him to spend time reading books from the library of her late husband, President William Henry Harrison, in nearby North Bend, Indiana. His first teacher was a local girl who remembered being "dazed with the idea of going into the family as a teacher, as I was but 16 years old."

At fourteen, Harrison was sent to a school in Cincinnati, Ohio. There he came under the influence of Dr. Robert Hamilton Bishop, a dynamic history teacher who used original government documents to teach students to read, think and debate past and current events. Bishop befriended Benjamin much in the way Thomas Jefferson was once mentored by a college professor.

Later Harrison often contrasted the way most teachers taught with Bishop's conversational techniques of connecting with his students. To illustrate his point he usually used the quote, "Tis the custom of most school masters to be eternally thundering in their pupils' ears as though they were pouring into a funnel ... he should also hear his pupils in return." Harrison would then add, "The tank may be full, but if there is no tap how shall we draw from it?" The future president never forgot the validating influence a caring teacher could have on a student's life.

Harrison's father then sent his son to Miami University in Oxford, Ohio. In a series of letters, his mother shared her worries about the "many temptations incident to a college life." These included associating with bad boys, smoking cigars, not writing home enough, and her son's dietary and eating habits. One such letter concluded, "I pray for you daily that you may be kept from sinning and straying from the paths of duty.... I hope you will be prudent in your diet ... and abstain from eating cucumbers."

It was when Harrison was a student in Cincinnati that he met his future wife, Caroline Scott, whose father had been his chemistry and physics professor. Dr. Scott then became president of the Oxford Female Institute, and Caroline joined him there as a student and part-time art and music teacher. She and Ben soon began a courtship, sneaking off to dances and enjoying the music objected to by both sets of parents.

The couple became secretly engaged, but further studies and a lack of money stood in the way of marriage. Harrison needed an additional two-year law apprenticeship before becoming a lawyer so Caroline moved to Kentucky to teach music at a girls' school there. Once they wed, they moved to Indianapolis where Caroline built an art studio in their new home to teach ceramics and art classes. They also both taught Sunday school at a local church.

When the Civil War broke out in 1861, Harrison formed a regiment of Indiana infantry volunteers and steadily rose through the ranks to become a brigadier general. Despite his success as a soldier, he hated the bitter sectional rivalries dividing the country and fueling the war. At its conclusion, Harrison returned to his law practice, entered Indiana politics, and was elected to the United States Senate where he became a strong advocate of federal aid to education.

Senator Harrison believed the best way to unite the still bitterly divided country was through public education. In 1884, he proposed the following amendment to the National Aid to Common Schools Act: "No money shall be paid out under this act to any State or Territory that shall not have provided by a law a system of free common schools for all of its children of school age, without distinction of race or color either in the raising or distributing of school revenues or in the school facilities afforded." The amendment passed, but the bill was defeated.

Four years later, Harrison was elected president. He used his first message to Congress to advocate the need for federal funding for education, writing,

> National aid to education has heretofore taken the form of land grants, and in that form the constitutional power of Congress to promote the education of the people is not seriously questioned. I do not think it can be successfully questioned when the form is changed to that of a direct grant of money from the public treasury. Such aid should be (authorized) by some exceptional condition. The sudden emancipation of the slaves of the South, the bestowal of the suffrage which soon followed, and the impairment of the ability of States where these new citizens were chiefly found to adequately provide educational facilities presented not only exceptional, but unexampled conditions.... It is essential, if much good is to be accomplished ... that the methods adopted should be such as to stimulate and not to supplant local taxation for school purposes.

Congress soundly rejected his reasoning. Following the Supreme Court's *Plessy vs. Ferguson* ruling that legally allowed public school children to be segregated by race, Congress seemed more determined than ever to not provide federal aid to education. Despite the rebuff, Harrison continued promoting the benefits of public schools. In one of many speeches on the subject, he declared,

> The public school is a most wholesome and hopeful institution. It has an assimilative power possessed by no other institution in our country where the children of the rich and poor mingle together on the playground and in the schoolroom. There is produced a unity of feeling and a popular love for the public institutions that can be brought about in no other way. God bless and promote public schools.

On the anniversary of George Washington's first inauguration, Harrison proposed displaying the United States flag in every public school classroom.

He hoped such a public demonstration of patriotism would create a shared sense of national unity for students from coast to coast. Public schools took up his challenge, and flags continue to be found in American classrooms to this day.

Caroline Scott Harrison also strongly supported female education. When asked to head up the Women's Medical Fund for the Johns Hopkins Medical School, she agreed on the condition the school "promote education and medical careers for women." The university accepted and other medical schools followed. For the first time in the nation's history, women were allowed to become medical students. Until her health broke, the first lady also found time to teach ceramics and have French classes taught in the White House for the daughters and wives of cabinet members interested in furthering their education. Caroline Harrison died in the final months of her husband's presidency shortly before he was defeated for reelection.

Following his single four-year term, Benjamin Harrison traveled to California where he lectured on constitutional law at Stanford University before retiring to his home in Indianapolis. The leading champion of public education in the United States and its greatest spokesperson died never having attended public school a day in his entire life. Eating cucumbers did not seem to be a contributing factor to his death.

Benjamin Harrison on Public Schools, Public Education, and the Common Ground They Provide

"The public schools are worthy of your most thoughtful care. It is there that children meet on common ground. It is there class distinctions are wiped out. It is the great America institution."

"Here on these benches and on these playgrounds the people of rich and poor mingle together and the pampered son gets his airs rubbed off with the vigor of his playmates."

"Our educational institutions beginning with the primary common schools and culminating in the great universities of the land are the instruments by which the future citizens of this country are to be trained in the principles of morality and in the intellectual culture which will fit them to maintain, develop, and perpetuate what their fathers have begun."

"Any child, however humble, can pass through our public schools and climb to any position of usefulness and honor he has the ability to attain."

"Education was early in the thought of the framers of our constitution as one of the best, if not the only guarantee of their perpetuation."

"How shall one be a safe citizen when citizens are rulers who are not intelligent?"

"Cherish it in your community the common schools of your state."

"If in any of the states the public security is thought to be threatened by ignorance among the electors, the obvious remedy is education."

Caroline Harrison Interview with Nellie Bly:

"I devote two mornings weekly to painting lessons, and one morning to a literature class.... We have three literary classes; and we have a Women's Club.... Besides the Women's Club we have the Fortnightly Club and the Merrill Library Club named in honor of our teacher, Miss Katherine Merrill, a remarkably gifted women. Our success is due to her teachings."

Ida Saxton and William McKinley
"No Startling Tales Are Told of His Precocity"

William and Ida Saxton McKinley were the last White House residents to live in the executive mansion in the nineteenth century and the first to live there in the twentieth century. After McKinley's election, reporters traveled to his childhood hometown to interview former teachers and playmates. The succinct understatement of one reporter captured the essence of the future president as a student: "No startling tales are told of his precocity." His best childhood friend was blunter: "I never thought Bill would be president."

McKinley did not grow up on a farm or receive his education in a one-room schoolhouse. When he was a young boy, he briefly attended the village school in Niles, Ohio. But his family then moved to Poland, Ohio, because it offered McKinley and his eight brothers and sisters a better education, a larger elementary school, and a local high school academy. By the time he was fifteen, McKinley proudly referred to himself as a "Latin scholar," but school reports described him as a "solid and thorough, rather than a showy student." The same adjectives might be used to describe his later political profile.

Following his high school graduation, McKinley briefly attended Allegheny College, but health and financial problems caused him to drop out. As the seventh child in a large family, he needed to work. Like his great-grandfather and two sisters, he went into teaching. The seventeen-year-old college dropout found a position at a one-room country schoolhouse not far from his parents' home.

McKinley received twenty-five dollars a month for teaching fifty students of all ages and skill levels. Some weeks he boarded with his students' families, but other times he walked several miles to and from school to stay at home with his parents. He hoped to earn enough money to return to college, but when the Civil War broke out in 1861, McKinley was faced with a decision. He

William McKinley taught in this one-room schoolhouse when he was only seventeen years old. When the Civil War broke out in 1861, McKinley decided to quit teaching and confront bullets and possible death on the battlefield rather than continue teaching his fifty unruly students (McKinley schoolhouse, Poland, Ohio — author collection).

could continue teaching fifty unruly students every day or confront bullets and possible death by going to war. McKinley promptly enlisted in the army.

When the war ended, he moved to Canton, Ohio, at the urging of his older sister Anna who taught there. She encouraged him to enter the legal profession, which he did. McKinley was a successful lawyer by the time he met and married Ida Saxton. She was a cashier and manager at her father's bank and taught Sunday school at the local Presbyterian church.

Ida Saxton received the best private school education available as the daughter of one of Canton's wealthiest businessmen. It was the time people came to call the Gilded Age. Those who had money wanted to display their wealth in homes, education, and travel. Ida was sent to boarding schools first in New York, and then in Cleveland, before attending a finishing school in Media, Ohio. Mr. Saxton then hired a teacher to take Ida, her sister Mary, and some of their friends to Europe "to visit the historic sites and those referring to literature and art." Their six month grand tour of Ireland, England, Scotland, France, Belgium, the Netherlands, Germany, Austria-Hungary, Switzerland,

and Italy was designed to complete their education and prepare them for prosperous marriages.

Following her wedding to William McKinley, Ida continued teaching Sunday school at the nearby Presbyterian church while her new husband taught Sunday school at the local Methodist church. This arrangement continued until they moved to Washington when McKinley was elected to Congress.

On a trip to Petersburg, Virginia, in 1885, McKinley made perhaps his most famous pre-presidential speech. The town near the Confederate capital of Richmond was the site of some of the bloodiest fighting during the late Civil War. There, using the poetry of Whittier, McKinley echoed the words of President Harrison and the role of education in bringing the country together:

> A School-house plant on every hill
> Stretching in radiate nerve-lines thence
> The quick wires of intelligence;
> Till North and South, together brought,
> Shall own the same electric thought;
> In peace a common flag salute;
> And, side-by-side, in labors free
> And unresented rivalry,
> Harvest the fields wherein they fought.

Following his election as governor of Ohio, McKinley was elected president of the United States in 1896 and then again in 1900. His opponent in both elections was William Jennings Bryan. Like McKinley, Bryan was educated in small-town America, not in the rural one-room schoolhouses of the past. Mr. Bryan's teacher-father wanted his son to have "the best education that the generation afforded." He planned on Bryan attending England's Oxford University, but financial reverses made that impossible. Instead Bryan was sent to local colleges where he studied Latin, Greek, political science and economics, without neglecting the spiritual side of his life. Following his wedding, he and Mrs. Bryan, like the McKinley's, both taught Sunday school until his election to Congress. In their presidential contests, voters twice choose the C student McKinley over the A student Bryan.

On the most important educational issue of the day, the *Plessy vs. Ferguson* Supreme Court ruling segregating students by race, McKinley remained silent. He was a transitional president, the last elected in one century and the first in another. As more people moved from farms to cities, waves of immigrants continued arriving in America. More women and men, blacks and whites, immigrants and American-born workers entered the urban workplace. Schools and the country were changing. McKinley recognized those changes in an address he gave in Columbus, Ohio, but provided no suggestions on how to meet them.

Old methods and standards may be good but they must advance with the new problems and needs of the age. The collegiate methods of the Eighteenth Century will not suffice for the Twentieth, any more than the packhorse could meet the demands of the great freight traffic of today. This age demands an education which, while not depreciating in any degree the inestimable advantage of high intellectual culture, shall best fit the man and woman for his or her calling, whatever it may be.

McKinley did not live to see the changes he predicted. He was assassinated in 1901.

William McKinley on Education

"How priceless is a liberal education! In itself what a rich endowment! It is not impaired by age, but its value increases with use. No one employ it but its rightful owner. He alone can illustrate its worth and enjoy its rewards. It cannot be inherited or purchased. It must be acquired by individual effort. It can be secured only by perseverance and self-denial. But it is as free as the air we breathe.... A liberal education is the prize of individual industry. It is the greatest blessing that a man or woman can enjoy, when supported by virtue, morality, and noble aims."

"Our hope is in the public schools and in the university. Let us fervently pray that they may always be generously supported."

"The free man cannot long be an ignorant man."

Ida Saxton McKinley

"People ought to travel to see how much there is to learn and read."

PART THREE

The Twentieth Century

Edith Carow and
Teddy Roosevelt
"We Call the Man Fanatic"

By the time Teddy Roosevelt entered Harvard College as a seventeen-year-old freshman he had hardly spent a day in school. His poor health, small size, and family travels kept him out of regular classrooms during most of his childhood. The only classroom he spent any time in as a child, was for a dance class he attended with his neighbor, good friend, and future wife Edith Carow. Edith, like Teddy, was primarily homeschooled. One Harvard classmate who saw Roosevelt in the college's gym described his physical condition as "a youth in the kindergarten stage of development." Roosevelt's mind was another matter. He received honors in all classes except Greek and graduated magna cum laude ranking 21 in a class of 161. Still, college was a disappointment to him.

Roosevelt's reason for attending Harvard was its strong reputation in the natural sciences, but he found the teaching uninspiring and the rigid curriculum a "total failure." He enjoyed hands-on experiments, but was unable to connect with any of the professors who were more interested in professing than teaching. Despite his lifelong passion and enthusiasm for the natural sciences, no professor in the department seemed to notice or take an interest in him. One classmate remembered, "A boy could go completely to pieces and there was no one whose job it was to know anything about it."

Harvard students were warned in the undergraduate weekly newspaper during Teddy's freshman year, "Don't take it upon yourself ... to ask questions or offer observations in recitations. Your questions would bore the students, and your observations would bore the tutors." Initially, Roosevelt ignored the advice; but after asking three questions during one natural history class, the most prominent professor in the department bluntly cut him off saying, "See here, Roosevelt, let me talk, I'm running this course."

More than his questions were silenced. For as intellectually curious, verbal, and social a student as Theodore Roosevelt was, the teacher-centered classroom was stifling. Years later, Harvard's president was asked if he remembered Roo-

When Teddy Roosevelt was a student at Harvard University he taught Sunday school for three years at the nearby Christ Episcopal Church in Cambridge, Massachusetts. He was fired when it was discovered he was not an Episcopalian (Christ Episcopal Church, Cambridge, Massachusetts — author collection).

sevelt the student. He vaguely recalled a "feeble" youth with "prominent teeth." A faculty member remembered Roosevelt as "an average B man ... not in any way distinguished." It may have been the last time in his life Teddy Roosevelt was called "average." His loss to the natural sciences was a gain for American politics.

During his years at Harvard, Roosevelt found time to teach a weekly Sunday school class. For three and a half years his class was held at Christ Episcopal Church, directly across from Harvard Yard and Massachusetts Hall where John Adams once lived as a student. Despite being raised in the Dutch Reformed faith, his teaching was well received and his classes well attended until a new rector discovered he was not Episcopalian. Roosevelt was told to convert or give up the class. The future president quit, but not before pointing out that he believed the rector was being narrow-minded. The last half of his senior year, Roosevelt continued teaching Sunday school, but in one of Cambridge's poorest neighborhoods. There his students were not only more diverse, they were encouraged to ask questions and actively participate.

Harvard in 1876 was like many old colleges of the time — an elitist blend of a snobby high school and a glorified country club. Unlike the land grant universities that began during and after the Civil War, most of these exclusive older colleges continued catering to descendants of their original constituents. Students there who took academics too seriously were generally looked down on. One observer wrote, "Socially, they had no chance." A popular Harvard song at the time exclaimed, "We deem it narrow-minded to excel. We call the man fanatic who applies.... We long to sit with newspapers unfurled, indifferent spectators to the world."

For Teddy Roosevelt, who loved reading and had a passion for learning, the adjustment must have been difficult. A Harvard acquaintance later wrote, "Most of his classmates simply did not like him." Yet Roosevelt became a respected New York City police commissioner and a successful western rancher, governor of New York and a colonel in the army, assistant secretary of the navy, vice president and then president of the United States. Along the way, he earned both the Medal of Honor for military service and the Nobel Peace Prize. Roosevelt later wrote of his college years, "There was very little in my actual studies that helped me in after-life. There was almost no teaching of the need for collective action, and ... collective responsibility." He regretted that he and his classmates were never taught or encouraged "to join with others in trying to make things better for the many by curbing the abnormal and excessive development of individualism in a few."

By the time Roosevelt became president in 1901, the United States, and even Harvard College, was changing. Blacks from the South were joining the waves of foreign immigrants filling the urban classrooms. Some welcomed the newcomers, others did not. Just twenty years earlier, Roosevelt's graduation class from Harvard had no Blacks, no Hispanics, no Italians, no student names ending in a vowel, no Jews, only three Catholics, none of them descendants of Boston's Irish immigrants, and no students from outside the continental United States.

As president, Roosevelt became the first White House resident to invite a black American to dine at the executive mansion. His guest was Booker T. Washington, perhaps the most respected educator in the country. Many southern newspapers condemned the event as a "damnable outrage." Roosevelt told a friend he felt "contemptuous indifference" to the backlash, but he was surprised and embarrassed by their bigoted reaction.

During the middle of Roosevelt's second term, the San Francisco School Board removed all ninety-one Japanese students from its public schools in order to segregate them from white students. Board members declared segregation a necessity in order to prevent a rising tide of illegal aliens, especially Asian immigrants, from crowding white students out of schools. The fact that the schools were not overcrowded and that many of the students and their families had lived in America for generations did not deter their decision. The news sparked anti–American rioting throughout Japan where the segregation of Japanese students was seen as a racial and cultural slur.

Roosevelt told his son, "The infernal fools in California, and especially in San Francisco, insult the Japanese recklessly and in the event of a war it will be the Nation as a whole which will pay the consequences." The president had no direct power to influence a locally elected school board, but Roosevelt quietly worked to resolve the crisis.

He asked Congress to naturalize Japanese citizens already living in the United States and lobbied California legislators to vote against statewide anti-immigrant legislation. Roosevelt assured a Japanese friend, "I shall exert all the power I have under the Constitution to protect the rights of the Japanese people who are here." In his annual address to Congress, Roosevelt publicly denounced the racial segregation of the Japanese students. "To shut them out from the public schools is a wicked absurdity when there are no first class colleges in the land, including the universities and colleges of California, which do not gladly welcome Japanese students and on which the Japanese students do not reflect credit. We have as much to learn from Japan as Japan has to learn from us; no nation is fit to teach unless it is also willing to learn."

Roosevelt directed the federal government to bring suit against the San Francisco School Board but also quietly invited its members to the White House. He promised to drop the federal lawsuit and to work to further restrict Japanese immigration if the school board reversed their segregation decision. The segregation order was dropped, Japan agreed to voluntarily curb immigration, but relations between the countries remained strained and continued to deteriorate.

Prior to the school segregation crisis, the United States and Japan had a history of positive, even cordial relations; but just forty-five years later, the war

Teddy Roosevelt feared with Japan came to pass. Some trace the spark lit at the time of the San Francisco school segregation crisis to the flames that consumed Pearl Harbor.

Theodore Roosevelt on Education

"The free public school, the chance for each boy or girl to get a good elementary education, lies at the foundation of our whole political situation. In every community the poorest citizens, those who need the schools the most, would be deprived of them if they only received school facilities proportioned to the taxes they paid. This is as true in one portion of our country as another."

"In all education we should widen our aims. It is a good thing to produce a certain number of trained scholars and students; but the education superintended by the state must seek rather to produce a hundred good citizens than merely one scholar, and it must be turned now and then from the class book to the study of the great book of nature."

"Education should not confine itself to books. It must train executive power, and try to create right public opinion, which is the most potent factor in the proper solution of all political solution and social questions. Book learning is important, but it is by no means everything."

"Education such as is obtained in our public schools does not do everything towards making a man a good citizen; but it does much."

"A man who has never gone to school may steal from a freight car; but if he has a university education, he may steal the whole railroad."

"A muttonhead after an education at West Point — or Harvard — is still a muttonhead."

Helen Herron and William Howard Taft

"To Live and Die a Professor"

In 1909, William Howard Taft, a proud graduate of Yale College succeeded Harvard's Teddy Roosevelt in the White House. Education was always important to Taft. Both his parents had been teachers. His wife Helen Herron went to private schools and college before becoming a teacher at the private school she once attended. The future first lady liked teaching but quit after two years because of the low pay and the challenge of disciplining students. She would have preferred a career in music which she described as "the inspiration of all my dreams and ambitions, but her parents wanted her to have a more traditional female career. By the end of the nineteenth century, the majority of teachers had become women.

Taft's childhood home overlooking Cincinnati shared a hilltop with the large public elementary school he attended. His mother and her sister had been students at Mary Lyon's Female Seminary in Holyoke, Massachusetts, the nation's "first permanent American institution for higher education of women." Taft's mother insisted he, his younger brothers, his sister and two older step-brothers from a previous marriage excel in their studies. She was a "driving force" in the community promoting the introduction of kindergarten classes in the city's public schools. At home, she carefully supervised her children's study time and homework.

When it came to grades, his father was even more demanding than his mother. Young Taft was a popular child, a good athlete, and a hardworking student, but only the last mattered to his father. Taft stood fifth in his grade school class of nearly forty students. By high school graduation, he was second. One teacher told him he was the brightest of any of his classmates and if he did not give in to his laziness, he might be successful. Taft's father never tired of quoting that teacher. The day following Taft's election to the White House, he returned to Cincinnati to lay the cornerstone for a new high school. He dedicated his first speech as president-elect to praise the public school education he had received.

It might be said that his parents and wife, public schools, and Yale made the man. A high school essay Taft wrote captured the changing times in which he lived:

> Co-education ... shows clearly that there is no mental inferiority on the part of the girls.... Give woman the ballot, and you will make her more important in the eyes of the world.... This will strengthen her character.... Every woman would then be given the opportunity to earn her livelihood. She would suffer no decrease in compensation for her labor on account of her sex.... In the natural course of events universal suffrage must prevail throughout the world.

These were radical thoughts in the early 1870s, but he learned the truth behind those words from his first teacher — his mother — and his extraordinarily bright wife, Helen Herron Taft. Helen excelled as a student at Miami University in Ohio in history, literature, science, and German. Taft once wrote his wife, "The thought of you has so much intellectual flavor and sweet sentiment.... You are my dearest and best critic and are worth so much to me in stirring me up to best endeavors." Helen Taft had a passion for learning that continued beyond college and extended throughout her entire life. She continued taking university classes in history, current events, and art even after the family moved to Washington, D.C.

When it came time to decide which college Taft himself would attend, there was no question. Taft's older brothers were Yale men, and his father was the first alum ever asked to serve on its board of trustees. At Harvard, the athlete was the most important campus hero; but at Yale more serious students like Taft were beginning to be more accepted. Despite his easygoing nature and popularity, he would occasionally threaten physical violence to persuade disruptors of his studies to move on. As if to prepare his father for the worst, he wrote home, "A fellow can work hard all the time and still not get perfect marks." Taft proved the point. Despite all his diligence, Taft only graduated second in a class of one hundred and thirty-two. A small consolation may have been improving on his father who graduated third in his own Yale class. The family honors for having the highest academic grades at Yale went to William's brother Peter, who subsequently suffered a complete nervous breakdown and died in a sanitarium.

Taft joined the Acacia fraternity when he was at Yale, the same fraternity of William Jennings Bryan, his opponent for president in 1908.

Taft was elected president in 1908, and gave what many believe, "the most disgraceful inaugural address of any president" in our history. Ignoring the constitutional mandates of the Fourteenth and Fifteenth amendments granting African Americans citizenship and the right to vote, Taft declared attempts to provide suffrage to southern blacks "a failure." He further stated, "It is not the disposition or within the province of the Federal Government to interfere with the regulation by the southern states of their domestic affairs." His inaugural address relegated responsibility for dealing with the rising tide of lynching, murders, harassments and intimidations against southern blacks to the "domestic affairs" of the southern states. Taft concluded his address by urging "intelligent, well-to-do, and influential" white southerners to "encourage the industrial education of the Negro." Many believed his presidential endorsement of "industrial education" for African Americans, in effect, sought to discourage the majority of black Americans from pursuing higher education. Shortly after his inaugural speech, Taft returned to his own college declaring, "I love Yale as I love my mother ... whatever is due ... the honor that came to me, I believe is due to Yale." Prior to, during, and after his presidency, Taft never used his political or personal influence to open the doors of Yale, or other schools, to blacks, women, or other minorities. He seemed to recognize and sincerely appreciate the importance of college for some people, but not others.

After leaving the White House and its $100,000 salary, Taft returned to Yale to accept a position for $5,000 a year as a professor of law. He was not a wealthy man but happily told friends, "I expect to live and die a professor." Early in his career, Taft had been a professor and dean at the University of Cincinnati Law School. While there, he was approached about becoming Yale's president but declined, feeling his liberal religious beliefs would offend the college's conservative financial supporters. He was also approached about leading Dartmouth, Johns Hopkins and other colleges and universities, but his heart remained at Yale.

Taft taught at Yale for eight years, regularly attending faculty meetings, athletic events, and school dances. Dancing came easily to the athletic Taft, but teaching proved difficult. Shortly before teaching his first class, he spoke to the editors of the *Yale News*: "The profession of teaching is a very different one from law or the functions of a judge on the bench. I have cultivated highly that ability to look wise, and if that sufficed on the teacher's platform I should have an easy sailing. I have cultivated that heat of the advocate before a court and I have shown that assumption of knowledge to a client, which a physician exhibits to his patient. I would be happy if these were all that was necessary." The former president discovered they were not.

Like many teachers, Professor Taft taught the way he learned best, through lecture and recitation. Despite his depth of knowledge, breadth of experience, and extraordinary interpersonal skills, students found him "surprisingly dull." He taught from the book, and since most Yalies could read, they found his class uninformative and uninspiring.

He, in turn, found a significant number of students intellectually lazy, all too willing to embrace the easiest way to complete assignments, and quick to cheat when the opportunity presented itself. Compounding the problem was Taft's tendency to arrive late to class and find the classroom empty. Unlike his White House cabinet, he discovered college students seldom wait for anyone, including ex-presidents of the United States. Yale's president visited the class and told the students they could not leave unless Taft was at least fifteen minutes late. His intervention sent a clear message to Taft's students. Their professor was a pushover, or he would have made the announcement himself.

Taft wanted everyone to recite, but he consistently lost half of the class the moment he called on his first student. Once he folded his large alphabetical class list in half to fit his lectern, he never turned it over again. Students immediately knew which half of the alphabet would be asked to participate. Their calculations did not stop there. Names facing upward only had a one-in-ten chance of having to answer a question during class. Most of the class quickly relaxed. Taft reinforced non-participating behavior by not recording those who spoke, repeatedly relying on verbal students to answer questions, and failing to give credit to those correctly reciting. The risk and rewards of non-preparation proved too tempting for students. Finally, taking pity on the frustrated former president, several students privately informed him what was going on. He laughed uproariously admitting he knew something was wrong but could not figure it out.

Students coached Taft on what he needed to do, and his teaching improved. He soon developed an equitable method of calling on everyone, began using open-ended case studies to encourage students to think, implemented regular writing assignments, and began giving untimed quizzes and final exams. As his confidence increased, he also began sharing personal experiences and stories that engaged his students through connections, illustrations, and examples.

By the end of Taft's first year of teaching he could honestly state, "You don't know, without experience, what a refuge from the sea of life this university has become." Taft embraced Yale, and the school embraced him. He helped coach the freshman debate team, attended student banquets, cheered for college teams and soon became a living legend on campus. Yet he found he was overwhelmed by paperwork. Reading, grading and writing personal comments on 120 to 200 papers a week devoured his time. Even using spare moments "on the train, in hotels, and in private homes," he could never stay ahead of the paperwork. In time, he used teacher assistants, but still created all exams, wrote individual comments, and monitored all student grades.

Cheating still troubled him. Taft thought a great deal about the problem, wondering what it said about a student who thought cheating necessary to succeed. He directly addressed the issue only once with his students. "To go to college and then not take the trouble to prepare your lessons is a foolish thing. When your children go to college you will find it hard to reconcile such practices on your part with the standards that you will wish them to follow.... Gentlemen, when you get as old as I am you will have observed that a man who cheats generally does so because he needs to." Taft could make no worse indictment of a person's character, but the cheating continued.

Taft planned to stay at Yale, but in 1921 he was appointed chief justice of the United States. Still, his association with the school continued. He often returned as a trustee and guest lecturer, and always surprised former students by remembering their names. Taft only missed three of his many college reunions. One of the former president's last public appearances was at Yale where he told his appreciative audience, "It is really a great pleasure to come back again to this fountain of youth."

For Taft, the education he received from Yale's professors and students provided some of the happiest times in his life. Yet, like many graduates of Ivy League colleges at the time, he did not believe higher education was for everyone. He explained, "Higher education is well for those who can use it to advantage, but it too often fits a man to do things for which there is no demand, and unfits him for work there are too few to do." The former president refused to believe such thinking was racist or elitist, believing that any national policy directly addressing race counterproductive. He defended himself by saying,

> Personally, I have not the slightest race prejudice or feeling, and recognition of its existence only awakens in my heart a deeper sympathy for those who have to bear it or suffer from it, and I question the wisdom of a policy which is likely to increase it. Meantime, if nothing else is done to prevent it, a better feeling between the Negroes and the Whites in the South will continue to grow, and more and more of the White people will come to realize that the future of the South is to be much benefited by the industrial and intellectual progress of the Negro.

The Tafts' only daughter earned a doctorate in history from Yale University, and later served as the dean and acting president of Bryn Mawr College. One of Taft's brothers founded his own prep school in Connecticut. First Lady Helen Herron Taft remained a lifelong learner. Like her mother-in-law, she crusaded to bring kindergarten classes into public education. Few presidential families celebrated education more than the Taft family, and few presidents recognized the importance of a college education more than William Howard Taft. Yet in many ways, his feelings on race and education were more rooted in the past than in the future.

Helen Herron Taft on Teaching

"I like teaching ... I really enjoy it. It is certainly a good discipline in patience ... I should not be so tired if when I came home from school I could only collapse and rest. I am in a chronic state of being tired out. I do not get sick, but I have just strength enough for it and no more."

"I do not dislike teaching when the boys behave themselves. I even feel that I rather like it, if I only felt that I could someday make more money."

"Every object used in kindergarten must be considered first as a key to the outer; second as an awakener to the inner world."

Ellen Axson, Edith Bolling Galt, and Woodrow Wilson
"To Transform Thoughtless Boys into Thinking Men"

When Woodrow Wilson was a student at Princeton, he wrote his father, "I have made a discovery; I have a mind." He was not joking. It had taken him years to figure out how to channel the way he learned into an acceptable configuration his teachers could understand. Wilson had been slow to speak and read as a child, started school late, and had already dropped out of one college. Most of his early life he struggled with a developmental learning disability that made school challenging. At Princeton, things improved, but he never made a strong impression on his teachers or they on him. He published two articles in a college literary magazine and one in a national magazine, but failed to graduate with honors or near the top of his class.

Still, university life agreed with him. He studied at Johns Hopkins, taught at Bryn Mawr and Johns Hopkins, then at Wellesley, before returning to Princeton as a professor. His first position in academia was at the newly opened Bryn Mawr College for Women. Cary Thomas, the school's female president, insisted that its curriculum and instruction be as academically vigorous as that found at any male college. She hired Wilson with the understanding he would complete his doctoral studies. Since school had always been a struggle for him, he resisted her demands. Eventually he negotiated a "special arrangement" with Johns Hopkins University allowing him flexibility to complete the program. Wilson's letter of petition explained he was a "nervous" student who "cut a sorry figure" with exams. He promised to succeed if given a chance. The school gave him that chance, and he did succeed.

It may have been at Johns Hopkins that Wilson began thinking seriously about teaching. The university "put postgraduate education and special training for teachers on a higher plane than had ever been known in America up to this time." Wilson's teachers seemed to follow the model of Yeats, who believed education not the filling of a pail, but the lighting of a fire. Even Wilson's classmates were impressive. One of them was John Dewey, an educational reformer who helped modernize and transform the nation's public school curriculum.

Earlier Wilson had dropped out of the University of Virginia Law School, but his time there had not been wasted. At Hopkins he seemed to connect the idea of a lawyer facing a jury to a teacher facing skeptical or indifferent students. Wilson began to revel at the "absolute joy in facing and conquering a hostile audience ... or thawing out a cold one." He told his wife that lectures should be real oratory, "the art of persuasion; the art of putting things so as to appeal irresistibly to an audience." But he was not a propagandist and was not troubled when students reached different conclusions than his own. What he most wanted was for them to think, to decide, to take positions, then support and defend them. Bad teachers he believed "had a genius for selecting the weakest forms of expression." The spoken word excited him, and he committed himself to using words in a way that would not allow him to be dull or boring in the classroom.

Wilson taught at Princeton for twelve years, becoming one of the most admired professors on campus. His verbal and mental skills captured the imagination of students who were known to interrupt lectures with cheers and stamping feet. Eventually, his classes were moved to the chapel in order to accommodate the overflow of students.

During his first year of teaching, he flunked one out of every thirteen students he taught. Almost no one received an A, but he was still voted Princeton's most popular professor. Wilson hated grading tests, partly because he felt personally disappointed and hurt when students did not do well. Once when asked how many students were at Princeton, he replied about ten percent. Students enjoyed his dry sense of humor, but their lack of academic effort troubled him.

As a professor, he worked hard to win over his students and usually succeeded through careful preparation, careful organization, and careful presentation. One student remembered, "He was the most inspiring college lecturer I've ever heard ... with his vivid pictures of incidents and characters." Another wrote, "His method was to give rapidly a description of the topic for the day with its lights and shades, its leading actors, its relations to former topics, its significance in relation to the whole subject. Then arousing our keenest interests, he proceeded."

For Wilson, the most important part of a lesson was its first minute. He happily exclaimed to a colleague one day, "I've decided on my opening sentence. That means the battle is won." Wilson worried a great deal about how to engage, energize, and encourage student thinking. Most students recognized his efforts, respected his knowledge, and enthusiastically embraced his lectures.

In 1896, he was selected as the faculty speaker at the college's sesquicentennial celebration. Representatives from colleges and universities associated with Princeton from across the nation were invited. One snobbish president from an old liberal arts college in southwestern Pennsylvania introduced himself using all his formal, pompous, secular, religious and academic titles. He then asked what position Wilson held at Princeton. Wilson replied, "I'm a teacher."

In 1902, Woodrow Wilson was unanimously elected president of the university. He quickly announced, "I will not be president of a country club. Princeton must either be an educational institution or I will not remain." Wilson's predecessor once declared to the faculty, "Gentlemen, whether we like it or not, we shall have to recognize Princeton is a rich man's college and rich men do not come to college to study."

Years in the classroom taught Wilson that few undergraduates were there to study. He noted, "Too many college students give their initiative and enthusiasm to other things and bring jaded minds to their classes." As an example of the problem, he told the story of a student who complained about an exam. "I don't think it is fair, sir. It makes a fellow think."

Wilson believed that a school's mission should be to "transform thoughtless boys into thinking men." It was a radical idea. In the early years of the twentieth century, most of the oldest established colleges in America continued to be primarily social clubs for sons of privilege. Princeton's new president, however, believed a college "false to its trust" if it did not demand thinking, real critical thinking. Working with faculty and trustees, he moved to reform three areas of college life: the curriculum, the methodology of teaching, and student living and dining arrangements. As he later wrote, "If you want to make enemies try to change something."

Woodrow Wilson married twice, and the education of both his wives reflected the times in which they lived. Each had been homeschooled. His first wife, Ellen Axson, was educated by her father because there were no public schools in Georgia when she was a child. His second wife, Edith Bolling Galt, was taught by her grandmother because her father believed sons, but not daughters, should be educated.

Ellen Axson eventually attended the Rome Female College in Georgia where she proved to be a superb student in mathematics, composition, literature, languages, and art. She hoped to attend Nashville University to become a teacher, but after passing the entrance exams did not have the needed tuition money. She returned to her former school and took postgraduate courses in French, German, and art. But her art instructor convinced her to begin selling her artwork and use the money for further schooling. She did, and was able to travel to New York to study at the Art Students League.

During her own studies, Ellen found time to become a teacher in some of the city's worst slums. Her classroom was over a saloon and her students were African American children who were taught reading, writing, math and Bible studies. It was not an easy job, but she was good at it. Ellen wrote Wilson whom she had met before moving to New York, "any small risk or unpleasantness connected with teaching" was outweighed by the pleasure it gave her and the good she was doing. Following a trip to Europe, she came home and they married. Later in life, when their three daughters were raised, Ellen returned to her art and became an accomplished professional painter. She exhibited and sold her popular watercolors donating all the money earned to a school for needy children in her hometown of Rome, Georgia.

When Wilson was hired to teach at Princeton, Ellen was horrified to hear students and faculty speaking openly about the widespread cheating there during examinations. She soon began working with students to create an honor code to combat the problem. Few thought it could work, but it did. Princeton's Honor Code became a model for other schools across the country.

Once he became president of Princeton, Wilson implemented many of his educational reforms despite strong resistance. In one year he doubled the size of the Princeton faculty and increased its diversity by hiring the first Catholic, and then, its first Jewish professor. He drew the line, however, at welcoming black students or black faculty members. Wilson explained the whiteness of Princeton in 1904 by writing, "The whole temper and the tradition of the place are such that no Negro has ever applied for admission, and it seems unlikely that the question will ever assume a practical form." Actually, three students of color had studied at Princeton by the end of the eighteenth century, but none graduated. A respected African American instructor taught at the institution by the end of the nineteenth century, and two African American men had received master's degrees there. But to Woodrow Wilson, it was unimaginable that Princeton would ever be anything but an all-white institution.

Most of the new faculty Wilson hired embraced his activist teaching philosophy, but he was less successful getting students to accept the college's revised curriculum. Some students complained, "Princeton was not the place it used to be … men were actually talking about their studies." In an address to the student body, Wilson announced that if they wished to stay at "the most charming Country Club in America," as Princeton was called, they "must pass their examinations."

Wilson continued teaching, although administrative duties forced him to frequently cancel classes. His lectures remained as popular as ever, but some students stubbornly withheld a full commitment to their studies. A fellow professor overheard two discussing Wilson's latest lecture. One said, "Did you ever in your life hear anything equal to that?" The other student replied. "I never did. He lives up to his reputation. Believe me, he is a world's wonder." Then he added, "And do you know the best part? He cuts half the lectures."

Woodrow Wilson dramatically "elevated the intellectual life of campus." But his Princeton days were numbered when his reforms began intruding on the social lives of the sons of wealthy donors. He told his brother-in-law, "What I am opposing is privilege. They would let me do anything in educational reform, but here I am attacking social privilege.... These people are not fighting me out of reason; they are fighting me on the basis of privilege, and privilege never yields." Wilson was right. Pressure soon forced him to resign from the university. Reform politicians, however, nominated him to run for governor of New Jersey, and he won.

Two years later, Wilson was elected president of the United States. People asked him how a "mere college president could meet and deal with politicians." He explained, "All he had ever seen in the politics of New Jersey or in the politics of the United States had never equaled what he learned about politics in his dealings with the Princeton trustees." Still he added, "It is a fine system when some remote severe school master could become president of the United States." John Adams and many other teacher presidents would agree.

Woodrow Wilson's Ten Rules of Teaching

- "The human mind has infinite resources for resisting the introduction of knowledge."
- "The mind does not consist in tasks performed, but in powers gained and enhanced."
- "The chief and characteristic mistake [of teaching] ... is devoting our selves to instruction and not enough to the life of the mind."
- "A certain percentage of students will always look upon their course work as unwanted intrusions into their personal lives and resent any time demands it makes upon them."
- "The knowledge that is supplied in school is not put there as if the student is merely a vessel to be filled to the top. The mind does not live by instruction. It is no prolix gut to be stuffed."
- "Wherever you have a small class and students are intimately associated with the study of an interesting subject, they catch the infection of that subject."
- "What we should seek to impart ... is not so much learning as the spirit of learning."
- "The educated mind is more apt to contribute light than heat to a discussion."
- "It is easier to move a cemetery than to effect change in a curriculum."
- "You must have a little spark in order to have a great blaze."

Wilson on Education

"I believe that there has been in all our universities in years past too much spirit of schoolboys; not because the men there have not really been interested in their studies, but because the processes of the University kept them schoolboys in their attitude toward their studies."

"Government resting upon the will and universal suffrage of the people has no anchorage except in the people's intelligence."

"It is an entirely wrong conception of the college to assume we are aloof and sheltered. We in the college are a part of the seething life of humanity; and there is an obligation not to withdraw ... but to make the college itself and all its life and energy a part of the redemptive processes of humanity."

Florence Kling and Warren G. Harding
"Naturally Smart"

Teddy Roosevelt went to Harvard, Taft went to Yale, and Woodrow Wilson went to Princeton. By the 1920 presidential election, America was in the mood for a simple man. They found him in the humble, handsome, and simple Warren G. Harding. Some would say Harding had much to be humble about. Shortly before his death he told a friend, "I know my limitations. I know how far removed from greatness I am." He was right. But he was just what the country wanted after the three giants who preceded him. Harding's sincere humility and handsome features endeared him to the country. Only when the corruptness of his administration was exposed following his death 882 days into his presidency did the public have second thoughts about him. Harding earned the sad distinction of being the first president in American history to have a sitting cabinet member imprisoned for bribery.

Warren G. Harding was born in Ohio to his doctor father who had once been a teacher. His mother was a nurse-midwife who taught Sunday school. The future president was able to read even before going to the same brick schoolhouse his grandfather had built and where his father once taught. Like most nineteenth-century students, Harding grew up reading tales from the McGuffey readers about American heroes such as George Washington and Abraham Lincoln. His own childhood heroes were Napoleon Bonaparte and Alexander Hamilton. Later, he added Julius Caesar. Yet as a student, he displayed no intellectual curiosity, academic discipline, or desire to be on the world stage.

His friends later recalled, "He was not the precocious type of youngster" but managed to "pull through his examinations." His father once said, "He studied his lessons, I don't know when. I never caught him at it and it used to worry me, so I asked his teacher what Warren was doing to bring in such decent reports when he didn't seem to work. 'Oh, he's just naturally smart,' his teacher said."

The "naturally smart" boy entered Ohio Central College when he was fourteen. He was a popular student better known for being tall, dark, and handsome than for displaying any academic enthusiasm. His college roommate wrote that Warren was "good at cramming." He would ignore the subjects he did not enjoy until exam time. Then he would "sit down with his face to the wall, head in hands, and soak [the subject] up.... When he was through, he would jump up with a yell and shout, 'Now darn it, I've got you' and slam the book against the wall."

Harding's mathematics professor never tired of telling his Ohio students that they were not as smart as those he once taught in Delaware. Warren decided to take up the "challenge." He "stayed up far into the morning hours studying." The next day when he was called on to recite, he happily engaged in a duel with his professor, "demonstrating propositions for two solid class hours without an error." The inquisition ended when Warren asked, "Is that as good as they do in Delaware?" The weary professor conceded it was. He never again compared his Ohio students to those in Delaware, and Warren Harding never again came to class prepared.

The two highlights of Harding's college career were extracurricular. He became the editor of the school newspaper, and he played alto horn in the school band. It was those activities that provided him his happiest times at school. Despite having to quit more than once in order to earn the seven dollars a semester needed for tuition, he still managed to graduate with a bachelor of science degree at seventeen years of age. Warren was one of three 1882 graduates from his school. No record was kept on whether he ranked academically in the top, middle, or bottom of his class. But due to his fine public speaking skills, he was chosen to give the school's commencement address. No one could recall later what he said.

Following college Harding wrote, "I did what was very much in practice at the time — turned to teaching, in my abundant fullness of knowledge." His good looks, charm, and confidence helped him easily find a job at a one-room country schoolhouse just two miles from his childhood home. Despite his considerable assets, he failed as a teacher. Harding was the oldest of eight children and was used to being looked up to by younger children and admired by adults. His students, however, found no reason to like or admire him since he was unable to establish or maintain discipline. They quickly took to ignoring, taunting, or laughing at him.

As his teaching career drew to a close, Harding wrote his aunt,

I am still fighting ignorance with fair success. Of course, there are some chronic kickers, but I deem THAT the best evidence on MY SUCCESS. Next Friday, one week, i.e., the 23rd inst., forever my career as a pedagogue will close, and — oh, the joy! I believe my calling to be in some other sphere and will follow out the belief. I sincerely hope my winter's labors are not lost, but that those with whom I have labored are somewhat benefited. How often it is that one's most arduous toils are without appreciation! I will never teach again without better [a good deal, too] wages, and an advanced school.

Warren Harding was the last president to teach in a one-room schoolhouse. After leaving teaching, he sold insurance, managed a baseball team, played in a band, became editor of a small-town newspaper and eventually entered politics. Later, whenever the subject of teaching was mentioned, he recalled, "It was the hardest work I ever performed."

Harding never earned his students' respect and never learned how to control their outrageous behavior. He had similar problems with his cabinet when he was president. He once said in the White House, "I have no trouble with my enemies. I can take care of my enemies in a fight. But my damn friends, they're the ones who keep me walking the floor nights."

He married Florence Kling, his sister's strong-willed music teacher. The formidable Florence had none of the discipline problems her husband had teaching. Florence had been an excellent, very determined student at the boarding schools she attended and later studying piano at the Cincinnati Conservatory of Music. She nearly always got what she wanted, including the presidency for her unambitious husband. When they walked into the White House on the day of his inauguration, she declared, "Well, Warren Harding, I have got you the Presidency. What are you going to do with it?" His response was, "May God help me." Barely two and a half years later, he died from exhaustion and heart failure.

During his brief time in the White House, Harding became the first president to travel south and give a speech connecting the nation's race problems with education. In 1921, he boldly told a segregated audience in Alabama he was going to speak on the race problem, "whether you like it or not."

In his speech he declared, "Let the black man vote when he is fit to vote, prohibit the white man voting when he is unfit to vote." Harding then stated "equal educational opportunities" must be provided for both races.

It is a matter of keenest national concern that the South not be encouraged to make its colored race a vast reservoir of ignorance.... If we mean the things we say about democracy as the ideal political state.... Every consideration, it seems to me, brings us back to the question of education. I would like to see an education that would fit every man, not only to do his particular work as well as possible, but to rise to a higher plane if he would deserve it. For that sort of education, I have no fear whether it be given to a black man or a white man. From that sort of education, I believe black men, white men, the whole nation, would immeasurably benefit.

Harding concluded his remarks, "The nation could not enjoy the promise of prosperity until the matter of race was addressed." The *New York Times* reported, "Negros in the audience" provided "loud and lusty cheers," but he received only "scattered" applause from the "white section" of his listeners.

Despite his remarks, Harding's white hosts still awarded him an honorary degree at the local segregated college.

Throughout his short presidency, Harding never forgot his time as a classroom teacher. He took every opportunity to praise teachers, describing himself as a "lifelong friend of the teaching profession." In one speech he proclaimed, "By experience and association I know the school teaching profession. I know the aspirations of the teaching world, and believe as cordially as anyone in America in recognizing the calling, as it merits both befitting compensation now, and comfort and security in retirement after an honored and valued public service." The former teacher never lived long enough to experience the "comfort and security" of his own retirement. He died at fifty-seven years of age.

Warren G. Harding on Education

"Every student has the ability to be a successful learner."

"The strength and security of the nation will always rest in the intelligent body of its people. Our education should implant conceptions of public duty and private obligation broad enough to envisage the problems of a greatly distraught world."

"I would lift up a Macedonian calf in behalf of our schools and colleges, to men and women who feel the urge to public usefulness. More even than money and endowments, our educational establishments need the devout and unselfish sustaining support of people moved by instincts of patriotism and service."

Warren Harding on the Teaching of History in the Post–World War I Era

"The teaching of history will have to be conducted, if it is conducted wisely, on different lines than have marked it in the past. There has been too much disposition among both the writers and students of history to deal with the different nations of the western world, as it were, in separate compartments; to assume that one may study and understand the history of one nation without particularly devoting himself to the relations of that particular nation to the others. Undoubtedly, we shall from this time forward have a much more adequate conception of the essential unity of the whole story of mankind; and a keener realization of the fact that all its factors mush be raised and appraised if any of them are to be accurately estimated and understood. I feel strongly that such a broader view of history, if it can be planted in the community's mind of the future through the efforts of educators and writers, will contribute greatly to uphold the hands and strengthen the efforts of those who will have to deal with the great problem of human destiny, particularly with that of preserving peace and outlawing war."

Grace Goodhue and Calvin Coolidge

"A Professionally Trained Teacher"

The death of Warren G. Harding brought Vice President Calvin Coolidge to the presidency in 1923. Coolidge never taught, but being a practical New Englander, he got a teaching license just in case he ever needed one. In his autobiography, he reminisced about his old school and the path many people from small-town America once took to teaching.

> The little stone school house which had unpainted benches and desks wide enough to seat two was attended by about twenty-five scholars. Few, if any, of my teachers reached the standard now required of all public schools. They qualified by examination before the town superintendent. I first took this examination and passed it at the age of thirteen and my sister Abbie passed it and taught in a neighboring town when she was twelve.

Coolidge's parents met as students in school. His mother died on her thirty-third birthday when Calvin was twelve. His father, a former school superintendent later married one of his son's former teachers. Coolidge was never an outstanding scholar, but he liked teachers and married one himself. She was Grace Goodhue, who taught at the Clarke Institute for the Deaf in Massachusetts. Like her future husband, Grace was a Vermonter who attended public schools without becoming an academic superstar. She was described as a "neglectful" student.

Grace Goodhue was one of the first women admitted to the University of Vermont, but devoted most of her time there to her sorority. Shortly before graduation a friend got her interested in working with the hearing impaired. After earning her bachelor of philosophy degree, Grace traveled to Massachusetts to study and then teach at the Clarke Institute, a school made famous by Alexander Graham Bell and other outstanding educators of the deaf.

Despite being an average student, she became an outstanding teacher once she wed her intelligence and her enthusiasm toward reaching and teaching her students. She was a "lively extrovert, with an unquenchable taste for good times, an infectious laugh and a knack for endearing herself to others." She brought her energy and warm personality to her classroom, first with students in the primary grades and later with middle school students. The school's director later wrote, "She was a professionally trained teacher who knew their language, [and] took time to understand all people. Her love of deaf children was lifelong and she strongly believed they could be taught to talk, and must be given full command of all communications." Another colleague recalled that her students "loved her.... She understood them, and ... felt the teaching of deaf was a vocation to which one could give one's whole being. She had an instinctive understanding of their needs as well as a very practical knowledge of what was required."

It was when she was teaching at the institute that she began dating the shy, taciturn Calvin Coolidge. A girlfriend teased Grace, "Now that you have taught the deaf to hear, you've set your sights on teaching the mute to speak." Coolidge was quiet, but in private he could be articulate, eloquent, and thoughtful. He gave Grace a beautiful illustrated children's book for her students inscribed with a note, "I wonder if your students realize what a good teacher you are." Coolidge found in this teacher of the deaf someone who understood his own silence.

They married in 1905. Grace retired from the classroom, transferring her

Grace Goodhue Coolidge was a teacher at the Clarke School for the Deaf in Massachusetts. As first lady she visited the school with her husband and remained a supporter of education for the hearing impaired throughout her lifetime. Calvin Coolidge earned his own teaching certificate when he was thirteen. His sister taught in a one-room schoolhouse when she was twelve (photograph courtesy Clarke Schools for Hearing and Speech, Northampton, Massachusetts).

personal and professional gifts to her husband. At the time of her wedding, Grace wrote a letter to her best friend providing an insight into herself, and perhaps Calvin Coolidge. "My mother ... claims I have no feelings, because I don't talk about them. I sometimes think that those who can speak of them don't always have the most sensitive ones."

The week Calvin and Grace Coolidge returned from their honeymoon, he began campaigning for election to the local school board. It was the only election he ever lost. A friend told him he had voted for his opponent because the other man had children. Coolidge replied, "Give me time." One month short of their first anniversary, Grace delivered their first son.

Coolidge was ambitious. During the next ten years, the quiet student whom almost none of his classmates seemed to notice was elected first to the state house of representatives, and then the mayor of Northampton, Massachusetts. From there he was elected to the state senate, and rose to become the president of the senate before being elected lieutenant governor. He was soon governor of Massachusetts and then vice president of the United States. Fifteen years after being defeated for the school board, Harding's death brought the Coolidges to the White House. He was reelected by a landslide in 1924.

Grace Coolidge was probably the only woman thrown out of the White House who later returned as first lady. Her earlier unceremonious exit happened when she was a chaperone for the Northampton High School senior field trip. On their visit to the executive mansion, Grace saw Helen Taft's grand piano "with ivory finish ... trimmed in gold to match the motifs in the Blue Room." Grace spontaneously sat down and played the students a tune. A White House security guard promptly escorted the group, and their chaperone, off the grounds. Grace never forgot the incident. She looked for the piano when she became first lady, but it was gone with Mrs. Taft.

People called President Coolidge "Silent Cal," but he gave more speeches and held more press conferences than any of his predecessors. One of his favorite talking points was about the importance of education. Recognizing the growing migration of southern blacks to American cities, he asked Congress to appropriate nearly half a million dollars "to help pay for the education of five hundred colored doctors needed each year." Calvin Coolidge also became an outspoken advocate of increased respect and pay for teachers. He seemed to understand and value teachers, perhaps because he married one who understood and valued him.

As first lady, Grace Coolidge never lost her commitment to the hearing impaired. She personally led tour groups through the mansion when they included visitors with hearing impairments. Perhaps remembering her earlier encounter, she encouraged students, teachers, and chaperones to touch the furniture and ask questions. She also welcomed Helen Keller, William Howard Taft's brother and sister-in-law, and many other hearing-impaired guests to fully participate in the social life of the White House.

In later years, Mrs. Coolidge became a trustee, then president, of the board of the Clarke School where she once taught. In the process she raised millions of dollars to fund their education programs. In time Smith College, Syracuse University and the University of Massachusetts offered joint degrees to Clarke graduates helping to fulfill her dream of equal educational opportunities for students with hearing impairments.

Grace Coolidge raised the profile, the status, and the expectations of what a first lady could do in the White House. She became the first wife of a president to receive honorary degrees for her humanitarian efforts. At the time of her death in 1957, her friend the future president John F. Kennedy declared, "As a fellow trustee of the Clarke School for the Deaf in Northampton I have strong personal recollection of her untiring devotion and labors throughout her life to this most worthy cause."

The director of the Clarke School may have captured best the essence of the former first lady's proudest claim to fame declaring, "The world has lost its most famous teacher of the deaf." Grace Coolidge helped to open up the world not only for the hearing impaired, but to the wives of future presidents on the potential for good the role of first lady offered them.

Grace Coolidge on Teaching and Teachers of the Deaf

"For many years it has been my privilege to keep closely in touch with the work done in the highly specialized field of education for deaf children and I am increasingly amazed at results obtained by combined efforts of teachers and pupils. I know of no profession more challenging nor of one which yields greater returns."

"What kind of person shall I say makes the best oral teacher? Someone who believes every deaf child can learn to talk and who wants to help him."

"The question is often asked, 'Does it not take a great deal of patience to teach the deaf?' The answer is, not more than is brought to the task of teaching hearing children. To see the face of a deaf child light up when a new idea is brought to him and he learns to put that idea into spoken and written form is a satisfying return for the effort put forth by the teacher."

Calvin Coolidge on Education

"If society lacks learning and virtue, it perishes."

"College is not to educate the individual, but to educate society."

"Education must not only give power but direction. It must minister to the whole student or it fails."

"There is given to legislators and magistrates a mandate forever to cherish and support the cause of education and institutions of learning."

"There are now no pains too great, no costs too high, to present or diminish the duty enjoined by the constitution of the Commonwealth that wisdom and knowledge, as well as virtue, be generally diffused among the body of the people."

"The individual may not require the higher institutions of learning, but society does. Without them civilization as we know it would fall from mankind in a night."

Coolidge on "the Noblest Profession"

"The cause of America is the cause of teaching, but of education with a soul, a trained intellect but guided over by enlightened conscience."

"The days of the Revolution ... teaching was to a considerable extent in the hands of the clergy. Institutions of learning were presided over by clergymen. The teacher spoke with the voice of authority. He was treated with deference. He held a place in the community that was not only secure but high.... That dual character little exists now, but the principle is the same. Teaching is the same high calling, but lacking now in the comparative appreciation."

"In an address I made at a Harvard College commencement I undertook to direct attention to the inadequate compensation paid to our teachers, whether in the universities, public schools, or the pulpits of the land. It is perfectly clear that more money must be provided for these purposes, which surpass in their importance all other public activities."

"We pay a good price to banks that guard our money. We compensate liberally the manufacturer and the merchants; but we fail to appreciate those who guard the minds of our youth."

"Government must adequately reward the teachers in schools.... These ... pillars of liberty and equality, have been neglected and left behind.... They must be restored to the place of reverence they formerly held."

"The sterling character of teachers of all kinds has kept them at their task even though we have failed to show them due appreciation. Unless a change is made and a new policy is adopted, the cause of education will break down. It will either become a trade for those little fitted for it or abandoned altogether, instead of remaining the noblest profession which it has been and ought to be."

"The profession of teaching has come down to us with a sanction of antiquity greater than all else. So far back as we can peer into human history there has stood a priesthood that has led its people intellectually and morally. Teaching is leading."

"Education is the result of contact. A great people is produced by contact with great minds."

"They minister not alone to their students, they minister to all humanity."

Lou Henry and Herbert Hoover

"A Whole New World of Ideas"

Herbert Hoover liked teachers and they liked him. His mother had been a teacher in Iowa before he was born and she was determined that her children would receive a good education. But his father died when Bert was six and his mother died three years later. After his parents' death, Bert was separated from his brother and sister who were sent to live with different relatives. Hoover's schoolteacher tried to adopt the orphan, but the family decided to send him to Oregon to be raised by his uncle. There Hoover attended the Friends Pacific Academy where his uncle, a former teacher, served as the school's principal. Following his graduation, the future president worked at several jobs and attended night school, where a teacher discovered his "natural aptitude" for mathematics. With his teacher's support, the seventeen-year-old Hoover enrolled at the newly opened Stanford University in California. Bert was not an A student, but he was a hard worker and was befriended by Dr. John Branner, his geology professor. Dr. Branner hired him as his teaching assistant and introduced him to Lou Henry, the only woman at the university majoring in geology. Lou had taught third grade, and her mother had also been a teacher. She later became Mrs. Herbert Hoover.

During her own childhood, Lou's schooling was frequently interrupted as her family moved from Iowa to Texas, back to Iowa, then to Kansas, and finally to California. Despite the challenge of always being the new girl in school, the moves provided Lou and her nature-loving father opportunities to discover fresh camping and fishing sites wherever they lived. Lou loved being outside, enjoyed both winter and summer sports, and later became a lifelong supporter of the Girl Scouts and their outdoor camping and education programs.

Mr. Henry believed "a girl could do anything a boy could do" and encouraged his daughter to develop her full academic and athletic talents. Lou became a scholar-athlete, and a self-assured leader at the public schools, private schools, and academies she attended. The future first lady loved learning about mathematics, history, and geography, and someday hoped to teach those subjects. But after graduating and holding one brief teaching job, she was unable to find a permanent teaching position. Lou then enrolled at Stanford University where in 1898 she became "the first woman in the United States to earn a degree in geology."

After his own graduation from Stanford, Hoover took whatever jobs he could find throughout the United States and as far away as Australia, but he continued to write Lou. When he was offered a good-paying engineering job in China, they married and quickly sailed for Asia. With Lou's help, Hoover earned an international reputation that took them around the world many times. The future president and first lady became passionate readers of fiction and nonfiction to fill their "hours of waiting for things to happen on ships, railways, and canal boats." Hoover later wrote, "While textbooks are necessary for learning, it was those other books which stimulated imagination and a better understanding of life. They made the whole world a home. They broadened my scope and made me feel a part of the mighty stream of humanity."

Hoover's reputation as an engineer, and his humanitarian efforts to prevent starvation in Europe following the First World War, earned him an appointment as secretary of commerce in the Harding-Coolidge administrations. Without ever holding public office, Hoover was elected president in 1928. The book-loving president discovered that the White House library Abigail Fillmore created seventy-five years earlier had disappeared through years of neglect. Working with the American Booksellers Association, Hoover selected 500 books for a new library made of the best of American literature "to be enjoyed by many other inhabitants of the White House."

In 1929, the Hoovers celebrated his birthday at their mountain retreat in the Shenandoah Valley. During the celebration, an eleven-year-old neighbor from a nearby hollow presented the president with a possum as a birthday present. The Hoovers discovered that the boy and his seven brothers and sisters had never attended school, seen a map, heard a radio, or watched a movie. He and his family had never even traveled beyond their mountain hollows. The birthday possum brought the Hoovers face to face with illiterate children living in third world conditions in the heart of America.

The president and first lady decided to build a school, hire a teacher, and provide their poverty-stricken neighbors an education. With as little publicity as possible, the president contacted several wealthy friends and arranged for land to be purchased and a school to be built. A teacher was hired from Kentucky's Berea College for $125 per month. The President's Mountain School enrolled students ranging in age from five to eighteen. At night the parents and grandparents of the students were also taught. The school's first teacher, Christine Vest, remembered that her "most faithful ... adult night school pupil ... was Mr. George Burraker, the father of nine children. He could read simple print but could not write, read script, or read numbers. He loved using the blackboard and his first wish was to learn to write his first name."

Miss Vest also later recalled, "I stewed and fretted over what my approach would be ... to teach these children of varied ages and experience.... How could I stimulate their interest in the very essentials of learning?" She found her answer in the Sears-Roebuck catalogue. Miss Vest introduced her students to reading, writing, and arithmetic by using pictures of shoes, tools, and dresses from the catalogue. "The girls selected the dress they liked and we learned the word DRESS. Later the numbers made up the price, then to write the word, and so we went until they could read and write and knew their numbers. We branched out to other books and later regular grade work, but always, if interest began to wane, I produced the catalogue for inspiration."

Perhaps Miss Vest's greatest ally in attracting students to the school was introducing them to twentieth-century technology. "The radio was one of the greatest mysteries they encountered. I tried many times in my feeble way to explain its workings— to all it was truly a magic box." The President's Mountain School soon became the local social center, hospital, barber, tailor shop, and church for local families.

At the end of the school term Miss Vest wrote, Mrs. Hoover visited bringing,

> a picnic lunch with extras for the children and we all had a good time under the big oak tree. After lunch, she went inside to watch them have their regular class work. She seemed very pleased with what she saw and the children enjoyed displaying the knowledge and skills they had learned.... The children had a genuine affection for Mrs. Hoover. They appreciated the school but were genuinely fond of her. When she was out horseback riding, the parents loved having her stop in for a visit. She learned all their names quickly and when I talked to her of the school and the people, it was on a first name basis for each one.

The school continued in operation until the Shenandoah Park was founded and the government moved the families away from the mountain to other schools. Miss Vest later reminisced,

> Mr. Hoover's school ... opened up a whole new world of ideas [for them].... "Some of the children made normal progress in school, but some of the older ones did exceptionally well. As soon as they were ready, I tried to put them in a regular grade. I also tried to let the fast ones go at as rapid a pace as possible. When they moved from the mountain because of the park, the older ones went to work and the younger ones found their places in the regular schools where they moved. I often wondered what their lot would have been if they had not had all this presentation before leaving their mountain.

Lou and Herbert Hoover came from humble roots, but education gave them the world. They recognized the importance of reading and getting an education. And due to that recognition, and a birthday possum, the Hoovers used the model of the nineteenth-century one-room school-house to bring more than one generation of Appalachian families into the twentieth-century.

Herbert Hoover on Teachers

"Who does not remember with a glow some gentle woman who with infinite patience and kindness drilled into us those foundations of all we know today?"

Lou Henry Hoover on Public Education

"We believe that the democratic influence of a good public school in a good community gives a much better training than the unavoidable exclusiveness of even the best private schools."

Eleanor and Franklin Roosevelt
"I Never Forgot a Damn Thing She Ever Taught Me"

Franklin and Eleanor Roosevelt were distant cousins privately tutored at their respective New York homes before both were sent away as young adolescents to boarding schools. Franklin began attending the Groton School thirty-five miles outside of Boston when he was fourteen. Fifteen-year-old Eleanor was sent across the Atlantic to Allenswood School on the outskirts of London. Except for a convent school in France that expelled her when she was six for making up stories and lying, Eleanor never attended any other school. The school experiences of the two cousins proved to be dramatically different. Eleanor was an orphan who had always felt like an outsider, but at Allenswood she emerged as one of the school's most popular students. Franklin had been the star of his family and friends his entire life. At Groton, he felt like an "interloper" and found himself an "outcast."

The only man who was ever elected president four times remembered his school days with these words: "I always felt entirely out of things." His headmaster did not disagree, writing, "There has been a good deal written about Franklin Roosevelt when he was a boy at Groton, more than I should have thought justified by the impression that he left at the school." Even when Roosevelt was at the height of his presidential popularity, a classmate declared, "I can't understand this thing about Frank. He never amounted to much at school." Eleanor Roosevelt recalled that things went "wrong" for her husband at school. His classmates "didn't like him ... he was never of the inner clique."

Franklin Roosevelt arrived at Groton two years later than most of his classmates who by then had already formed close friendships and adjusted to the school culture. Hazing of newcomers was an accepted part of school life, and Franklin quickly became a target of older boys. Despite difficulty with spelling and leaving words out of compositions, he was rated academically a "slightly better than average scholar." But his strange accent from traveling and living abroad, slight height and weight, and lack of athletic ability did not help him be accepted. Football was the premier sport at Groton, and Franklin was not good at it. He had never played on a team sport, and it showed. Abandoning football, he ended up playing baseball, describing his teammates in a letter home as "about the worst players in the school." The primary rewards for his athletic efforts were injuries.

In letters home, a very adolescent Franklin Roosevelt did everything he could to persuade his parents to bring him home from boarding school. Selected quotes from his letters include:

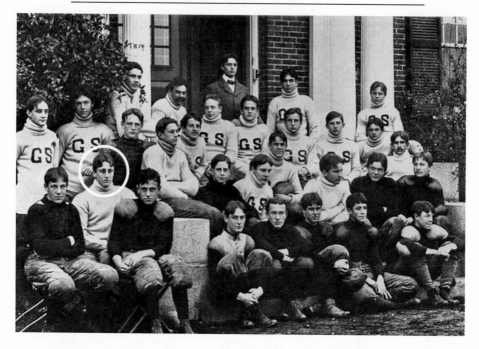

Franklin Roosevelt at Groton Prep School in 1899 always felt like an outsider. Here (face is circled) he poses with his baseball teammates whom he described as "about the worst players at school." Eleanor Roosevelt recalled things went terribly "wrong" for her husband there. His classmates "didn't like him ... he was never of the inner clique" (photograph courtesy FDR Library).

"My Dear Mama and Papa:

It feels very familiar to be back here, rather sickening."

"I have been given two black marks [demerits] since I came back ... given for no fair reason."

"One of the new boys got half way across the river and got very tired. We had to hold him up by his hair until a canoe came to the rescue."

"I'm hoping to get pink eye so I can come home."

"Thank you very much for the grapes, they are delicious. Please do not send anymore, because Mr. P says that they make too much mess on the floor."

"I was given a black mark [demerit] yesterday that was not deserved."

"I do not intend to overwork myself as I did last term."

"Last Monday was a red letter day for me ... we had the Class II high kick ... at every kick I landed on my neck on the left side so the result is that the whole left side of my body is sore and my left arm is a little swollen."

"I shall begin studying next Monday."

"Lot's of fellows are going to fail ... as old A ... has given us an awful lot more than we can possibly do."

"I have managed to keep reasonably uninjured my only casualties were having the wind knocked out twice and a kick over the appendix."

"I forgot to mention in my last letter, that I together with most have just taken the most outrageous ... exam which has ever been known in the history of education. Not only was it unfair, but the marking was atrocious ... the old idiot A ... refused to pass me as is customary when one almost passes."

"The trouble is that one must write on entirely original subjects and everything must have a point to it."

"I do not understand why I do not have an A ... as [the teacher] ... told me himself that I had an A. I intend to speak about it as I do not wish to be cheated out of it if I really deserved it."

"I have managed to get 3 or 4 black marks [demerits] this week, but I had good fun, quite worth them!"

His parents were sympathetic but did not take him out of Groton. Throughout his time at the school, he got along better with adults and younger students than peers. Perhaps because of his lack of popularity, the attention of teachers and the headmaster became especially important to him. To the annoyance of fellow students, he tirelessly tried to court and please adults. For the rest of his life he kept in regular contact with Endicott Peabody, his former headmaster, saving all their correspondence and even having him officiate at his wedding. As president, Roosevelt often invited him to the White House and affectionately quoted "my old schoolmaster" in his fourth inaugural address. Peabody may have been the only friend Franklin made at boarding school.

Eleanor Roosevelt was the ugly duckling who became a swan at school. She learned to find her voice there. Despite its English location, Allenswood students were required to speak only French in and out of class, whether the conversation was academic or social. Her headmistress and favorite teacher, the very French Mademoiselle Souvestre, recognized, invested in, and nurtured Eleanor's potential until it became a reality. Unlike her future husband, Eleanor was embraced and celebrated by fellow students. School and her teachers taught her to believe in herself, but it was Mademoiselle Souvestre who became the single "most significant influence on her intellect and emotion."

Souvestre wrote that the future first lady has "the warmest heart I ever encountered.... She is full of sympathy for all ... [with] an intelligent interest in everything she comes in contact with.... As a pupil she is very satisfactory but even that is of small account when you compare it with the perfect quality of her soul." Souvestre's recognition of Eleanor Roosevelt's wonderful combination of head and heart strengthened both. Not since the death of Eleanor's father when she was ten had anyone recognized her special gifts.

Mademoiselle Souvestre was not just a remarkable judge of character; she

Eleanor Roosevelt is one of many students in this group shot at the Allenswood School in England in 1900. Unlike her future husband, however, Eleanor was embraced and celebrated by students and teachers at her school. She later became a teacher herself and declared, "I like it better than anything else I do" (photograph courtesy FDR Library).

was also a great teacher. She had the enthusiasm found in most successful teachers and she had it times four: enthusiasm for learning, enthusiasm for teaching, enthusiasm for her students, and enthusiasm for life. One student remembered that her lessons were "informed by that infection of ardor, that enlivened zest, which were the secrets of her success as a schoolmistress.... The dullest of her girls were stirred into some sort of life in her presence, to the intelligent girls she communicated a Promethean fire which warmed and colored their whole lives."

Under her teacher's challenging but encouraging influence, Eleanor's self-confidence soared. She later wrote, "I felt that I was starting a new life, free from all my former sins and traditions ... this was the first time in all my life that all my fears left me. If I played by the rules and told the truth, there was nothing to fear." For a girl with a reputation for not always being truthful, or at least "afraid sometimes to tell the truth," school provided Eleanor a fresh beginning. School taught Eleanor Roosevelt to think and speak for herself.

She was assigned to tutor slower students and discovered a gift for teaching. Eleanor had "an insatiable appetite for knowledge, and an instinctive talent and enthusiasm for imparting it to others." After her marriage to Franklin and the birth of their children, she followed in the footsteps of Mademoiselle Souvestre and began teaching history and literature at a private girl's school in New York City. She loved teaching and told a reporter, "I like it better than anything else I do."

As a teacher, Eleanor Roosevelt patterned her teaching after her own school experiences, inspiring students to think critically and to view things from many different viewpoints. She brought literary and historic characters to life by telling students, "That is what the book says. Now how would *you* put it?" Frequent field trips were scheduled where students could discover new things for themselves, learn by doing, and be immersed in what they had studied. She wrote the head of one welfare agency, "I would like them to see the worst type of old time tenement. They need to know what bad housing conditions mean and then I would like them to see as a model a tenement in a bad neighborhood and on up to something really good in the way of houses for the moderately salaried groups." Students were repeatedly challenged, "Be somebody.... Be all you can be," and "Education ends only with death." One former pupil later recalled, "I never forgot a damn thing she ever taught me."

Eleanor Roosevelt continued teaching when Franklin Roosevelt became governor of New York. But after his election to the presidency, security concerns for her students caused her to leave the classroom. She declared at the time, "I teach because I love it.... I should prefer to be a school teacher, in certain ways that is what I would be best qualified to do." Privately she confided to a friend that leaving teaching was the hardest thing she ever did.

Once in the White House, the Roosevelts welcomed public school teachers and educators of all races and backgrounds to the executive mansion. Mrs. Roosevelt on behalf of her husband also traveled to schools, especially public schools in the poorest parts of the nation, to celebrate teachers and teaching and encourage students to succeed academically. Despite her busy schedule, the former teacher annually traveled to the tiny West Virginia town of Arthurdale to pass out diplomas to graduating students during her twelve years in the White House. President Roosevelt once joined her there to give out the diplomas himself. Following his death, she continued visiting schools, wrote about education, and lectured at Brandeis University. By then, many had begun calling her the First Lady of the World.

After she died in 1962, her home in upstate New York was opened to the public. It remained just as she had left it, filled with pictures of her family and signed photographs of innumerable kings, queens, presidents, prime ministers, and one unforgettable teacher — Mademoiselle Souvestre. In a life crowded with remarkable people and achievements, Eleanor Roosevelt never forgot the teacher who gave her the confidence and the courage to succeed. She warmly wrote of Mademoiselle Souvestre, "All my life I have been grateful for her influence."

Eleanor Roosevelt on Education

"Teachers are all important."

"A democracy must provide for public education since it is a form of government that without education cannot succeed."

"I wish that as a nation we would think first of teachers in terms of character, personality, and the special gift of imparting enthusiasm for acquiring knowledge. The basis of good national education is good teachers ... worthy of adequate pay and security.... If they can accumulate degrees and write books along any line, well and good, but the first requisite should be their ability to inspire youth."

"It is never enough, it seems to me, to teach a child mere information. In the first place we have to face the fact that no one can acquire all there is to learn about any subject. What is essential is to train the mind so that it is capable of finding facts as it needs them, train it how to learn."

"I think what we really need is far better teachers in the primary grades so that at a much earlier age ... we will be able to evaluate the ability of our children, and their natural trends."

"If the child's curiosity is not fed, if his questions are not answered, he will stop asking questions."

"When you are genuinely interested in one thing, it will always lead to something else."

"Facts after all are a small part of education.... Learning as you go—gives life its salt."

"Teachers' salaries in this country should be the concern of every community."

Franklin Roosevelt on Teaching, Teachers, and the Young

"The profession of teaching must become dignified as the foundation of modern democratic life. The teachers of the Nation must receive not only adequate pay, but must have a standing in the community which will make their position that of the highest possible influence for the good."

FDR Address to the National Education Association on Teaching and Democracy

"The teachers of America are the ultimate guardians of the human capital of America, the assets which must be made to pay social dividends if democracy is to survive."

"We have believed wholeheartedly in investing the money of all the people on the education of the people. That conviction, backed up by taxes and dollars, is no accident, for it is the logical application of our faith in democracy."

"Man's present day control of the affairs of nature is the direct result of investment in education. And the democratization of education has made it possible for outstanding ability, which would otherwise be lost to make its outstanding contribution.... We cannot afford to overlook any source of raw material. Genius flowers in the most unexpected places."

"No government can create the human touch and self-sacrifice which the individual teacher gives to the process of education. But what government can do is to provide financial support and to protect from interference the freedom to learn."

"No one wants the Federal government to subsidize education any more than is absolutely necessary. It has been and will continue to be the traditional policy of the United States to leave the actual management and control of schools and their curricula to state and local control."

"There is probably a wider divergence today in the standard of education between the richest communities and the poorest communities than there was one hundred years ago; and it is, therefore, our immediate task to seek to close that gap — not in any way by decreasing the facilities of the richer communities but by extending aid to those less fortunate."

"The ultimate victor of tomorrow is with democracy, and through democracy with education."

Bess Wallace and Harry S Truman
"Nobody Thought That He'd Go Far"

One of Harry Truman's teachers wrote of the man who succeeded Franklin Roosevelt in the White House in 1945, "We all liked Harry, and he always got his lessons, but ... we never thought ... nobody thought that he'd go far at all." Another teacher put it more simply, "He was not the quickest to learn." An elementary school classmate added, "He wore glasses and didn't play our games. He carried books, and we'd carry a baseball bat. So we called him a sissy." Truman responded,

> I was never popular. The popular boys were the ones who were good at games and had big, tight fists. I was never like that. Without my glasses I was blind as a bat, and to tell the truth, I *was* kind of a sissy. If there was any danger of getting into a fight, I always ran.

Truman's words are surprising considering his feisty reputation as president for never backing down from a fight.

Harry spent the first part of his life on a farm in rural Missouri. His family was not wealthy, but like many nineteenth-century Americans, Truman's mother insisted the family move to town so her children could get a better education. Somehow she found money to buy Harry the expensive thick glasses he needed to see and also to pay for piano lessons. A love of reading and music transformed Harry's life, connecting him to people and places beyond the prairies, hills, and small towns of Missouri. Music and reading also carried him beyond the jeers of other boys who teased him unmercifully for carrying sheets of music to his music lessons or books to the library — his two favorite destinations.

It was at the new grade school he attended in town that he met his future wife, Bess Wallace. She was everything he was not. Bess was a star student, athletic, popular, and from a wealthy family. They went through high school together, but she was able to continue her education at an exclusive girl's finishing school. Truman had no money to go to college, but he read enough books to fill a library. Despite a genuine thirst for knowledge and a love of history, he received no honors or awards at his high school graduation. He had grown up afraid of guns and had never been in a fight his entire life, but his goal was to attend the United States Military Academy. Only a military scholarship might allow a poor farm boy from Missouri to attend college. But bad eyesight kept Harry out of West Point, ending his hopes for higher education.

Truman never forgot the pain of wanting to continue in school but not having the money to pay for it. The boy who could not get into West Point did finally become a soldier in World War I by cheating. He memorized the eye chart. Later as an artillery officer he was ordered to teach his men the "fundamentals of artillery fire." Most officers were college educated, but their schooling failed to provide them the simple communication skills needed to teach their soldiers the basics. Truman wrote,

> It seemed to be the policy of all high ranking artillery officers to make a deep dark mystery out of the firing of a battery. They taught us logarithms, square root, trigonometry, navigation and logistics, but never did tell us that all they wanted to do was to make the projectile hit the target.... Afterward when they made me a firing instructor in France, I told the boys right off what we were trying to do and explained at some length that all the trimmings were to make the first shot more accurate — after that it was just like any other shooting.

Truman understood the importance of clear, direct communication in teaching, and later in politics.

As president of the United States, one of Truman's greatest accomplishments was in implementing the GI Bill that helped pay the college expenses of over four million veterans of World War II. Like Truman, most of these men did not have the financial resources to attend college. Many college and university presidents opposed the plan, fearing that older students would lower academic standards. The opposite proved to be true. The motivated veterans enthusiastically took full advantage of the educational opportunity afforded them, and academic standards in colleges actually rose during their attendance. Those successful college graduates became the foundation for America's prosperous middle class.

After leaving the White House, Truman traveled to Europe and received an honorary degree from Oxford University. The former president whose formal schooling stopped at high school was warmly saluted with a standing ovation at Christ Church College where England's elite had been educated for five centuries. That evening at the white-tie reception, Truman kept his remarks short, declaring, "Every child is entitled to a first-rate education." His own life and the success of the GI Bill provided powerful proof to his statement.

Two years later he accepted an invitation to visit Yale University, not "to do lectures for publication" but to "give our graduates more sense of what their lives are worth — how to spend them for value." He was "an immediate hit with students and faculty." He also gave a series of lectures at Columbia University, but it was at Truman's presidential library in Independence, Missouri, where Harry Truman once again became a real teacher.

The former president's knowledge and love of history, his "enthusiasm for learning" and his ability to communicate with his audiences connected Truman to his library visitors, whether they were Missouri elementary school students or graduates of the nation's greatest colleges and universities. Few teachers, or presidents, were more effective at getting their point across or being understood than Harry S Truman — the same Harry Truman nobody in his school thought would go far.

Harry S Truman on Teachers, Reading, Schools and Education

"We had wonderful teachers.... All of them made a contribution to the knowledge and character of the students."

"Readers of good books, particularly books of biography and history, are preparing themselves for leadership. Not all readers become leaders. But all leaders must be readers. Many readers become historians and teachers. They are ... among the greatest assets to this republic."

"The bulwark of our free institutions, of course, is based on a public school system where every person, no matter what his station, may have access to education. Our public school system has been a shining success in the history of the nation and I know it will continue to be just that."

"I think the fundamental purpose of our educational system is to instill a moral code in the rising generation and create a citizenship which will be responsible for the welfare of the nation."

"My first, second and fourth grade teachers made more impression on me than all the rest put together. I skipped the third grade."

"I think we need to spend more time and money to make *good* teachers, both men and women. No one has more influence on the young mind except his mother."

"It makes not much difference what sort of building you're in when you are after knowledge, but it does count entirely on who teaches you."

"I have an idea that 100 schools with 1,000 students are of much more value to the country than two schools with 50,000 students."

"The GI Bill of Rights proved conclusively that young men ... after some experience thirst for learning and that they are willing to work hard and at some disadvantage for an education."

"When the pioneers came into the Ohio-Mississippi-Missouri valley the first thing they thought of after shelter and safety for their families was education for their children."

"My definition of an education is the lighting of that spark which is called a 'thirst for knowledge.'"

"Personal contact with instructors of character is absolutely essential."

"We can't blame the schools—the trouble is really at home."

"Teachers are overworked — they are underpaid."

Mamie Doud and Dwight Eisenhower

"A Lackluster Student"

Dwight Eisenhower shared none of Harry Truman's, Eleanor Roosevelt's, or Herbert Hoover's fond memories of school and teachers. He once wrote, "The darkness of the classrooms on a winter day and the monotonous hum of recitation are my sole surviving memories. I was either a lackluster student or involved in a lackluster program." Even though Eisenhower attended Abraham Lincoln Elementary School, and later the James Garfield Elementary School in his home state of Kansas, neither stirred academic ambitions in the future president. Still, like Lincoln, Eisenhower earned his reputation as a leader during a time of war. And like Garfield, he served as a college president before being elected to the presidency of the United States.

Near the end of his long, event-filled life, Eisenhower could still vividly recall the shock of leaving home to attend elementary school. "I was transported from the family circle of a small frame house where every figure was familiar into an immense brick building populated by strangers of varying ages. This upheaval in my way of life ... was far more cataclysmic than any changes to follow." As an adult, Eisenhower traveled around the globe and played a pivotal role in many of the most historic events and wars of the twentieth century. Yet, he believed nothing was as earth-shattering to him as his journey from home to school.

Reading was an important part of Eisenhower's childhood. He wrote,

> At one point a suggestion was made that I should "skip" a grade. This was not a tribute to my subject mastery. I suspect that it was simply recognition that I lived in a home where learning was put into practice. The ability to read in a good clear voice and correctly ... was necessary if each of us was to maintain his self-respect in a daily family rite. The reading of the Bible, although principally done by our parents, was shared with the boys. A simple rule applied when one of us took over: The honor ended if a mistake were made. This put each of us on our mettle. Undoubtedly, too, it simplified our classroom task of reading aloud. The words in our school readers were in far larger print than the family Bible and were not so polysyllabic. So, I may well have had some advantage over my classmates. The suggestion that I skip a grade was never put into effect. My conduct was not the equal of my reading ability.

Eisenhower's conduct and academic ability was not a foreshadowing of future life successes. He liked and excelled in only a few subjects.

> In grammar school, spelling was probably my favorite subject either because the [spelling] contests aroused my competitive instincts or that I had learned that a single letter could make a vast difference in the meaning of a word. In time I became almost a martinet about orthography, inclined to condemn as beyond redemption a man who confused principle with principal.... Arithmetic came next because of the finality with which an answer was either right or wrong.

He hoped to attend the United States Naval Academy at Annapolis. A low score on a competitive exam blocked that dream, but qualified him instead to attend the army academy at West Point. The Point prides itself on harassing and breaking nonconformist students. Eisenhower took pride in bending and breaking rules. A collision was inevitable. In his graduation class of 164, he ranked 125 in discipline, but the army remained his home for nearly four decades.

Despite his low marks in discipline, the only time Eisenhower may have actually risked expulsion was caused by an argument with a teacher over a mathematical equation. In his integral calculus class, Eisenhower was asked to solve a complicated problem the teacher had briefly explained, quickly written on the board, and then erased. Eisenhower had not been paying attention because it was clear to him the instructor had merely memorized the lecture with little if any understanding of the thinking behind it. After an hour, Eisenhower created his own mathematical formula and solved the problem.

His teacher accused him of cheating by writing the answer down and making up phony steps to get there. Eisenhower refused to back down. He insisted his solution was shorter, simpler, and correct. A loud argument ensued causing a senior member of the math department to investigate the disturbance. After reviewing both formulas he announced Eisenhower's "superior to the one being used in the department" and ordered it added to the curriculum. Rote learning, regurgitation, and blind obedience were all parts of the hidden curriculum at West Point. Eisenhower's critical thinking skills and independent streak alienated some tradition-bound instructors, but in time helped make him a successful military officer.

He slowly rose through the army ranks, helped by his outgoing personality, athletic abilities, and analytical mind. When he was stationed in Texas, he met his future wife Mary Geneva Doud, who was visiting from Colorado. She was popularly nicknamed Mamie, and like her husband, had never devoted her time or energies to scholarship. One biographer wrote, "She liked school, but excelled more in school related activities than in classroom work." Her granddaughter was more direct. She wrote, "Mamie was at best a mediocre student."

A leg injury at West Point redirected Dwight Eisenhower's love for athletics from playing football to coaching it. His later success as a football coach allowed him to make friends wherever he was stationed. At one point, he was briefly a military instructor at the Army Tank School, but again got into trouble for his untraditional thinking. During World War II his personality and brains helped him be appointed as the supreme commander of the Allied Expeditionary Forces that successfully defeated Nazi Germany.

Following the war in 1948, Eisenhower became president of Columbia University in New York City. One of his goals was to visit every classroom, lab, office, and corner of the campus, but he quickly found that security guards, janitors, and secretaries barred his entrance. Despite being one of the most famous men in the world, not even Dwight Eisenhower could get past such entrenched gatekeepers. He had more success as a guest lecturer in classes and genuinely came to enjoy the students and faculty. Yet, there was one part of the job he hated—faculty meetings. Privately, he said he would rather fight another war than sit through one more faculty meeting. He described them as his "special hell" since every topic seemed to degenerate into "less and less consequential" discussions. He recognized the chief asset of any school was its faculty, but he never got used to the amount of inconsequential talk such highly talented individuals generated.

Eisenhower spent his military career surrounded by many southern-born racially bigoted officers. The tolerant racial attitudes of Columbia's faculty provided him a broader viewpoint of race in America. Despite his dislike of faculty meetings, he came to recognize and deeply respect the wisdom and power of teachers as instructors and role models. One of his subsequent leadership initiatives was to strengthen Columbia University's respected Teachers College, believing good teachers were necessary to build and maintain a strong nation.

His time at Columbia was cut short when President Truman asked him to become commander of the NATO military forces in Europe. A few years later, he returned to the United States and was elected president in 1952 and again in 1956. Ike, as he was popularly called, confronted many national and international issues during his time in the White House, including the legally mandated end of racial segregation in America's public schools.

After years of ignoring the disparities of educational opportunities between black and white students, the Supreme Court thrust the issue into President Eisenhower's reluctant hands. Eisenhower later wrote, "On May 17, 1954, the United States Supreme Court, in a unanimous opinion, made one of the most historic judgments of its existence. It reversed the 1896 *Plessy versus Ferguson* decision [of] 'separate but equal' public educational facilities for children of the white and Negro races." Eisenhower was "flabbergasted ... at the size and scope of the ruling," but quickly agreed to enforce the legal mandates.

As president, Eisenhower had already ordered racially segregated schools on military bases integrated "from top to bottom." But following the Supreme Court ruling, he also instructed the federally controlled Washington, D.C., city government to "take the lead in desegregating its schools as an example to the entire country." Peaceful desegregation began, but the governor of Arkansas resisted complying with the order at the Little Rock High School. Eisenhower nationalized the Arkansas National Guard and called out the United States Army's 101st Airborne Division to prevent "unlawful interference" with the federal court's order. The president made it clear that legal racial segregation of public school children was at an end.

Earlier in his army career, Eisenhower had opposed the racial integration of the army. Privately he thought the Supreme Court decision "wrong," but he enforced the ruling because it was the law of the land. Many people denounced his actions, but he had the support of others, including his wife Mamie. She had already done her own small part for integration. When she realized black schoolchildren were not allowed to participate in the annual White House Easter Egg Hunt, she immediately ordered the celebration integrated.

Another event during Eisenhower's presidency dramatically impacted education. When the Soviet Union launched the first man-made satellite to circle the earth, many Americans felt threatened by the scientific achievement of the nation's major military and political rival. Eisenhower persuaded Congress to pass the National Defense Act providing direct federal aid to education under the guise of teaching science in schools. Over the next four years, nearly one billion federal education dollars were spent, matched by state governments, to build and equip new public schools and expand the teaching of science at all grade levels. By linking education to the nation's defense needs, Eisenhower broke the logjam that for over a century had kept direct federal aid from reaching the country's elementary and secondary schools.

Eisenhower promised and confidently predicted,

> Federal help in building schools will not mean federal control. After these new schools are built, after the bricks are laid and the mortar is dry, the federal mission will be completed. All control and use of those schools will be in the hands of the

states and of the localities.... I will have no federal money in higher education as long as there is one iota of federal control coming with it.

Time and politics would prove President Eisenhower wrong.

Eisenhower on Schools and Universities, Teachers and Education

"Any man that underestimates the importance of the American teacher in world affairs is misleading himself. Under our system, high government policy expresses the considered will of the people, and the will of the people, in the last analysis, is compounded out of the convictions, the idealisms, the purpose fostered in classrooms of the nation's schools."

"A distinguishing characteristic of our nation — and great strength — is the development of our institutions within the concept of individual worth and dignity. Our schools are among the guardians of that principle."

"Education is one of those local functions that we should guard jealously because I found in every totalitarian state that I know anything about, one of the earliest efforts was to get charge of the educational process."

"The pursuit of truth, its preservation and wide dissemination; the achievement of freedom, its defense and propagation; these purposes are woven into the American concept of education."

"Individual freedom, all the basic rights of free speech, worship, self-government, are the very core of all our deepest desires and aspirations. The universities must point the way to perpetuation of these and be alert in warning us against all the insidious ways in which freedom can be lost.... If the things we fear as threats to our venerated system are trends brought about by faulty leadership, by shallow thinking, and by sheer neglect, it seems to me that only through education, led by our great universities, are we going to get back on the right track."

"In a nation which holds sacred the dignity and worth of individuals, education is first and foremost an instrument for serving the aspirations of each person."

"The federal role should be to merely facilitate — never to control."

"I see no hope for the future except through education."

Eisenhower's Advice to Young People and Presidents:

"Always try to associate yourself closely with and learn as much as you can from those who know more than you, who do better than you, who see more clearly than you."

Jacqueline Bouvier and John F. Kennedy

"If You Study Too Much, You're Liable to Go Crazy"

In 1960, John F. Kennedy, the youngest man ever elected president, followed Dwight Eisenhower into the White House. John, who became popularly known as Jack or JFK, was a bright man with an "uneven" school record. He went to the Edward Devotion Public School in Brookline, Massachusetts, from grades one through three and quickly earned a reputation there as a daydreamer. His first-grade teacher stopped by his house to discuss Jack's "idleness" with his mother. The future president defended his behavior by explaining, "You know, I'm getting along all right, and if you study too much, you're liable to go crazy." It was a philosophy he clung to at the five public, private, and parochial schools he attended in three different states as his parents searched for an educational environment that suited him. Poor health and behavior problems compounded his educational odyssey.

One headmaster complained he "conspicuously failed to open his schoolbooks." Kennedy did well in subjects he liked, such as history and English, but was "mediocre at best in languages, which required the sort of routine discipline he found difficult to maintain." His mother wrote, "What concerned us ... was his lack of diligence in his studies, let us say, lack of 'fight' in trying to do well in those subjects that didn't happen to interest him."

Mrs. Kennedy also remembered, "Jack couldn't or wouldn't conform. He did pretty much what he wanted, rather than what the school wanted of him." One teacher told his father that Jack was likable yet exasperating to teach; he never knew whether to hug or kick him. In his senior year at the Choate School, Kennedy was threatened with expulsion for misbehavior, but finally graduated fifty-six in a class of one-hundred and ten. Jack dropped out of more than one school for health problems, including Princeton University. He eventually graduated from Harvard. By most academic standards, he would be considered a late bloomer.

Jacqueline Bouvier also had school problems; but they were not academic. Jackie earned excellent grades, but her teachers found her difficult to handle, prone to mischievous behavior, high-strung, defiant, arrogant, and talkative. At the elite private schools she attended, she regularly earned a reputation as the "naughtiest girl" in class. While Kennedy's behavior at school made him popular with peers, Jackie's classmates considered her a "brat." She had no close friends and preferred solitary activities such as reading, writing, and drawing. Her art teacher believed she had real talent and had "to work hard to keep up with her."

But when group work was required, Jackie tried to dominate and bully other children. As a result, she was teased and taunted, angered easily, and frequently displayed temper tantrums.

Jackie attended Vassar College before transferring to Smith College which allowed her to study at the Sorbonne in France and display her genuine talent for languages. She and Jack Kennedy married in 1953 and, by the time they moved to the White House, were the parents of two small children. Jackie created a school on the top floor of the executive mansion where her oldest daughter and other children her age attended. Over the years a number of presidential children had been taught in the mansion, but this became the White House's first racially integrated school.

When Jack Kennedy was growing up, family loyalty and approval always took priority over academics. As one of the older children in a family of nine, his most influential sibling regarding his lackadaisical school attitude may have been his sister Rosemary. She was closest to him in age, attractive and likable, but unable to learn. Some labeled Rosemary slow or developmentally disabled. Eventually doctors diagnosed her as mentally retarded. After a failed experimental operation, she was permanently institutionalized. As long as Rosemary was home, Jack had always made a special effort to include her in all activities. His uneven academic performance had always allowed Rosemary to not be alone in her academic struggles.

Shortly after her unsuccessful operation, Rosemary's family created a foundation "to provide leadership in the field of mental retardation." The Kennedy Foundation was the first in the nation to offer support, research, and funding to study the causes and treatment of mental retardation. That same year, John Kennedy was elected to Congress, and six years later to the United States Senate. He proved to be a different kind of public servant, one of the first elected politicians to champion education programs for the physically and mentally handicapped. Kennedy joined the board of directors of the Clarke School for the Deaf where he became friends with Grace Coolidge. He also became an advocate and spokesman for families affected by cerebral palsy, but he never forgot his sister Rosemary or others like her.

Once he was elected president, Kennedy declared, "We as a nation have neglected, too long ... the mentally retarded. It affects all of us, and it affects us as a country." In one of his first press conferences he stated, "Although we have made great strides in the battle against disease, we as a nation have for too long postponed an intensive search for solutions to the problems of the mentally retarded." Kennedy followed up his rhetoric with action, creating a National Institute of Child Health and Human Development to research mental retardation and the treatment and care of the retarded. He asked his advisors to find out what other nations were doing in the field and discovered they were years ahead of the United States in the education of the mentally impaired. He immediately increased funding to the Office of Education's programs assisting exceptional children and became the first president to ask for, receive, and distribute federal funds to states to train teachers in what became known as special education.

Increased funding, specialized teacher training, and additional research became integral parts of programs Kennedy targeted to meet the needs of children with exceptionalities. Sargent Shriver, married to the president's sister Eunice, later said, "For the first time in history mental retardation — the least understood, most feared and most neglected scourge of mankind — came under the guns of the chief executive of the most powerful government of the world."

JFK soon appointed a presidential assistant to guide all legislation focusing on mental retardation through Congress, and he became the first president to address the National Association for Retarded Children. During his presidency, the first White House Conference on Mental Retardation was convened to encourage states to create special education departments. Sargent Shriver presented the keynote speech, Eunice Kennedy Shriver helped organize the event, and the president addressed the conference.

Eunice Kennedy Shriver, founder of the Special Olympics, proudly remembered her brother's leadership. "He never turned down anything we asked him to do about, or for, the mentally retarded." Some complained she and the president pushed too hard and too fast. Her blunt attitude seemed best summed up by the unapologetic statement, "If we hadn't done this, we wouldn't have gotten the retarded anything. They've been in dungeons too long."

No president had ever before taken such an interest in promoting educational opportunities for exceptional children or their teachers. Kennedy signed bills into law creating university affiliated facilities to provide "specialists on mental retardation" at community clinics, "mental retardation research centers, and increased funds for training teachers of the mentally retarded." The new legislation also offered incentives to encourage individual states to modernize and update their treatment and education of the retarded. On a more personal level, he gave standing orders that he wished to meet any national poster child for the retarded and their families when they visited the White House. His younger brother Edward later wrote of Jack, "He was a man of special grace who had a special care for the retarded and handicapped."

President Kennedy did not forget that exceptional children became adults. His sister Eunice proudly pointed out that he became the first president "to change the Civil Service laws to let the retarded work" in government — even in the White House. When asked about the wisdom of hiring a person with a mental disability, Kennedy's reply was direct and to the point: "If he can do the job, it's fine with me."

His example and attitude opened minds and hearts. Other presidents and first ladies reached out to the handicapped, Grover Cleveland to the blind and Grace Coolidge to the hearing impaired. But Kennedy was the first to use the presidency to educate the public and to provide public funds to train teachers in the field. His respect, attention, and commitment toward exceptional children helped bring them, their families, and teachers into the mainstream of American society.

Even after President Kennedy's death, his family continued his crusade. In 1974, Jean Kennedy Smith, JFK's youngest sister, founded Very Special Arts dedicated to encouraging adults with disabilities to fully participate in the arts. In 1990, his brother Edward, a longtime United States senator, co-sponsored the American with Disabilities Act. The law brought "forty-three million disabled Americans into the mainstream" of schools and the workplace. And in 2008, Edward Kennedy joined with his son, Congressman Patrick Kennedy, in sponsoring the Mental Health Parity Act, which mandated insurance companies cover to mental as well as physical illnesses.

Following President Kennedy's assassination in 1963, his mother Rose Fitzgerald Kennedy dedicated her autobiography not to her son the president, but to Rosemary, her retarded daughter. She wrote,

> This book is dedicated to my daughter Rosemary and others like her — retarded in mind but blessed in spirit. My vision is a world where mental retardation will be overcome, where we no longer mourn with mothers of retarded children, but exult and rejoice with parents of healthy, happy youngsters. Then, and only then, can we say, in the words of St. Paul: "I have fought the good fight. I have finished the course. I have kept the faith."

The words were Rose Kennedy's. But the vision she wrote about was shared by her entire family, even the son who had been a "dreamer" in school, and as president "couldn't or wouldn't conform" to the rules that had governed the mentally handicapped for centuries.

JFK on Teachers and Education

"The healing of children doomed in the past to the shadows— the comforting of their families on whom the burden falls with special severity ... is surely a work worthy of all our efforts and sacrifices."

"[A teacher's] influence is not in bombs or wealth or national fame; nor is it dependent on political parties, pressure groups or sheer force of numbers. But the fact remains ... the teaching profession will in the long run have more to say about the future of this country and the world than [those] on the battlefield ... [and those] in the council room."

"I would respectfully suggest that present methods for recruiting teachers might be reexamined — to attract the best students, to select the best graduates.... Once the teachers are recruited and hired, more can be done to improve the methods of teacher promotion. We must find better rewards for our better teachers; we must make actual use of probationary periods to retain only those with satisfactory performances and we must demonstrate concretely to you beginners in the fields that real opportunities for advancement await those whose contribution is of the highest caliber."

"Our citizens must cooperate in the effort to achieve better teacher salaries.

No profession of such importance in the United States today is so poorly paid. No other occupation group in the country is asked to do so much for so little. No amount of new classrooms, television, and training and recruitment techniques can attract and retain good teacher as long as their salaries are beneath the responsibility and dignity of their profession."

"It is not enough ... that our schools merely be great centers of learning, without concerning themselves with the uses to which that learning is put in the years that follow graduation."

"'Knowledge is power,' said Francis Bacon; it is also light. In the dark and despairing days ahead, our youth shall need all the light the teaching profession can bring to bear on the future.... Teachers of America, we who hope for the future peace and security of our nation, and for the wisdom and courage of our leaders ask once again that you bring candles to illuminate our way."

"That public education is in a state of crisis today is well known. There is less agreement on the cause and on the cure. I can only hope that those who recognize the urgent need of improving public education in this country will not exhaust their efforts in looking for a scapegoat, but will join in attacking the problem at its roots."

"The most direct, rewarding and important investment in our children and youth is in education.... We need to strengthen our nation by investing in our youth. The future of any country which is dependent upon the will and wisdom of its citizens is damaged, and irreparably damaged, whenever any of its children are not educated to the full extent of their talents, from grade school through graduate school."

"Civilization, according to the old saying, 'is a race between education and catastrophe.' It is up to us to determine the winner."

"If our nation is to meet the goal of giving every American child a fair chance — because an uneducated child makes an uneducated parent, who in another day produces another uneducated child, we must move ahead swiftly ... and recognize that segregation in education ... brings with it serious handicaps to large proportions of the population."

"The pursuit of knowledge itself implies a world where men are free to follow out the logic of their own ideas. It implies a world where people are free to solve their own problems and to realize their own ideals."

"We cannot continue to pay our college faculties and school teachers less for improving the minds of our children than we pay plumbers and steamfitters for improving our homes."

"It is no exaggeration to say that the struggle in which we are now engaged may well be won or lost in the classrooms of America."

"A free nation can rise no higher than the standard of education set in its schools and colleges."

"Our progress as a nation can be no swifter than our progress in education."

"Our ultimate goal must be a basic education for all who wish to learn."
"Without education you can't win."

Excerpt from the Undelivered Speech President Kennedy Intended to Make in Dallas, November 22, 1963, the Day of His Assassination

"The advancement of learning depends on community leadership for financial and political support — and the products of that leadership are essential to the leadership's hopes for continued progress and prosperity.... Only an America which has fully educated its citizens is fully capable of tackling the complex problems and hidden dangers of the world in which we live."

Claudia Taylor and Lyndon Johnson
"Scars on the Hopeful Face of a Young Child"

Lyndon Johnson, who succeeded John F. Kennedy in the White House in 1963, was no privileged son of Harvard or Princeton. Johnson graduated from Southwest Texas State Teacher's College. Both his parents had been teachers, and his first school was a simple one-room schoolhouse in a poor part of Texas with no electricity or indoor plumbing. He was the last president to attend a one-room schoolhouse.

As a student, Johnson could not keep his mouth shut or his hands and feet to himself. He was hyperactive before the word was invented. Teachers could not keep him in his desk or stop him from arguing with them or his fellow students. He was a verbal bully who loved being the center of attention and could out-argue teachers, classmates, and his parents. Yet despite such behavior and being the youngest child in his class, he consistently earned the highest possible grades.

Johnson's family was not wealthy, but when he became a teacher himself, nothing prepared him for the poverty he found in his first teaching job at a school on the Texas-Mexico border.

I shall never forget the faces of the boys and girls in that little school, and I remember even yet the pain of realizing and knowing then that college was closed to practically every one of those children because they were too poor. And I think it was then that I made up my mind that this nation could never rest while the door to knowledge remained closed to any American.

He taught in a crowded classroom filled with thirty-two fifth-, sixth-, and seventh-graders. Johnson was also appointed the school principal, started a literary society, a school debate team, and made regular home visits to parents unable or unwilling to come to school. At one point he asked his mother to send him 250 packages of toothpaste so he could teach his students how to brush their teeth. Much of his $125-a-month salary was spent buying school supplies, athletic equipment, and musical instruments the school did not have. When he discovered the elderly janitor could neither read nor write, Johnson stayed after school to teach him. One student later wrote that having Mr. Johnson as a teacher "was like a blessing from the clear sky."

As president, Johnson remembered his students and declared a national war on poverty, fighting it on two fronts: education and civil rights. In a televised address to Congress on the Voting Rights Act, he recalled,

> My students were poor and they often came to class without breakfast, hungry. They knew even in their youth pain and prejudice. They never seemed to know why people disliked them. But they knew it was so, because I saw it in their eyes. I often walked home late in the afternoon, after the classes were finished, wishing there was more that I could do. But all I knew was to teach them the little that I knew, hoping that it might help them against the hardships that lay ahead. Somehow you never forget what poverty and hatred can do when you see its scars on the hopeful face of a young child. I never thought then, in 1928, that I would be standing here.... It never even occurred to me in my fondest dreams that I might have the chance to help the sons and daughters of those students and to help people like them all over this country. But now I do have that chance — and I'll let you know a secret — I mean to use it.

And use it he did. One of the first pieces of legislation he passed was the Education of Children of Low Income Families Act. Johnson followed that with the groundbreaking Elementary and Secondary Education Act, signed in the one-room schoolhouse he once attended with his first teacher sitting at his side. Honored guests included the students he once taught. Johnson declared, "Education is the only passport from poverty [and] ... I believe deeply that no law I have signed or will ever sign means more to the future of America."

Congress had passed just six significant bills relating to education since the administration of Abraham Lincoln. President Lyndon Johnson signed sixty new education bills into federal law. In his first two years in office, he increased the Department of Education's annual budget from one and a half billion to four billion dollars. Most of the increased funding was steered to keeping low-income students in school and to helping them succeed academically. But Johnson and his wife did not stop there.

Claudia Taylor Johnson, popularly known as Lady Bird, was also a trained teacher. She too attended a one-room Texas schoolhouse and was the last first lady to do so. But, unlike Lyndon, her grades *and* behavior were exemplary. Until she went to high school, her classmates were the poor children of migrant workers and tenant farmers. At fifteen, Lady Bird began attending a junior college before transferring to the University of Texas where she became an honor student earning both a college degree and her teaching certificate.

As first lady she invited experts on child development to the White House to share their research on the best way to fight poverty. They told her poor children had to be reached *before* they attended school. About that time President Kennedy's sister Eunice and her husband Sargent Shriver proposed a preschool program to prepare poor children for school called Operation Head Start. President and Mrs. Johnson enthusiastically embraced the idea.

Head Start was introduced at a White House reception to almost universal acclaim. Mrs. Johnson wrote in her diary, "The Head Start idea has such hope and challenge. Maybe I could focus public attention in a favorable way on some aspects of Lyndon's poverty programs." She was soon traveling around the country publicizing the program and meeting with participating families and teachers. At one point she spoke about the program's implication for future school success at Princeton University's Institute for Teachers of the Disadvantaged. The role of education in America and its connection to the nation's universities was changing. Head Start became one of her husband's greatest edu-

Lyndon Johnson once taught 32 fifth-, sixth-, and seventh-graders in a crowded classroom on the Texas-Mexican border. A former student wrote, having Johnson as a teacher "was like a blessing from the clear sky." Pictured is President Johnson in 1965 signing the Elementary and Secondary Education Bill into law in front of the one-room schoolhouse he attended. His first teacher, Kate Deadrich Loney, sits at his side, and his former students were among the honored guests. Johnson believed education the only passport from poverty (courtesy the Lyndon Johnson Library and Museum; photograph by Yoichi Okamoto).

cational legacies, and much of its success was due to the support given it by Lady Bird Johnson.

In some ways Lyndon Johnson never left the classroom, partly because he never forgot the students he had met there. More than once during his presidency, he returned to the school where he began his teaching career. There, as president of the United States, he declared,

> I had my first lessons in the high price of poverty and prejudice right here. Thirty-eight years later our nation is still paying that price.... Until every Mexican-American child has the right to go through grade school and high school and college, and get all the education that he can or will take, I shall not be satisfied.... Until the day comes when we no longer hear the hum of the motor before dawn hauling off the kids in a truck to a beet patch or cotton patch in the middle of the school year and give them only two or three months of schooling, I will not be satisfied.... And when they have that right, when they have that opportunity, from "Head Start" to a college Ph.D. degree, a great many of them will exercise it — they will profit from it — we will have a better and a stronger, and, what is very important, a more prosperous and happier America.

Lyndon and Lady Bird Johnson gave a head start to millions of economically deprived students who might never have had an opportunity to succeed without educational support from the White House. As a teacher and as president, Lyndon Johnson remembered lessons his students had taught him. In one of his most famous speeches on education he acknowledged, "In that [first] year, I think I learned far more than I taught. And the greatest lesson was this one: Nothing — nothing at all — matters more than trained intelligence. It is the key not only to success in life, but the key to the meaning of life."

LBJ on Education:

"Education is mankind's only hope. Education is the imperative of a universal and lasting peace.... Education is the key that unlocks progress in the struggle against hunger and want and injustice wherever it may exist on the earth. It is the path, which now beckons us toward the planets and stars. Above all else, it is the wellspring of freedom and peace."

"I left college as a sophomore to become the principal of a six teacher school and I drew the magnificent, munificent salary of $125 a month!"

"The classroom — not the trench — is the frontier of freedom now and forever more."

"I came from a family that is interested in public life and education. My mother was a teacher and my father was a teacher."

"If we, of this generation, are to assure greatness for our nation, survival for our freedoms and honor for ourselves, we must make provision in our land — and in all lands where men are free — for education of the first class on all levels."

"I propose we begin a program in education to insure every child the fullest development of his mind and skills."

"Education is not a problem. Education is an opportunity."

"To lead inquiring and impressionable minds into the great treasure house of knowledge that the world has accumulated is of itself a priceless privilege."

"In the life of an individual, education is always the unfinished task. And in the life of this nation, the advancement of education is a continuing challenge."

"I urge that we now push ahead with the number one business of the American people — the education of our youth."

"We must make special efforts to overcome the handicap of poverty by more individual attention, by creative courses, by more teachers trained in child development."

"I am going to use every rostrum to tell the people that we can no longer afford the great waste that comes from the neglect of a single child."

"We have entered an age in which education is not just a luxury permitting some ... an advantage over others. It has become a necessity without which a person is defenseless in this complex, industrialized society."

"Today Head Start reaches into three out of every four counties where poverty is heavily concentrated and into every one of the fifty states. It is bringing more than education to children. Over half the youngsters are receiving dental and medical treatment. Hearing defects, poor vision, anemia, and damaged hearts are being discovered and treated. In short, for poor children and their parents, Head Start has replaced the conviction of failure with the hope of success."

"The achievements of Head Start must not be allowed to fade. For we have learned another truth which should be self evident — that poverty's handicaps cannot be easily erased or ignored when the door of first grade opens to the Head Start child."

"Education is the most economical investment that we can make in the nation's future."

"I want to be the president who educated young children to the wonders of their world."

"Elementary and secondary education are the foundation of our education system."

"Few Americans face such continuing challenges and respond as well as do the teachers of America. Upon their shoulders we have placed a heavy responsibility. The education that they impart to our young people is the basis of our prosperity, it is the basis of our security, and really is the basis of freedom itself."

"I believe strongly, as I have all my adult life that no profession means more to the future of our country than the teaching profession."

"Our work to enrich education finds its focus in a single person: the classroom teacher, who inspired each student to achieve his best.

Claudia Taylor Johnson on Education and Learning

"Education is the most lasting investment anyone can make."

"Teachers cannot teach alone; students cannot learn alone; education must be a family affair."

"Education brings learning, but it is useless unless it also brings a courageous attitude toward life."

"The continuing expression of an inquiring mind can mean more in terms of success than all the service symbols of status."

Pat Ryan and Richard Nixon

"I Had a Saint of a Teacher"

Richard Nixon followed Lyndon Johnson to the White House in 1969. In reminiscing about his school years he wrote, "I have always found that the best teachers were those who graded the hardest, just as the best dentists are those who aren't afraid to hurt you in order to clean out the cavities." Nixon had definite ideas on education. He dedicated a full chapter in one of his final books to "Teachers," recalling several personal favorites. "My fifth grade teacher, Miss Burum, launched me on a life long love affair with geography [and] my seventh-grade teacher, Lewis Cox ... sparked the interest that led me to become a history major in college."

Nixon's grandmother, wife, brother, and brother-in-law were all teachers. Richard Nixon was a well-behaved, serious pupil who earned consistently high grades. His first grade teacher described his class work as excellent, but also noted he was "a very solemn child." A longtime classmate remembered, "I don't recall ever hearing him laugh." As a young man, Nixon taught Sunday school and met his future wife in a Sunday school classroom where they were both auditioning for a play. She was Pat Ryan, a first-year teacher working at Nixon's former high school. Like many of her students, Richard Nixon fell in love with her at first sight.

Pat Ryan excelled academically in the public schools she attended. She graduated cum laude from Southern California University in 1937 and was soon earning $180 a month as Whittier High School's new business education teacher. Pat's education professors noted in her evaluations her "splendid attitude toward young people," her ability to get "good results from them" and confidently predicted, "She will be able to handle any class situation that may arise." She earned their "highest and unqualified recommendation," and did not disappoint them.

Miss Ryan faced challenges confronting many young teachers, not from her students, but from older faculty members who viewed her idealism and enthusiasm with suspicion. The superintendent who hired her had once been her high school principal, and many believed she got her job through favoritism. Still, within a short time, she won over faculty and students by a careful balance of friendliness, high expectations, and strict classroom discipline.

In many ways her youth and attractive appearance made her a star, but she made a point to never "outshine" or compete with other faculty members. One former pupil recalled,

> I have to laugh when I recall how the boys thought [she] would be a cinch as a teacher. They thought here was a new teacher who was so attractive, full of enthusiasm and pep she couldn't be a hard teacher. But it turned out ... she was a real disciplinarian, and the course wasn't just fun and games.

Another student remembered how quickly she earned everyone's respect:

> She always arrived in the classroom well ahead of time and stood at the door to greet us by name. By the same token she expected clockwork punctuality from us and we absorbed the gentle hint that questions directed to her should be prefaced with her name. Tardy students were warned by a direct look which hurt more than any lecture she could ever give. Miss Ryan followed the book. She allowed no compromise, no errors, no second-rate job. Perfection and high standards were the only thing she accepted. Despite her warm friendliness, if mistakes were made, she expected assignments to be done over. She also made herself available to her students in and out of class.

A former student wrote, "I can never remember her sitting down in class. She constantly went up and down the aisles and seemed somehow always to know what everyone was doing."

Another student said,

> She was approachable, friendly, and outgoing.... We liked her enormously because she never talked down to the students, always meeting them on an adult level, never intimidated *by* them. She enjoyed her life and work. Her classroom door was always open as she graded papers every day until five making herself available for extra help or to talk over problems.

Like Lyndon Johnson, Pat Ryan took a special interest in her Mexican American students. English was not their first language, and their parents needed them to earn money to supplement the family income. Many migrant workers pulled their children from school at harvest time to work from morning to night. As a student herself from a poor working family, an exhausted Pat Ryan often struggled to stay awake during her own high school classes. When she was a teacher, she worked with parents and students to keep her students in school to continue their education.

Nearly thirty years later, a student remembered Miss Ryan as the teacher who changed her life.

As a grade schooler I was overweight and had a million freckles. Homely would have been a kind description [but] I had a saint of a teacher. She sensed I was miserable and asked me to stay after school so we could talk. She told me to stop thinking of freckles as disfiguring because many people considered them wholesome if not downright attractive. She encouraged me to lose weight. As for boys who made cruel remarks, she said they were just trying to get my attention. "Smile and be pleasant" she advised. "Soon they'll be smiling back." I took her advice and I will never be able to repay her. She changed my life.... That teacher's name was Miss Ryan. Today she's known as Mrs. Richard Nixon.

The future first lady taught for four years at Whittier High School. In an interview in the school newspaper, she reminded students and fellow teachers to "never lose your enthusiasm — merely direct it — and that same enthusiasm will take you where you want to go." Pat Nixon's own inner strength carried her through the birth of two daughters, and her husband's career as a congressman, senator, vice president and then president of the United States. As a popular first lady, she visited 29 counties and traveled 123,245 miles meeting thousands of people who spoke hundreds of different languages from nearly every continent.

After her husband resigned from the presidency in 1974, she accepted only one request to speak again in public. She dedicated the Pat Nixon Elementary School in her California hometown. Like America itself, the school's population had become increasingly diverse and was now composed of African American, Asian, Hispanic, and white students. Patricia Ryan Nixon told students and teachers, "I am proud to have the school carry my name. I always thought that only those that are gone had schools named after them. I am happy to tell you — I'm not gone." Several years later she gave the school a wishing well made of hand-painted tiles with a small plaque reading, "May All Your Wishes Come True."

Pat Nixon willingly departed the public stage when President Nixon left the White House, but Miss Ryan had not gone. The kindness, time, and enthusiasm she invested in her students and her high expectations continued to inspire them even after her death in 1993. They remembered their former teacher not just because of the subjects she taught, but because she connected with them as human beings. The epitaph on her tombstone reads, "Even when people can't speak your language they can tell if you have love in your heart." The words eloquently described the world-traveling first lady and the teacher from Whittier High School.

Richard Nixon on Teachers, Schools, and Education

"In the final analysis, it always comes back to the teachers."

"In too many communities today, teaching is the most underpaid, unappreciated profession."

"Any program of educational reform should put the primary emphasis on the quality of teaching. While we cannot expect our children to love all of their teachers, it is vital that they respect them and that their teacher be worthy of that respect."

"Schools should discipline and strengthen the mind, teach young people how to think about and solve problems, and make them realize the world did not begin the moment they were born."

"What concerns me is not the breadth of education, it is the depth."

"Students do not need friends, they need teachers."

Patricia Ryan Nixon on Teaching, Being a Care Giver, and Being the First Lady

"Caring for others creates the spirit of a nation."

"Life is sort of sad, so I tried to cheer everybody up."

"Helping a person gives one the deepest pleasure in the world."

"If you put your whole heart into something, and work for it, you usually end up liking it."

Betty Bloomer and Jerry Ford
"We Do Not Need That Kind of Character in Our Girls"

In 1971 a Connecticut judge issued the following statement, "Athletic competition builds character in our boys. We do not need that kind of character in our girls." Many people disagreed with his statement. Just four years later President Gerald R. Ford signed the Title IX Act into law. It read in part, "No person in the United States shall, on the basis of sex, be excluded from participation in, be denied the benefits of, or be subject to discrimination under any educational programs or activity receiving federal assistance." That same year, Ford also signed the Education of all Handicapped Children Act opening American classrooms to handicapped children. Ford worried about the financial cost of both pieces of legislation, but strongly supported the ideas and ideals behind them. Few laws have had a more positive impact on the lives of schoolchildren, schools, and parents.

When Ford was a student attending the public schools of Grand Rapids, Michigan, he struggled to find the balance between academics and athletics. He had considerable help from his parents. The future president remembered,

Athletics, my parents kept saying, built a boy's character. They were important, but not nearly as important as attaining good grades. My parents made sure I did my homework and pressed me to excel. In chemistry and other science courses, I received average grades. In Latin, which I disliked, it was a struggle to earn C's. Math was not too difficult. In the courses I really enjoyed, history and government, I did very well. At the end of my junior year, I made the National Honor Society and ranked in the top 5 percent of our 220 member class.

On the other side of Grand Rapids, Betty Bloomer was also developing her academic and athletic talents in the city's public schools. She described herself as a "demon swimmer," a "terrible tomboy" and the "bane of my big brothers' existence. I trailed them around and tried to make them let me play football and hockey." Betty, her brothers, and her youthful neighbors terrorized their neighborhood. "We tipped over everybody's garbage pail, whitewashed everybody's porch, and soaped everybody's windows. We did things so terrible I would be furious if my children had ever tried them." Eventually the future first lady combined her rowdy athleticism with her love of music by becoming a dancer. Betty began dancing lessons when she was eight and learned every kind of dance from Latin American rhythms, to ballet, tap, acrobatic, and modern. By the time she was fourteen, she was a dance teacher herself.

In school she was a good student who enjoyed her math, Latin, and French classes; but when the last class bell of the day rang, she raced to the dance studio. Betty later wrote, "There was no kind of dance that didn't fascinate me. I'd hear about some boy who'd been out West among the Indians and learned a rain dance, and I'd go after him and make him teach it to me. I was insatiable.... Dance was my happiness."

After graduating from high school, her mother allowed her to spend her summers at Bennington College in Vermont, studying dance eight hours a day with many of the nation's greatest dance teachers. She called it ecstasy, despite the fact that by the end of the day, "we could walk up the stairs for dinner, but we couldn't walk down again. Our thigh muscles had knotted up, and our knees wouldn't flex, and the pain was so bad we had to sit on our tails on a landing and slide down, step by step, jarring ourselves as little as possible."

Martha Graham was the teacher she most admired at Bennington. Later she studied with her in New York. Betty later wrote,

> It's almost impossible to describe the impression made by Martha Graham on a girl who came straight out of high school. I worshiped her as a goddess. She was a tough disciplinarian ... but ... I admired that kind of strictness. You can't be a dancer without it; not only your body but your mind must be disciplined.

Graham told Betty she had a future in dance "but would have to give everything else up." Betty loved dancing but was not willing to give up family and friends, or devote her entire life to it. Her dreams took her to Vermont's Bennington College and then to New York City, but other dreams brought her home to Michigan. Dance remained a large part of her life. In Grand Rapids she taught dance at the YMCA and at the local hospital where she taught children crippled with polio and those immobilized in plaster casts how to move and dance to music.

To Gerald Ford, whom his friends called Jerry, athleticism took him in another direction. In high school he played center on the city championship football team and was named to the all-city squad. At the University of Michigan, he was named outstanding freshman player, but he sat on the bench his sophomore and junior years as an All-American playing his position took the team to two national championships. Ford remembered, "Not playing was tough, but I learned a lot sitting on the bench." As a boy, he struggled with a bad temper that got him into trouble at home and at school. His mother taught him to control his temper, or it would control him. Two years on the bench gave Jerry Ford plenty of time to practice what his mother had taught him. The way he handled being benched impressed his coach and fellow players as much as his fine athletic skills.

His senior year, Ford played in every game and was voted most valuable player. Academically, he ranked in the top quarter of his class. He was a solid but not a great student. Ford later wrote,

> If I had to go back to college again — knowing what I know today — I'd concentrate on two areas: learning to write and to speak before an audience. Nothing is more important than the ability to communicate effectively.... I was horribly unprepared for my Freshmen English course. Every weekend I would labor over the 1,000 word theme due on Monday morning. At the end of the year, I earned a C in the course — and was glad to get it.

Like Betty Bloomer, Jerry Ford had to make a choice regarding his future. He was offered contracts to play professional football for either the Green Bay Packers or Detroit Lions, but he turned down both offers. Ford wanted to study law, and his athleticism and positive attitude helped him reach that goal. The coach who had benched him for two years recommended him for a job as assistant football coach at Yale University, home to one of the best law schools in the country. Ford got the coaching job. Eventually he was allowed to take some law classes, was formally admitted, and graduated in the top twenty-five percent of his law class.

Ford coached two future United States senators, William Proxmire and Robert Taft Jr. at Yale. Proxmire described Ford as a "natural at coaching," explaining, "Coach Ford was very very conscientious. The players ... saw in Ford not only diligence, but a good first rate mind." Taft remembered Ford as an effective coach and powerful role model: "Some coaches were hot heads, always shouting, but Coach Ford was very calm and spoke to your intelligence. He taught the basics, blocking and tackling, by *telling* you how and *showing* you how."

Patience and character won out over the hot tempered student of Ford's childhood. Following graduation from Yale, Jerry Ford returned to Grand Rapids, and met and married Betty Bloomer. He ran for Congress, taught law, and eventually rose to the presidency of the United States. Jerry and Betty Ford may have been the most athletic presidential couple to ever live in the White House; perhaps the ideal president and first lady to open the gymnasium, classrooms, and playing fields to American girls and boys through Title IX and the Education of Handicapped Children Act.

Jerry Ford on Education

"No group in our country is more in need of supportive services than the handicapped. Our handicapped citizens have demonstrated time and again that, given a fair break, they can lead as full and productive lives as other citizens."

"Corrective measures in early childhood can reduce the severity of a handicap. Young children should be screened for handicaps, and when found, should be corrected.... The problem of mental retardation deserves our attention, not only for the sake of six million afflicted Americans and their families but for all of us. The majority of retarded citizens can become productive members of society."

"Our school systems must be strengthened, so that they can provide the appropriate education which both the law and our conscience say may not be denied to retarded or otherwise handicapped children. By appropriate education, I mean training in academic, vocational, and social skills which will enable these children to live up to their highest potential. And never let us underestimate how high that potential is."

"In a free society, like our own where education is open to many, not just the few, the university's life, liberty, and learning must not be abstract but rather must relate to reality. A sound liberal education should be the key to preparing young people, men and women, for a full life beyond their student years."

"Looking back, I realize I was lucky to have competed in sports. As a football player, you have critics in the stands and critics in the press. Few of them have ever centered a ball, kicked a punt or thrown a touchdown pass with 100,000 people looking on, yet they assume they know all the answers. Their comments helped me to develop a thick hide, and in later years whenever critics assailed me, I just let their jibes roll off my back."

Betty Ford

"I feel that God gives us these children and expects us to do the best we can with them for a certain amount of time."

"Jerry and I believe that if you can save the life of one person — just one — then you have accomplished your life mission."

Rosalynn Smith and
Jimmy Carter

"Stretching Our Minds and Stretching Our Hearts"

Many presidents and first ladies have taught Sunday school, from Benjamin and Caroline Harrison and William and Ida Saxton McKinley to George and Barbara Bush, and their son George W. Bush. Jimmy Carter began teaching Sunday school as an eighteen year old midshipman at the United States Naval Academy and continued teaching well into his eighties. His first students were nine- to eleven-year-old daughters of servicemen in Annapolis, Maryland. Following graduation, he taught other navy men "between the torpedo tubes" of his submarine. When he retired from the navy, he returned to his tiny hometown of Plains, Georgia, and began teaching the boys' pre-teen Sunday school class once taught by his father. His wife Rosalynn taught the girls' class.

Carter's rise in politics began as a crusading member of the county school board supporting racial integration of local schools, and as a state senator fighting for educational reform, but politics never took him far from the classroom. When he became governor of Georgia, he taught a Sunday school class near the state capital. After his election to the presidency in 1976, whenever possible, he taught at the Baptist church nearest the White House. Following his term as president, he returned to Plains taking over the adult Sunday school class at the Maranatha Baptist Church. Carter also traveled weekly to Atlanta where he served as a professor at Emory University, but he continued teaching his Sunday school class for over three decades in Plains.

His Sunday school class attracted thousands of visitors to Plains (population 650) from around the globe. Congressmen and governors, homemakers and sharecroppers, young and old, Democrats and Republicans, Christians, Jews, Muslims, and atheists of all colors and ethnic backgrounds sat side by side to learn from the teacher the locals call "Mr. Jimmy."

Rosalynn Smith went to the same elementary and high school in Plains attended by Jimmy Carter. She was a straight-A student, becoming the valedictorian of her graduating class, an honor that eluded her future husband. When she was still in the elementary grades, teachers asked her to help teach mathematics to the younger students. She wrote in her autobiography, "I loved school as a young child. My favorite teachers, all women, were my idols." By the time Rosalynn reached seventh grade, she wrote,

> I began to realize that the boundaries of the world extended beyond our sheltered and isolated community.... We had a young teacher who was beautiful and who I thought knew more than anyone I have ever met. She was extremely interested in

current events and prodded us to read the newspapers and listen to the radio, to stretch our minds about the world.... For the first time in my life I began searching newspapers to discover a world of interesting people and faraway places.

Despite their small public school in one of the poorest parts of the country, the Carters were taught by academically challenging teachers who actively involved them in learning. Jimmy Carter continued to use this method in his Sunday school class. In his book *Living Faith,* the former president wrote about his first rule of teaching.

> Involve the class in a give-and-take discussion. Questions back and forth keep us all awake and help us understand the subject. We have lively debates but few hurt feelings.... I have discovered during these years of teaching that it is far better to ... share the lesson on an equal basis with those who have come to join me. The most memorable experiences are when we meld into a common group.... We all have a feeling of being a part of a community of people trying to make sense of our lives and our world. Because of this diversity, I've had to go more deeply into other people's questions— some of which I have never raised in my own life.

Jimmy Carter has taught Sunday school since he was eighteen and continued teaching classes in Plains, Georgia, well into his eighties. President Carter and First Lady Rosalynn Carter were both taught in Plains by Miss Julia Coleman. Carter quoted Miss Coleman in both his inaugural address and the lecture he gave when he accepted the Noble Peace Prize. He later wrote, "I have never known a teacher who had such a profound impact on students as she did" (Jimmy Carter teaching at the Maranatha Baptist Church, Plains, Georgia — author collection).

One of the reasons Jimmy Carter became such an effective teacher was that he never limited his learning to school. His parents were his first teachers, but others also taught him. He lived at a time and in a place where students and schools were segregated by race. But as a child nearly all his playmates were black, and he sometimes attended the St. Mark AME Church where his neighbor, Bishop William Becker Johnson, was the minister. Bishop Johnson may have been the best educated, most respected man in the county. Despite his education and social standing, Johnson never used his impressive skills to talk down to or divide his congregation. His preaching and sermons were dedicated to bringing his community together.

Carter never forgot his visits to the AME church.

> Bishop Johnson would preach, and his character seemed to change during his sermon. He was ... a master of the English language, but he would shift to the vernacular ... when he wanted to emphasize a key point. His voice would become so soft that the congregation would lean forward to hear, and then he would erupt with a startling volume of sound. He used singsong rhythm on occasion, even when quoting scripture, so that long familiar words assumed a different meaning ... during the sermon, the sense of being brothers and sisters in Christ wiped away any thought of racial differences.

The land surrounding Plains, Georgia, is "marginally fertile" farm country, economically poor, and geographically isolated. The business district is hardly more than a half dozen storefronts surrounded by thousands of acres of sandy farmland and thick woods. Many residents never traveled more than a hundred miles from the place of their birth. But President and Mrs. Carter were both taught by one particular woman who showed them the world beyond their classroom. At Plains High School, which is now a museum, she served as their principal, superintendent, and high school English teacher. At one point, a student visiting the museum asked the former president if he had a favorite teacher. His quick response was "Miss Julia Coleman." He then explained:

> I had her beginning in eighth grade when I was in high school. Miss Julia taught primarily literature, English, reading, writing, and composition. She taught us about great books. She taught us about music. She would play classical records and she would give us a test on the name of the music and who wrote it. She made us memorize the great paintings of history and she would give us a test again. We would have to tell her the name of the painting and the artist. Miss Julia was always making us do new things and stretching our minds and stretching our hearts to learn about God's world and to learn about interesting and exciting things.
>
> I think there is no doubt that Miss Julie Coleman was my favorite teacher ... not only at Plains High School, but I went to four different colleges and universities ... of all those opportunities for education, she was still my favorite.... She devoted herself to understanding each of us individually. She knew our strengths and weaknesses. She knew what we liked and what we didn't like. And she saw in every one of her students something that was special, either a love for the outdoors, or a love for books, or a love for mathematics, or a love for sports.
>
> She tried to take what was there in each one of us and expand it every day with new and interesting projects.... We would learn how to memorize a poem ... spell new words, read a book, or ... act in a play. Miss Julia was special because she made everyone of us feel we were special, that she really cared about us. We were very proud when Miss Julia would say, "That was a good job, Jimmy."... She was trying to make it clear to us that we shouldn't put a limit on what we hope to do in life. We should

set our standards high, our goals high, and our moral values high to honor the principles that we learned in school and not be self limiting in our ambitions.

Even before he had Miss Coleman as a teacher, she had a major influence on him. As principal and superintendent, she "encouraged the teachers to promote reading." Student readers were given certificates entitled "Readers Make Leaders." When he was in the second grade, he was given such a certificate and a framed print of Thomas Gainsborough's *Blue Boy* for reading the most books of any second-grader. The portrait hung over Carter's bed until he went to college, reminding him that there were other boys, in other times and places, that were different from him, yet the same. When he was twelve, Miss Coleman informed him he was ready to read *War and Peace*. He later remembered,

> I was happy with the title because I thought finally Miss Julia had chosen for me a book about cowboys and Indians. When I checked the book out of the library, I was appalled. It was about 1,400 pages long and, of course, not about cowboys at all. But Tolstoy's novel turned out to be one of my favorite books.

In his inaugural address, Carter thanked his former teacher for introducing him to the world. Then nearly sixty years after she encouraged him to read *War and Peace*, the former president won the Nobel Peace Prize for his international peacekeeping efforts. In his acceptance speech in Oslo, Norway, he remembered his former teacher:

> I thought often during my years in the White House of an admonition that we received in our small school in Plains, Georgia, from a beloved teacher, Miss Julia Coleman. She often said: "We must adjust to changing times and still hold to unchanging principles." When I was a young boy, the same teacher also introduced me to Leo Tolstoy's novel *War and Peace*. She interpreted that powerful narrative as a reminder that the simple human attributes of goodness and truth can overcome great power. She also taught us that an individual is not swept along on a tide of inevitability but can influence even the greatest events.

Mr. Carter took the lessons he learned from Miss Julia to heart. She remains the only teacher ever quoted in both a presidential inaugural address and a Noble Peace Prize lecture. Human rights became a cornerstone of Carter's presidency and worldwide peacemaking efforts. If she were still alive, Miss Julia Coleman might well have said, "Good job, Jimmy."

Jimmy Carter on Miss Julia Coleman

"Despite its small size, with fewer than three hundred students in eleven grades, our Plains High School was superb. This was primarily because of Miss Julia Coleman, the school superintendent and best teacher I ever had. She walked with a limp, had failing eyesight, and never raised her voice to scold or in anger.... She was totally dedicated to her profession, evidently seeing something special in us rural children. I thought at the time that I was one of her pets because she knew I had a burning desire to go to the U.S. Naval Academy, but later I discovered that many others in my class had the same impression about themselves. Miss Julia was just as interested in preparing most of the graduates for their predictable lives as housewives, railroad and sawmill workers, or share-croppers."

"I believe I am the only president who has quoted a teacher in his inaugural address. She died shortly before that election. But she is alive in my memory to this day."

"I have never known of a teacher who had such a profound impact on students as she did."

Rosalynn Carter on Miss Julia Coleman

"We were all ... encouraged to make something of our lives.... Our very special school superintendent, let us know that nothing less than the best in our schoolwork was sufficient. We had to be prepared for the outside world.... Miss Julia's ambitions for us fired my imagination."

Rosalyn Carter has called her husband "a natural teacher."

Nancy Davis and Ronald Reagan
"The Last Kid Chosen"

Anne Frances Robbins Nancy Davis, who would become Mrs. Ronald Reagan, attended some of the nation's best private and public schools, but she was not a standout at any of them. The first three years of her schooling she attended the Sidwell Friends School in Washington, D.C., the same school where the Nixons and Obamas later sent their young daughters. Although her former classmates remembered nearly all the other students in their class, they could not remember the girl who became that nation's first lady. In interviews they said, "Never heard of her" or "I don't recall the name at all." A few even asked each other, "Who in the world was she?"

For much of her early childhood, Nancy Davis, as she began calling herself, seemed invisible despite that fact that her mother was a popular actress whose friends included some of the biggest stars in Hollywood. When Nancy was older, she moved to Chicago where her stepfather was a respected doctor and teacher. In her autobiography she wrote of him,

> As a teacher, he was known for being strict ... his students were always required to wear a tie and jacket to class ... [He] was a tough teacher ... but he made his students stretch to heights they hadn't always known they could reach.

As a student herself, Nancy did not stretch. Her primary interest was not in the direction of academics. She wrote,

> I can't remember when I wasn't interested in the theater, and in school my main interest was drama. I was only an average student at Girl's Latin School in Chicago, but I was class president two or three times, and I acted in all the school plays.... After high school, I went to Smith College, where I majored in English and Drama — and boys.

Ronald Reagan, like Nancy Davis, was not a star as a child or as a student. He wrote in his autobiography, "I was always the last kid chosen.... I was always the first to think: 'I can't make the team. I'm not as good as Jack or Jim or Bill.'" He continued, "I suppose it isn't unusual for school children to suffer feelings of inferiority and lack of self confidence — I'd be surprised if it wasn't one of the most common afflictions of childhood — but when it is happening to you, it can seem the biggest thing in the world, and for a while it caused me a lot of heartache." Despite the pain and insecurity of his childhood, Reagan grew up to become a successful sportscaster, a movie and television star, the governor of California and one of the most popular presidents in American history.

Reagan's mother tried to help her shy son by having him memorize short speeches to present at church functions. He dreaded speaking in front of people, but competition with his outgoing older brother pushed him to overcome his fears. He wrote, "I guess there was something competitive enough in me that made me want to try to do as well as my brother and I finally agreed." To his surprise, Reagan found he loved the attention and applause.

Then in high school he met the teacher who changed his life. Mr. B. J. Frazier wore thick glasses like Reagan; but he carried himself with none of the self-conscious shyness plaguing the adolescent. Frazier taught English and history in ways that nurtured creativity and encouraged confidence. Reagan remembered,

> Our English teachers until then had graded student essays solely for spelling and grammar, without any consideration for their content. B. J. Frazier announced he was going to base his grades in part on the originality of our essays. That prodded me to be imaginative with my essays; before long he was asking me to read some of my essays to the class, and when I started getting a few laughs, I began writing them with the intention of entertaining the class. I got more laughs and I realized I enjoyed it as much as I had those readings at church. For a teenager still carrying around some old feelings of insecurity, the reaction of my classmates was ... music to my ears.

When he discovered Mr. Frazier would be directing the school play, Reagan decided to try out for it. Nearly seventy years later he wrote,

> For a high school English teacher in the middle of rural Illinois, he was amazingly astute about the theater and gave a lot of thought to what acting was all about.... He'd teach us that it was important to analyze our characters and think like them.... Often his questioning made you realize that you hadn't tried hard enough to get under the skin of your character so you could understand his motivations.... The process, called empathy, is not bad training for someone who goes into politics [or any other calling]. By developing a knack for putting yourself in someone else's shoes,

it helps you relate to others and perhaps understand why they think as they do, even though they come from a background much different from yours.

The famous communication skills that allowed President Reagan to connect with the American people may have taken root in the classroom of B. J. Frazer.

Two years after meeting Mr. Frazer, Reagan began teaching Sunday school at a local church in Dixon, Illinois. He was only fifteen, younger than some of the boys he taught, but he seemed much older. Reagan never once dressed casually when teaching and came across as "supremely self-assured." By preparing himself and his lessons with care, he appeared mature beyond his years. In looking back, his former students were "genuinely surprised" to discover how young he had been. Years later they still recalled his lessons in their entirety. The leader of the girl's class later wrote, "I can still see the row of upturned faces as he sat on a table and held them all spellbound. There were no discipline problems."

Reagan used storytelling to illustrate his points, connecting the lives and testimonials of contemporary sports heroes to scripture lessons. His stories made biblical verses sound as if they had been written for each individual student.

> Dutch [as he was called] would start telling the story. Just when it got really interesting he'd say, "Oh, oh, to be continued. You have to come back next Sunday and I'll tell you the rest." We never missed.

He continued to teach for almost three years never missing a class. When he went to a church-sponsored college a hundred miles from Dixon, he returned every Sunday to teach until someone was found to replace him.

The future president was not a top-notch student, but his deep religious faith helped bring him to Eureka College — a small four-year liberal arts school operated by the Disciples of Christ. There he received a Needy Student Scholarship paying half his tuition. He majored in economics but was more interested in sports and the social part of college life than academics. Looking back he admitted, "I let football and other extracurricular activities eat into my study time with the result that my grade average was closer to the C level required for eligibility than it was for straight As. And I wonder what I might have accomplished had I studied harder."

There were many ups and downs for Reagan at college. At one particular low point he received a letter from B. J. Frazier who reminded him to not give up, to believe in himself, and to never stop believing in his future. The country was going through very tough economic times. Many of his classmates quit school, but Reagan stayed on to graduate.

During his college years, Reagan continued growing in confidence. He wrote in his autobiography,

> As governor of California, I presided over a university system regarded as one of the best. But if I had it all to do over again, I'd go back to Eureka or another small college like it.... I think too many young people overlook the value of a small college and the tremendous influence participation in student activities can have during the years of adolescence to adulthood.

The shy boy from Mr. Frazier's eighth-grade English and history class and the young girl nobody remembered from her primary school days grew up to become two of the most famous, influential people on earth. Students and teachers who saw Ronald Reagan walk into Mr. Frazier's room the first day of class may have seen only a small, quiet, boy with thick glasses, but B. J. Frazier saw more. He, and then Nancy Davis, recognized things in Reagan others did not. Nearly everyone was surprised at the giant of a man "Dutch" Reagan became, but B.J. Frazier and Nancy Davis were not among them. They expected nothing less.

Ronald Reagan on Education

"I have a warm spot for high school principals. I was in the principal's office in Dixon High School, and I wasn't there just to pass the time of day. Well, at one point he said to me, 'You know, I don't care what you think of me now, I'm only interested in what you think of me fifteen years from now.'"

"Professors should teach you how to think, not necessarily what to think. If a professor for some reason does impose his personal bias on his students then he should at the same time urge them to find someone of a contrary opinion, hear his reasoning and having heard both sides form his own opinion. I assume we still do accept that most issues have more than one side."

"True education is soci-

Ronald Reagan and his wife Nancy were not the most popular children at school. He wrote in his autobiography, "I was always the last kid chosen ... I was always the first to think: I can't make the team." Reagan was one of many White House residents whose life was positively turned around by a teacher. Later, he became a standout as a teacher himself. Reagan taught Sunday school for nearly three years at his church in Dixon, Illinois. A fellow Sunday school teacher remembered, "I can still see the row of upturned faces as he sat on a table and held them all spellbound" (First Christian Church, Dixon, Illinois — author collection).

ety's attempt to enunciate certain ultimate values upon which individuals and hence society may safely build. When men fail to drive toward a goal or purpose the drift is always toward barbarism."

"The teacher must not teach the young only what they want to learn. The experience of the human race must be offered. We must learn for example the price of just getting by — that we get from life exactly what we put in — no more — no less."

"We must study man's achievements as well as his failures. The problems we must solve today are the results of errors of the past."

"Perhaps young people aren't rebelling against our standards—they are rebelling because they don't think we ourselves are living by the standards we tried to teach them."

"Schools ... must be ... designed to impart sound discipline based on moral standards which will become self-discipline in the individual student."

"Having seen the domination of governments by a religious order and/or those nations where religious belief was dictated by the government, the framers of our Constitution made sure that our new nation would enjoy a separation of church and state. They simply meant that individuals would be free to worship as they chose; that government could not favor or discriminate against particular religions or denominations, nor could any denomination assume a role in government."

"St. Thomas Aquinas warned teachers they must never dig a ditch in front of a student that they failed to fill in. To clearly raise doubts and to seek and never find is to be in opposition to education and progress.... Our obligation is to help our young people find truth and purpose, to find identity and seek a goal."

"The advantage of a smaller school is that you can't be anonymous.... Also in small schools, the faculty has personal knowledge of you."

"Our nation is blessed with a pluralistic school system reflecting the great diversity of our people. We developed at the local school district level probably the best public school system in the world."

Nancy Reagan on Drug Education

Nancy Reagan used her position as first lady to promote education programs on the dangers and prevention of drug abuse. Her signature motto for the programs was "Just Say No."

"One of the things I learned from the drug programs is that parents are not always responsible."

"I hope I'm remembered for the drug program and the help to children."

Barbara Pierce and George H. W. Bush

"Faking His Way Through Reading"

George H. W. Bush and his wife Barbara Pierce Bush followed Ronald and Nancy Reagan to the White House bringing with them a strong national call for improving education and increasing literacy. As students, they had attended some of the finest private and independent schools available in the country, but were not always academically at the top of their classes.

Barbara Bush, like Nancy Reagan attended Smith College, where she described herself as "very social" but a "lousy" student. Barbara captained the soccer team at Smith before dropping out to marry George Bush. She admitted,

> I didn't like to study too much.... I'd hate to have anybody go through my records from freshman year. I was all right in high school, but when it came to Smith, I was a cliff-hanger. The truth is I just wasn't very interested. I was interested in George.

At the Milton School, and the Rye Country Day School in New York, and later the Ashley Hall Boarding School in South Carolina, she was popular and athletic, but academics were not a priority. She later said,

> When I was growing up, my father would say, "Why didn't you get an A?" I'd be so excited with a B plus. I would say to my kids, B? 'Hooray, you passed." There's this difference. My father expected quality; I expected to just get through.

Barbara Pierce's father was a Phi Beta Kappa scholar athlete, captain of the college football team, and a summa cum laude graduate from Miami University in Ohio. He then earned post-graduate civil and architectural degrees from MIT and Harvard before becoming a successful businessman. Barbara described her mother, a graduate of Oxford College in Ohio, as a "campus beauty" who seemed to have everything, but never seemed completely happy. Barbara contrasted her own life philosophy with her mother's by saying, "She always thought the grass was going to be greener some time, some other place. I don't believe that. I believe life is right now. I think my mother taught me that."

As a child Barbara felt closest to her father, who taught her that the three most important things a parent could give his children were "a fine education, a good example, and all the love in the world." She appreciated the example he set, and the love he gave her, but "a fine education" was another matter. One of her earliest bad/good school memories was of her first day of school when her mother "disappeared with no goodbyes. I felt abandoned. But I truly loved school so much I forgave her by the time I got home."

At school, other things quickly took precedence over her studies such as her physical appearance. "I was a very happy fat child who spent all my life with my mother saying 'Eat up, Martha' to my older sister and 'Not you, Barbara' to me." At school, the future first lady was the tallest girl in her class, overweight yet athletic. She described herself as looking like Porky Pig and protected herself by making jokes and being a self-described "tomboy." Barbara played football with the boys, and at dances danced with the other girls because she got to lead. Her mother told her, "You must not be the boy every time." But Barbara was afraid no boy would ask her to dance. "I didn't want to be left. Not me. I was five feet eight at the age of twelve." She was very self-conscious that her height "bothered the boys."

In school Barbara was a natural leader. Her friends described her as "confident, very confident" but also "sarcastic and mean"—a real "bully." They recalled she was quick to make fun of others and to zero in on their weaknesses. Her best friend remembered Barbara's favorite torment was selecting another girl in their class and giving her the "freeze treatment ... she would determine who was speaking to whom ... on the bus.... It would all be planned. Nobody's going to talk to June this morning. You'd sit on the bus with your friends and no one spoke to you."

When Barbara Pierce reached adolescence she was sent to a boarding school in Charleston, South Carolina. She described her new classmates as "a lot of fat, squatty girls.... I distinctly remember walking up the long flight of stairs to the third floor. I felt miserable for about four minutes until I got to know the other girls."

Barbara took classes that didn't appeal to her, and appeared in several school plays without "critical acclaim." She did manage some notable non-academic achievements. She set a school record for "speed knitting," and another for "swimming underwater — two and a half times across the pool." Despite having lost a great deal of weight, she also managed to eat "the most hot,

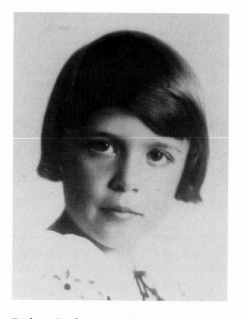

Barbara Bush, pictured as a seven-year-old, remembered feeling deserted her first day of school when her mother dropped her off "with no goodbyes. I felt abandoned. But I loved school so much I forgave her by the time I got home" (photograph courtesy the George Bush Presidential Library and Museum).

buttered biscuits in one meal without being caught." When she was returned home for Christmas she met George H. W. Bush.

George Bush was a popular, good-looking, superb athlete at the Greenwich Day School in Connecticut, and later at the Phillips Academy at Andover, in Massachusetts. He was particularly close to his older brother who was two years his senior. When his brother went off to boarding school without him, the future president became so agitated and upset, that his parents sent him along so they could be together. George was the youngest boy in his class, but being with his older brother more than made up for the academic and social challenges he faced.

The Andover faculty noticed that the only time the young student seemed to put forth a genuine effort, display enthusiasm, or show any emotions was in athletics. During class discussions, his principal contribution was to make jokes and wisecracks, but he always stopped before he got into trouble. Bush's greatest strength at school was in easily making friends with students and teachers alike. Within a short time, he established a C-plus average, which he and his parents seemed happy and content to accept.

George H. W. Bush was a popular, good-looking athlete as a student at the Phillips Academy in Andover, Massachusetts, where he loved soccer and baseball more than academics. By college, he earned a Phi Beta Kappa key for his scholarship (photograph courtesy the George Bush Presidential Library and Museum).

Bush's English teacher at Andover remembered,

His studies reflected more industry than brilliance.... My remaining impression is he just sat in my class and handed in his papers.... He showed no imagination or originality ... didn't contribute much ... a nice guy, but that's about it.

His coach and P.E. instructor remembered something different: "He was a very well liked kid." By the time he graduated, his senior yearbook saluted him as "Best All Round Fellow," president of the senior class, president of the Greeks, captain of the baseball team, captain of the soccer team, secretary of the Student Council, treasurer of the Student Council, and recipient of the "John Hopkins Perfect Attendance Prize." The $300 award was divided with the thirty other students who had not cut class or been tardy.

After fighting in World War II, Bush went to Yale University on the GI Bill where he did well academically, but especially enjoyed athletics. He and Barbara had married by that time and had their first child, George W. Bush, who would also grow up to become president. The senior Bush completed a four-year economics degree in two and a half years, but managed to also find time for sports. He was proud to survive what he called the "dismal science" of economics but admitted, "My real minors were soccer and baseball — especially baseball." In addition to serving as captain of Yale's baseball team, his grades and popularity allowed him to earn a Phi Beta Kappa key for his scholarship. At both Yale and at Andover, he seemed to epitomize "popularity, good attitude, and school spirit."

The Bushes moved to Texas, raised their growing family, taught Sunday school, and became active in the public schools where they sent their children. Despite being very bright, the Bush children sometimes struggled academically. Their oldest son George was diagnosed with aphasia, a language disorder that sometimes caused articulation problems. Neil, a younger son, was discovered to have dyslexia causing reading problems. Neil later remembered, "A reading disability isn't a class thing, it isn't racial, it happens to anybody. Unless a parent is supportive, well prepared, and recognizes the problem, a child can be lost forever. And my mother was very stubborn about it, lining up specialists, [and] making sure I saw them." All the Bush children eventually became successful students and graduated from excellent colleges and universities.

The Bushes never had the passion for academics that they did for athletics, but they understood the joy and importance of reading. Barbara described the Pierces as "omnivorous readers," so she was shocked to discover that Neil, who "was getting all As in school, including reading,"—"didn't have a clue" how to read. Barbara later wrote,

> I spoke with his teacher who told me I was dead wrong: Neil was one of her better students. I went to class to see the "great little reader" ... A student helped him with the first word, the teacher the next, and so it went. Neil had been faking his way through reading — not uncommon for children with reading problems— and no one had noticed.

As parents, she and her husband learned firsthand the surprises and struggles of having children who fall through the cracks at school.

When they moved into the White House, the Bushes brought their experiences and concerns about education and literacy with them. President George H. W. Bush called an education summit with the nation's governors and challenged them to set the highest possible academic standards to improve the quality of public education across the United States. He also signed into law the Americans with Disabilities Act, which expanded the Handicapped Children's

Act legally mandating public education for all students regardless of their disabilities or handicaps.

As first lady, Barbara Bush mounted a national campaign to promote reading and literacy, believing literacy the foundation for success in and out of school. She explained in public forums, on radio and television, and in libraries, and communities across the country, "I chose literacy because I honestly believe that if more people could read, write, and comprehend, we would be that much closer to solving so many of the problems plaguing our society."

Academics had not been at the forefront of their life as students, but as the president and first lady, George H. W. Bush and Barbara Pierce Bush put education and literacy at the very top of the country's national agenda.

George H. W. Bush at the Signing of the Americans with Disabilities Act ...

"Together we must remove the physical barriers we have created and the social barriers we have accepted. For ours will never be a truly prosperous nation until all within it prosper."

... and at a High School Commencement Address

"A student told me a while ago that high school is a great place to learn about personal risk-taking. I asked him, 'How do you figure?' And he said, 'Have you ever tasted cafeteria food?'"

Barbara Bush

"The home is the child's first school. The parent is the child's first teacher. Reading is the child's first subject."

"Persist in teaching your children! They are impressionable. They listen to us. If children don't listen to us, they will listen to TV, video games, and their friends—and they will get the wrong message."

"Another thing most of us were taught early in school that we shouldn't forget when you get older is: Help your classmates...help your fellow human beings."

"I'm cheering for teachers who are under-paid, under-praised, and overworked."

PART FOUR

The Twenty-First Century

Hillary Rodham and
Bill Clinton
"I Want to Be a Teacher or a Nuclear Physicist"

Bill Clinton was hired as a law professor at the University of Arkansas even before graduating from law school. The chair of the faculty hiring committee admitted it was unprecedented but explained, "He charmed us right out of our mortarboards." Clinton's impressive resume, his intelligence, and "wide range of interests" helped; but he also persuasively stated, "he would teach anything, did not mind working, [and] did not believe in tenure." The twenty-six-year-old Yale student did not lack confidence. He was "offered the job by a unanimous vote."

The hiring committee was convinced he would be an outstanding teacher, and in many ways he was. Most students liked him immensely, and he quickly became popular on campus. Clinton taught students the law rather than taught law to his students. Some teach because they love their subject or because they love teaching and working with students. Others teach to use their knowledge and position to intimidate, bully, or terrorize. Clinton fit into none of those categories. His knowledge was impressive. He had the pedagogical and communication skills to teach effectively, but he also seemed to genuinely like his students and enjoy interacting with them.

Clinton did not lecture or use the Socratic method of asking students questions. Instead he led class discussions where everyone was encouraged to participate and contribute. Teaching and learning to Bill Clinton was a cognitive dialogue. He seldom spoke with notes, taught using a conversational tone, and moved around the classroom like a moderator at a town hall meeting rather than a traditional professor. One student remembered Clinton as "enthusiastic and dedicated" and his class as "liberating and thought-stimulating." Word spread quickly that Professor Clinton made boring classes interesting and was an easy grader. Enrollment in his classes exploded.

He gave lots of As and Bs, some Cs, a few Ds, and no Fs. The downside was he took forever to grade papers and post grades. The dean investigated

179

because Clinton's grades seemed too high for a school where thirty percent of the freshmen traditionally flunked out. Clinton's strength was engaging students and not imposing his own views on them, but he "seemed to be juggling too many things at the same time." Aside from disorganization and his off-the-cuff teaching style, a faculty reviewer concluded that Clinton had the "qualities ... of a good teacher," in part because he had a genuine talent to involve his students in the class.

Clinton also mentored, tutored, and championed students of color at a time when his all-white faculty colleagues seemed indifferent or even hostile to them. African American students nicknamed him "Wonder Boy" not just because of his youthful appearance. One later explained,

> In the South at that time, whites would say one thing, but their deeds and words were often different ... he was not prejudiced. He did not ... treat you different from anyone else. That's why we called him Wonder Boy. It was a miracle ... he did not waiver in respect to his conduct with African American students.

Another factor made Bill Clinton stand out. He seldom missed an opportunity to denounce racism in or out of class. On his Arkansas campus at the time, such behavior was neither politically popular nor socially accepted; but Clinton seemed color-blind in his personal and professional treatment of students.

When Clinton was a child, he attended both public and parochial schools in Arkansas where he consistently excelled in academics but earned low grades in behavior and deportment because he talked too much. He constantly answered all the questions directed at him and all the questions asked of every other student. He drove his teachers and classmates to distraction.

Clinton was able to read by the time he was three, was "mature beyond his years," had a passion for books and music, but described himself as fat, clumsy, unathletic, uncool, and unpopular with girls. It may have been his love of music that taught him to discipline himself, make friends, and succeed in school. He later wrote, "I don't think I would have been president if it hadn't been for school music.... Music has had a powerful influence on my life, helping me to learn how to mix practice and patience with creativity, and how to be both an individual performer and a good member of a team."

Years later when Bill Clinton was teaching law at the University of Arkansas, his girlfriend from Yale, Hillary Rodham, visited him. During the visit, the dean encouraged her to apply for a teaching position and she soon joined the faculty. Students were impressed by her intelligence, but she intimidated some and caused resentment in others. Professor Rodham was clearly a brilliant woman. A male freshman in the first class she taught later wrote, "People were never indifferent about her. Some of the guys were not used to being taught and led by a strong woman. And there is no question she was a role model for some of the female students."

Hillary was a standout even when she was a young girl attending public schools in the comfortable middle-class suburbs of Chicago. Like Betty Ford and Barbara Bush, she enjoyed athletic competition playing hockey and softball, and teaching swimming and tennis. One of her two brothers recalled, "When she wasn't studying, she was a lot of fun. But she was always studying." She loved school, and her teachers seemed to love her. One sixth-grade teacher was so impressed with Hillary that she transferred to the junior high so she could teach her for two more years. In high school, Hillary's AP English teacher described her as having an "incisive and intuitive mind, a voracious appetite for challenge, boundless energy and a puckish sense of humor." Yet in most ways Hillary Rodham was a typical bright American girl who found the boys in her fifth-grade class "incorrigible" and remembered high school as a place where "we still found ways to isolate and demonize one another."

When Hillary Rodham began teaching law in Arkansas, her teaching style stood in sharp contrast to Bill Clinton's. She was demanding, precise, and exacting in her expectations. One student described her in the classroom as "thorough, intelligent, and articulate ... her lectures were forceful and organized, and she demanded the best from every student. She would invite discussions of all viewpoints and then follow a careful logical analysis to a concrete answer."

Clinton taught from the heart, Rodham from the head. A student who shared both professors later wrote,

> Rodham was less willing to waste time. Clinton rarely confronted students.... Rodham would come straight at students with difficult questions. She was more likely than Clinton to offer clear opinions on legal issues and not leave the class hanging ... and unlike Clinton.... Rodham wrote rigorous exams and was a tough grader."

He described her as "all business ... approachable, but serious."

Professor Rodham's high academic expectations exasperated some students. In one criminal law class, a student continually refused to answer the question being posed. He finally "threw up his hands and said, 'Why don't you leave me alone. What did you expect? I just went to school in Arkansas!'" She refused to accept his excuses until he answered the question she knew he was capable of answering. Rodham demanded that students give their personal best. No one was allowed to hide or slide. Students learned to rise to her expectations or avoid taking her class.

Although they had dramatically different ways of teaching, Clinton and Rodham both gave their best to their students. Like most teachers, they taught the way they had learned. After Bill Clinton became president in 1993, his secretary of education wrote, "A lot of people wonder how this guy from a rather poor family could become such a great student and strong supporter of education. Education is what made him, and he knew it."

Bill Clinton's love of education matched his wife's. Even as a child, Hillary Rodham thought about teaching and learning. In a sixth-grade essay she wrote,

When I grow up I want to have had the best education I could have possibly obtained.... I want to be a teacher or a nuclear scientist. Sometimes people ask me why I would want to be a teacher. The way I figure it ... the government and adults are always talking about how the children of today are the citizens of tomorrow. With this thought in mind, you have to have teachers to train young children.

In 2000, Hillary Rodham Clinton became the first first lady to be elected to a public office when she was elected to the United States Senate from New York. She was reelected in 2006, ran for president in the 2008 presidential election, and was appointed secretary of state by President Barack Obama in 2009.

In a commencement address at Agnes Scott College, Hillary told the graduates,

As you make this journey, consider ways of helping other[s].... Mentor someone. Tutor someone. Think about how you can teach, whether it be formally in a classroom or in some other setting, and broaden that horizon that is now ours to look far beyond our own shores.

The former professor and sixth-grade student who wanted to grow up and be a teacher or a nuclear physicist now had the world as her classroom.

Bill Clinton on Education

"A lot of young people learn in different ways."

"There is no bigger issue affecting our longtime security than education."

"We believe that every child can and must learn at world-class standards of excellence."

"With the help of lifetime scholarships, Pell grants, work study slots, and changes in student loans, everybody who wants to go to college can go."

"Study after study confirms what every parent knows—that smaller classes and better trained teachers, especially in the younger grades make a difference in what is learned and how much is learned."

"What should our shared values be? Everybody counts. Everybody deserves a chance. Everybody's got a responsibility to fulfill. We all do better when we work together. Our differences do matter, but our common humanity matters more."

Bill Clinton's Favorite Quote from Abraham Lincoln

"I will study and get ready, and perhaps my chance will come."

Hillary Clinton on Education

"Every child needs a champion."

"I loved school and was lucky enough to have some great teachers."

"Today education is the most important function of state and local government ... it is a principle instrument in awakening the child to cultural values."

"New research in childhood development establishes that a child's environment affects everything from I.Q. to future behavior patterns.... The case for quality early childhood education programs like Head Start is stronger than ever and we should be expanding them."

"Our children are getting good at filling in those little bubbles. But how much creativity is being left behind. How much passion for learning is being lost?"

"My struggles with math and geology convinced me once and for all to give up on any ideas ofbecoming a doctor or a scientist. My French professor gently told me, 'Mademoiselle, your talents lie elsewhere.'"

"I am particularly indebted to the many people who taught Sunday school and vacation Bible school. I can remember the lessons there, sometimes more vividly than what I have read or seen just last week."

Laura Welch and George W. Bush
"The Absolute Profession"

At George W. Bush's presidential inauguration in 2000, the reviewing stand was filled with hundreds of important people including former presidents and first ladies, the highest elected officials in the national government, cabinet members, military officers, family, close friends—and Laura Bush's second-grade teacher Mrs. Charlene Gnagy.

When Laura was just seven years old, she informed her parents that she wanted to be a teacher just like Mrs. Gnagy, and she never waivered from that goal. Although she earned good rather than great grades, Laura loved reading, school, and other children. In kindergarten she quickly learned all the names of all the students in her class so she could be their friends. Laura was an only child and described her childhood as "lonely," but school was a place where she was surrounded by children and teachers she liked.

Throughout her childhood, she enjoyed lining up her dolls in her bedroom classroom so she and her friends could teach them. Once her mother found Laura and her friends chatting outside her bedroom door as her student dolls sat alone in the "classroom." When asked why they were not teaching, Laura explained, "This is what our teachers do!" Later as first lady, she quoted James Baldwin's famous observation to teachers visiting the White House: "Children have never been good at listening to their elders, but have never failed to imitate them." She might have been referring to that earlier conversation with her mother.

Like many teachers, Laura felt "called" to the classroom, believing that children needed dedicated teachers in their lives. She believed and often said, "Teachers have a more profound impact on our society and culture than any other profession." When she entered Southern Methodist University she majored in elementary education. Despite four years of college and sixty hours of education credits, she never worked directly with children until her student-teaching semester her senior year. Laura was so overwhelmed and worried about finding a job when she graduated, she later admitted she could not recall who her college commencement speaker was or one word he said. The speaker was her future father-in-law George H. W. Bush.

Following graduation, when she was unable to find a teaching job, she took a clerical position at an insurance agency. Three months after the beginning of the school year, a third grade classroom opened up in the Dallas Public Schools and she was offered the position. She quickly took it and later wrote, "It was a predominately African American school, and it was a really good school. Our principal was very careful to make sure we had twenty students in the class, which was a great small number. But if you have never taught before, twenty was a lot."

Miss Welch liked her students but at times felt overwhelmed. "I don't think I was really prepared to teach." The school had no mentoring programs to help her adjust to the rigors of teaching. At the end of the school year, she moved to Houston where she was hired to teach second grade at the John F. Kennedy Elementary School. She remembered, "I particularly wanted to teach in a minority school. This was a mainly African American student population at JFK and I loved it. I think mainly I just learned about the dignity of every human and every child, and how important every single child is and how important each one of their lives are." She become so attached to her students she moved with them to the third grade, but worried, "In the subjects I was not good at or that interested in they were shortchanged, and the things I like, like reading, they got a double dose.... They probably didn't end up with good math skills. But it was fun."

After three years as a classroom teacher, Laura returned to school full time to work on a master's degree in library science. She became a children's librarian at a public library in Houston, but missed working in schools. The following year she became a school librarian, working again with an inner-city population. Ninety percent of her students lived at or below the poverty level and qualified for "free or reduced lunch prices," and eighty percent were Hispanic or Latino. One of her fellow teachers described their student population: "They were tough, and hard to teach and what they got in life was what they got at school.... Some of those kids ... thought books were foreign objects. She had to deal with discipline problems, kids who threw her books down. She was friendly and very loving but very firm. She had her rules ... and you followed them."

A number of her students' parents were alcoholics and drug addicts. At home, some of her students were raising younger siblings. Those who fought her the most seemed to need her the most. Without the ability to read, they would be condemned to live and die in the poverty in which they were born. Laura realized that literacy, teachers, and schools provided the only opportunity most of her students would ever have to secure a better future. It was while she was a school librarian that she met George W. Bush at a neighborhood barbecue.

Although they were both from Midland, Texas, they had only briefly attended the same schools and did not know each other. Three months after meeting at the barbecue, they married.

George W. Bush began school as an A student, enthusiastic, and conscientious. But when he was in second grade his younger sister Robin became ill and died of cancer. His personality changed and his grades dropped. By the time he completed third grade, a pattern had set in, and he was labeled an underachiever. Despite his above-average intelligence, he became and remained a C student. Reading problems and aphasia caused him to have difficulty recalling, understanding or articulating words, and he began using jokes and sarcasm to mask his speaking problems. Teachers described him as hyperactive and a bully, but his nice looks, clownish personality, love of

George W. Bush pictured with his sister Robin. He began school as an enthusiastic student earning A grades. When he was in the second grade, Robin became ill and died of cancer. His personality changed and his grades dropped. By the end of third grade, he was labeled an underachiever. Years later, he met and married Laura Welch, a second- and third-grade teacher, who understood the boy in the man, and the man in the boy (photograph courtesy the George Bush Presidential Library and Museum).

athletics, and willingness to flout authority made him popular with nearly everyone who met him.

He followed his father to Phillips Academy at Andover and then to Yale. Later, Bush earned an MBA degree from the Harvard Business School. Looking back on his school experiences, he wrote,

> I was never a great intellectual. I like books and pick them up and read them for the fun of it. I think all of us [the Bush family] are basically in the same vein. We're not real serious, serious readers. We are readers for fun.

In his autobiography he explained, "I was a solid student, but not a top one. I did well in the courses I liked, such as history, math and Spanish, and not so well in others, such as English." An Andover classmate wrote, "I'm sure he took some things seriously, but he was more interested in social standing than what grades he had to get." Another remembered, "George was always part of a small group of seven or eight guys, who were really, well, you'd have to call them the big men on campus. He was one of the cool guys."

It was when he was a student at Phillips Academy that Bush's attraction to the study of history took root. He later wrote,

> I discovered a new interest, one that has stayed with me throughout my adult life. It was sparked by a great teacher, Tom Lyons, who taught history. He has a passion for the subject, and an ability to communicate his love and interest to his students. He taught me that history brings the past and its lessons to life, and those lessons can often help predict the future. Tom Lyons' descriptions of events that shaped America's political history captured my imagination. Not only was he a great teacher, but also he was an inspiring man. Tom Lyons was a twenty-year-old football player at Brown University when he contracted polio. He would never walk again without crutches. The polio crippled his body but never hindered his enthusiasm for his subject or his profession.

George Bush appreciated the influence of teachers in his life. He never forgot his history teacher from his prep school days or that his wife had been a teacher. After becoming president he told a group of teachers visiting the White House, "I've had some first-hand experience with teachers in my life — I married one. Thank goodness."

Laura Bush's first solo trip as first lady saluted teachers, and she continued saluting them throughout her eight years in the White House. In one of many such appearances with teachers, she told them, "I know you don't hear often enough how much we appreciate you. I know, because I've been there." She never stopped emphasizing the value of reading and early childhood education or the importance of teachers in making a positive difference in the life of a vulnerable girl or boy.

George Bush, who in second- and third-grade had been labeled as a hyperactive, brash, mouthy bully, grew up and married a second and third grade teacher who understood and loved him. As first lady, Laura Bush called attention to the special needs of boys in schools and the declining numbers of males attending college,

I think we need to examine the way we are teaching children in elementary school. Are we asking boys to sit still when they really want to jump around? Is it because boys have fewer and fewer role models because such a large percentage of elementary teachers are women? ... If we can figure out ways to help address the education of boys—not denying girls, of course—maybe boys will continue through school and get good jobs.... Helping American's youth is about girls *and* boys.

One of the central programs around which President Bush built his presidency was his No Child Left Behind legislation designed in part to put a highly qualified teacher into every American classroom. Laura Bush worked to create a teacher training institute for women in Afghanistan and supported American teacher recruitment programs such as Troops to Teachers, Teach for America, and the New Teacher Project.

President and Mrs. Bush both believed a good teacher can make all the difference in a child's life. It was a belief shared by their daughter Jenna who followed her mother into the classroom as a public school teacher and reading specialist. Laura Bush, however, was the family member who may have captured the essence of teaching best when she declared at a teacher of the year ceremony, "Teaching is the absolute profession, the one that makes all others possible."

George W. Bush on Teachers, Schools, and Education

"A good teacher instills a sense of your own possibilities."

"Many schools in our country are places of hope and opportunity."

"Public schools are America's great hope, and making them work for every child is America's great duty."

"I know that as we battle the ills of society—poverty and hopelessness—education is the great beacon and the great hope."

"I believe strongly in the hope and promise of the public school systems all across America. And I know how important it is to thank your teachers; to thank those who come to your classrooms every day; to wish them the best; and to herald such a noble and important profession for the future of our country."

George W. Bush on the Anniversary of the Americans with Disabilities Act Signed by His Father

"The Americans with Disabilities Act [ADA] has helped tear down barriers for millions of people with disabilities. On the anniversary of this important legislation, our nation underscores our commitment to ensuring that all individuals have an equal opportunity to realize their full potential.... Over the course of nearly two decades, this Act has made our schools and workplaces more welcoming, helped change attitudes that once seemed unchangeable, and expanded opportunity of many exceptional Americans. The ADA is one of the most successful civil rights laws in our history and has been an essential part of countless American lives."

Laura Bush on Teachers, Schools, Reading, and Education

"We all know that the most important ingredient in a child's education is a good teacher."

"The early language experiences and education we provide our children shape the way they think and learn."

"One of my predecessors, Eleanor Roosevelt, persuaded the 81st Congress to proclaim a National Teacher's Day in 1953. Today that tradition continues."

"Our obligation to America's teachers is as clear and strong as our obligation to America's children. Teachers deserve all the knowledge and support we can give them.... Teachers are the heart and souls of our schools and deserve our support."

"There are few careers that have such a lasting effect on an entire generation and an entire nation. Teachers shape the minds of our children and the destiny of our country. Teachers fill children's lives with hope, learning and love — not just on school days, but every day of their life."

"As important as a good education ... are good teachers."

"We know that a lot of students who have the most problems are the ones who can't read. They're the ones who drop out or they're the ones who are frustrated and act out in school. Often they're boys.... I think we've neglected boys. As a society, we believe boys can take care of themselves, that boys don't cry, and that boys don't express emotion or shouldn't — that it's just not manly to do that. There are a large number of boys who are in trouble and go to jail, who are adjudicated. The choices they make really impact the rest of their life."

"Teachers comfort their students, [but] who comforts the teachers?"

"Great history teachers take required coursework and turn it into a thrilling experience."

"We owe so much to America's teachers. You have one of the most important jobs because you shape our future through your love of children and passion for knowledge."

"Teachers are the lifeblood of our nation's classrooms. These committed and dedicated professionals are helping to shape our children's future and our future. For that we owe them our highest regard, our highest respect."

"My advice is to consider a career in teaching. I believe teaching is the greatest community service. It's challenging yet deeply rewarding. The education we provide our children helps the way they think and learn throughout their entire lives."

"Schools are at the heart of helping America's youth."

Michelle Robinson and Barack Obama
"The Chance to Succeed"

Barack Obama was happy as a small child — even after his Kansas born mother divorced his African-born father when Barack was only two. By the time he was six, his mother had remarried an Asian man and Barack had a new stepfather from Indonesia. The family then traveled halfway around the world to live. In his new home, his mother taught English at the American Embassy in Jakarta. But she also taught Barack to be proud of his father's African heritage, his stepfather's Indonesian culture, and the all-American Kansan roots of his maternal grandparents, who lived in Hawaii. To keep him connected to his American home, his mother woke him every morning at 4:00 A.M. to teach him English and other subjects from American correspondence courses she had sent from the United States.

In Indonesia he survived childhood measles and chicken pox, unfriendly monkeys and crocodiles, and the disciplining smacks of his Indonesian teachers' bamboo sticks at the Catholic school he attended. Obama struggled to understand the language and culture of his classmates and often sat quietly by himself reading or drawing. Perhaps because he was the new boy, or a different color, or chubbier than the other children, he was sometimes teased and bullied.

Barack's happy disposition stayed with him, even when he moved to a new public school in fourth grade. There most of the students were Muslims. Some of his classmates were friendly, others were not, and he often found himself alone and ignored by students and teachers alike. When he was nine he came across a racist magazine story that upset and confused him. He later wrote, "Seeing that article was violent for me — an ambush attack." It unleashed questions about his own skin color, race, and prejudice that he had never thought about before. He did not say anything at the time, but he never forgot the story or the questions it raised.

By the time he was in fifth grade, his mother's second marriage had failed. When she was ending her marriage and finishing up a doctoral degree program in Indonesia, Barack was sent to live with his grandparents in Hawaii. They arranged for him to attend one of the island's best private schools where most of his wealthier classmates had been together since kindergarten. Once again he found himself trying to fit into another culture. He still seemed happy, but by the seventh grade he recalled becoming "such a terror ... my teachers didn't know what to do with me." When a classmate used a racial slur against him, he quickly bloodied the boy's nose.

During high school Barack seemed to get along with everyone, but later wrote, "I learned to slip back and forth between my black and white worlds, understanding that each possessed its own language and customs and structures of meaning, convinced that with a bit of translation on my part the two worlds would eventually cohere." He sought out black friends and read black literature, searching for "some hope of eventual reconciliation" with his different parts. He found some relief in playing basketball with white and black friends, writing, "At least on the basketball court I could find a community of sorts, with an inner life all its own."

Gradually Barack turned his growing confusion and anger against himself by smoking, drinking, and taking drugs. The last two years of high school his grades slipped, and he later wrote, "I had grown tired of trying to untangle a mess that wasn't of my making ... Junkie. Pothead. That's where I'd been headed." His mother visited him regularly from Indonesia and in his senior year confronted him about the drug arrest of one of his closest friends. Barrack tried to reassure her that everything was fine. But she told him he was fooling himself. She warned him he was wasting his talents and throwing away everything people had invested in him.

Obama refused to argue with her. He decided to go to college in California where he again coasted through his studies. His mother's words came back to haunt him when he heard her warnings coming from his new friends and professors. After attending a school rally where he was asked to speak against the apartheid policies of South Africa he decided to make a fresh start. He traveled across the country and enrolled at Columbia University in New York. For the first time in his life, Barack Obama began to study seriously.

In 1983 he graduated and took a high-paying job in business, but he soon felt restless and unfulfilled. Obama decided to search for a career that would fill the void he was feeling in his life. He looked at many jobs and finally found one that hired him as a community organizer in Chicago for $10,000 a year. Barack moved to the American Midwest where his mother and her parents had been born. There he was to find a new home and a focus to his life.

Three years of working in the city's poorest neighborhoods educated him about the disappointments, challenges, and legal frustrations of the people there. He decided to go back to school, become a lawyer, and return to Chicago armed with a law degree. Obama applied for and was accepted at Harvard University's Law School in Cambridge, Massachusetts. When the newly graduated lawyer went back to Chicago, he met, fell in love with, and married Michelle Robinson, a local girl with her own Harvard law degree.

As a child, Michelle lived with her parents and older brother in a rented one-room apartment in the home of her music teacher aunt. She attended the neighborhood public school. After skipping a grade there, she began taking classes for gifted students. Her brother remembered, "Our parents emphasized hard work and doing your best ... and once ... you get used to it you don't want to get anything but As and Bs." But Michelle added, like many smart kids, she lived in two worlds. "What I learned growing up is that if I am not going to get my butt kicked every day after school, I can't flaunt my intelligence in front of peers who are struggling with a whole range of things.... You've got to be smart without acting smart.

At thirteen Michelle began attending the Whitney M. Young Magnet High School in an industrial area with the downtown Chicago skyline as a backdrop. Michelle was a quiet student, nearly invisible to most students and teachers. Still she became a class officer and a member of the National Honor Society. After she became famous, however, few of her former teachers remembered her. She later said, "Not many people believed in the possibility of me."

Michelle was smart, but not a good test taker. She wanted to go to Princeton University because that was where her brother went. Her teachers discouraged her, and her high school counselor told her, "You can't go there — your test scores aren't high enough." The future first lady still remembers,

> No one talked to me about going to Princeton or Harvard ... or even going to college.... Every step of the way there was somebody telling me what I couldn't do. I applied to Princeton.... I went. I graduated with departmental honors. And I wanted to go to Harvard. But [was told] it was "probably a little too tough for me."

Michelle earned her law degree from Harvard five years ahead of her future husband.

Princeton had become co-educational, but in many ways was still the school of James Madison and Woodrow Wilson. "Michelle was one of 94 black students out of a total of 1,141 in the freshman class." Her family was not rich, and her parents had never gone to college; but with their help and work-study jobs, Michelle paid her own way. Two of her jobs involved education. She worked at a literacy program for neighborhood children and ran a child care center. After her marriage in 1992, she continued working. Eventually she became "vice president of community and external affairs" at the University of Chicago Hospitals and served on the school board of the university's Laboratory School.

After their marriage, Barack Obama entered politics and began teaching. For twelve years he taught constitutional law at the University of Chicago Law School. He liked teaching and was good at it. Obama said of his experience, "Teaching keeps you sharp. The great thing about teaching constitutional law is that all the tough questions land in your lap: abortion, gay rights, affirmative action. And you need to be able to argue both sides."

When he was elected to the state legislature, Obama was forced to schedule classes early Monday mornings and late Friday afternoons — times and days when most instructors would have a hard time filling up a classroom. Professor Obama's classes remained filled to capacity. One student remembered that the

Princeton University, where James Madison and John F. Kennedy had once been students, and Woodrow Wilson once taught. As president of Princeton, Wilson wrote, "The whole temper and tradition of the place are such that no Negro has ever applied for admission, and it seems unlikely that the question will ever assume practical form." Eighty years later, future first lady Michelle Robinson was one of Princeton's 94 students of color when the school enrollment stood at 1,141. She graduated with honors and later earned her law degree from Harvard University (Nassau Hall, built in 1756, Princeton University, Princeton, New Jersey—author collection).

class was "still packed ... at the crack of dawn." Another noted, "He was an excellent teacher ... very even handed in his approach to very sensitive topics."

A third wrote in his class evaluation,

> He wanted all voices to be heard in the classroom, and when there was a viewpoint that wasn't being expressed or students were too complacent ... he would push the contrary view himself. He encouraged dialogue and conversations.... Professor Barack Obama reminded me that whatever my beliefs were, I'd have to find a way to implement them in the real world if I wanted to make change happen. Good lesson, Great professor.... Oh, and I only got a B.

Students consistently rated Professor Obama among the college's best instructors. It was when he was teaching that he may have achieved his most impressive electoral "landslide." Most colleges and universities dating back to the Yale days of William Howard Taft allowed students to leave if the instructor was more than fifteen minutes late. The University of Chicago instituted the same policy. Once Barack Obama came forty-five minutes late to class, and his entire class "elected" to wait for him. Few professors in their entire teaching career receive such a "vote of confidence."

During his campaign for the presidency Barack Obama said,

> In the end, children succeed because somewhere along the way, a parent or teacher instills in them the belief that they can succeed.... From the moment our children step into a classroom, new evidence shows that the single most important factor in determining their achievement today is not the color of their skin or where they come from; it's not who their parents are or how much money they have. It's who their teacher is. It's the person who will brave some of the most difficult schools, the most challenging children, and accept the most meager compensation simply to give someone else the chance to succeed.

Half the presidents and first ladies have taught, all have been students. Barack Obama taught constitutional law at the University of Chicago Law School for twelve years. In this 2002 picture, he leads a class discussion on the *Bush versus Gore* Supreme Court decision. Six years later, he was elected president of the United States (©Scott Goldsmith 2002).

If President Obama's words are true, it is not surprising that half of our presidents and first ladies have been teachers— even if many struggled academically or socially as students on their journey from the classroom to the White House. Each and every man and woman, president and first lady, who made it to the White House had a parent or a teacher, or a parent and a teacher, who believed in them and gave them the chance to succeed.

Barack Obama on Education and Teachers

"The future belongs to the nation that can best educate its citizens.... We have everything we need to be that nation. We have the best universities, the most renowned scholars. We have innovative principals and passionate teachers and gifted students, and we have parents whose only priority is their child's education. We have a legacy of excellence, and an unwavering belief that our children should climb higher than we did."

"America's future depends on its teachers. And so today, I'm calling on a new generation of Americans to step forward and serve our country in our classrooms. If you want to make a difference in the life of our nation, if you want to make the most of your talents and dedication, if you want to make your mark with a legacy that will endure — then join the teaching profession."

"We are the nation that has always understood that our future is inexplicably linked to the education of our children — all of them. We are the country that has always believed in Thomas Jefferson's declaration that 'talent and virtue, needed in a free society, should be educated regardless of wealth or birth.'"

"It's the promise of a good education for all that makes it possible for any child to transcend the barriers of race or class or background."

"The source of America's prosperity has never been merely how ably we accumulate wealth, but how well we educate our people."

"This is the promise of education in America, that no matter what we look like or where we come from or who our parents are, each of us should have the opportunity to fulfill our God-given potential. Each of us should have the chance to achieve the American dream."

"The truth is being successful is hard. You don't have to love every subject you study. You won't click with every teacher. Not every homework assignment will seem completely relevant to your life right this minute. And you won't necessarily succeed at everything the first time you try. That's okay. Some of the most successful people in the world are the ones who've had the most failures. J. K. Rowling's first Harry Potter book was rejected twelve times before it was finally published. Michael Jordan was cut from his high school basketball team, and he lost hundreds of games and missed thousands of shots during his career. But he once said, 'I have failed over and over and over again in my life. And that is why I succeed.'"

Michelle Obama on Education and Teachers in Giving Students the Chance to Succeed

"I wouldn't be here if it weren't for the public schools that nurtured me and helped me along. And I am committed, as well as my husband, to ensuring that more kids like us and kids around this country, regardless of their race, their income, their status — their property values in their neighborhoods, get access to an outstanding education."

"I am a product of people who were investing every day in the education of regular kids who'd grown up on the south side of Chicago, kids on the north side, folks in the south, and in the west — young people not knowing their own power and potential."

"We all remember the impact a special teacher had on us — a teacher who refused to let us fall through the cracks: who pushed us and believed in us when we doubted ourselves; who sparked in us a lifelong curiosity and passion for learning. Decades later, we remember the way they made us feel and the things they inspired us to do — how they challenged us and changed our lives. So it's not surprising that studies show us that the single most important factor affecting students' achievement is the caliber of teachers."

"When we think about the outstanding qualities that make an outstanding teacher — boundless energy and endless patience; vision and a sense of purpose; the creativity to help us see the world in a different way; commitment to helping us discover and fulfill our potential — we realize: These are also the qualities of a great leader."

Bibliography

Preface

Clark, Tim. "The Classmates: Graduates from St. Paul's School in Concord New Hampshire." *Yankee Magazine*, May/June 2008.

Clinton, Bill. *My Life*. New York: Knopf, 2004.

Clinton Presidential Library docent interview, 28 December 2005.

Dean, John. *Warren G. Harding*. New York: Henry Holt, 2004.

Eisenhower, Dwight D. *At Ease: Stories I Tell My Friends*. New York: Doubleday, 1967.

Flaherty, Tina Santi. *What Jackie Taught Us*. New York: Perigee, 2004.

Hurley, Catherine, ed. *Could Do Better: School Reports of the Great and the Good*. London: Simon & Schuster, 1997.

Kennedy, Rose Fitzgerald. *Times to Remember*. New York: Doubleday, 1974.

Longo, James McMurtry. *The College Community as an Academic Village: Global Society and the Changing Nature of Higher Education*. Oxford Round Table, Oxford University, 2 July 2004.

McElroy, Richard L. *From George to George: American Presidents*. Vol. 11. Canton: Daring Books, 1982.

Miller, Merle. *Plain Speaking*. New York: Harcourt Brace, 1973.

"Obama's Remarks at the NAACP Centennial." *Politico*, 16 July 2009. Web, 20 July 2009, http://www.politico.com/news/stories/0709/25053.html.

Smith, Page. *John Adams*. Vol. 1. New York: Doubleday, 1963.

Martha Dandridge Custis and George Washington

Brady, Patricia. *Martha Washington: An American Life*. New York: Viking, 2005.

Ellis, Joseph. *His Excellency George Washington*. New York: Knopf, 2004.

Flexner, James Thomas. *Washington: The Indispensible Man*. Boston: Little, Brown, 1974.

Ford, Paul Leicester. *The True George Washington*. Philadelphia: J. B. Lippincott, 1904.

Foss, William O. *Childhoods of the American Presidents*. Jefferson, NC: McFarland, 2005.

Fritz, Jean. *The Great Little Madison*. New York: Putnam & Grosset, 1989.

_____. *James Madison: A Biography in His Own Words*. New York: Newsweek Books, 1972.

Jefferson, Thomas. *Autobiography, Notes on the State of Virginia, Public and Private Addresses, Letters*. New York: Library of America, 1984.

_____. *The Life and Selected Writings of Thomas Jefferson*. Edited by Adrienne Koch and William Peden. New York: Modern Library, 1998.

Mayzck, Walter H. *George Washington and the Negro*. Washington, DC: Associated Publishers, 1932.

Personal interview with docent. James Madison Museum. Montpelier, Virginia, 8 April 2006.

Rejai, Mostafa, and Kay Phillips. *The Young George Washington in Psychobiographical Perspective*. Lewiston, NY: Mellen Press, 2000.

Selzer, Steven M. *By George: Mr. Washington's Guide to Civility Today*. Kansas City, MO: Andrews McMeel, 2000.

Shorto, Russell. *Thomas Jefferson and the American Ideal*. New York: Barron's, 1987.

Small, Jim. "Letter to William Small from Thomas Jefferson." Ancestry.com, 1998. Web, 27 January 2011, http://homepages.rootsweb.ancestry.com/~smalljd/ri/ptj.htm.

Smith, Richard N. *Patriarch: George Washington and the New American Nation*. Boston: Houghton Mifflin, 1993.

Wiencek, Henry. *An Imperfect God: George Washington, His Slaves, and the Creation of America.* New York: Farrar, Straus and Giroux, 2003.

Women Breaking and Making Tradition at the University of Virginia. "The First Students, Part 2." University of Virginia Library, 16 December 2009. Web, 27 January 2011, http://lib.virginia.edu/small/exhibits/women/first_students2.html.

Abigail Smith, John Adams, and the Remarkable Smith Sisters

Adams, John. *Diary and Autobiography of John Adams, Volume 3, Diary 1782–1804, Autobiography Part One to October 1776.* Edited by L. H. Butterfield. Cambridge: Harvard University Press, 1961.

Bernstein, R. B., ed. *The Wisdom of John and Abigail Adams.* New York: Metro Books, 2002.

Gawalt, Gerald W. *My Dear President: Letters between Presidents and Their Wives.* Washington, DC: Library of Congress, 2005.

Harnsberger, Caroline Thomas. *Treasury of Presidential Quotations.* Chicago: Follett, 1964.

Kaminski, John P., ed. *The Quotable Abigail Adams.* Cambridge: Belknap Press, 2009.

McElroy, Richard. *From George to George: American Presidents.* Vol. 2. Canton: Daring Publishing, 1992.

Nagel, Paul C. *The Adams Women: Abigail & Louisa Adams, Their Sisters and Daughters.* Oxford: Oxford University Press, 1987.

_____. *John Quincy Adams: A Public Life, a Private Life.* New York: Knopf, 1997.

Nobel, Laurie Carter. "Abigail Adams." Unitarian Universalist Historical Society, 1999–2008. Web, 8 August 2009, http://www.uua.org/uuhs/duub/articales/abigailadams.html.

Pine, Joslyn, ed. *American Presidents' Wit and Wisdom.* Mineola, NY: Dover, 2002.

Smith, Page. *John Adams.* New York: Doubleday, 1963.

Taylor, Tim. *The Book of Presidents.* New York: Arno Press, 1972.

Thomas Jefferson

Castel, Albert. "The Founding Fathers and the Vision of a National University." *History of Education Quarterly* 4 (December 1964). Bloomington: University of Indiana Press, 2004.

Foss, William O. *Childhoods of the Presidents.* Jefferson, NC: McFarland, 2005.

Gordon Reed, Annette. *The Hemingses of Monticello: An American Family.* New York: Norton, 2008.

Harnsberger, Caroline T., ed. *Treasury of Presidential Quotations.* Chicago: Follett, 1964.

Mazyck, Walter H. *George Washington and the Negro.* Washington, DC: Associated Publishers, 1932.

Kane, Joseph. *Facts about the Presidents.* New York: H. W. Wilson, 1959.

Koch, Adrienne. *Jefferson & Madison.* New York: Konecky & Konecky, 2005.

O'Brien, Cormac. *Secret Lives of the U.S. Presidents.* Philadelphia: Quirk Press, 2004.

Personal interview with docent. Monticello Museum, 24 March 2006.

Richardson, James D., ed. *A Compilation of the Messages and Papers of the Presidents, 1789–1897.* Vol. 1. Washington, DC: Bureau of National Literature and Art, 1910.

Shuford, Tom. "Jefferson on Education: Can He Speak to Us Today?" *Education Week,* July 2004.

Wagoner, Jennings L., Jr. *Jefferson and Education.* Charlottesville, VA: Thomas Jefferson Foundation, 2004.

Wead, Doug. *The Raising of a President: The Mothers and Fathers of Our Nation's Leaders.* New York: Atria Books, 2005.

Dolley Payne Todd and James Madison

Alley, Robert S., ed. *James Madison on Religious Liberty.* Amherst: Prometheus, 1989.

Brant, Irving. *The Fourth President: A Life of James Madison.* Indianapolis: Bobbs-Merrill, 1970.

Foss, William O. *Childhoods of the American Presidents.* Jefferson, NC: McFarland, 2005.

_____. *First Ladies Quotation Book.* New York: Barricade Books, 1999.

Hunt, Gaillard. *The Life of James Madison.* New York: Doubleday, 1902.

Israel, Fred L., ed. *Taught to Lead: The Education of the Presidents of the United States.* Philadelphia: Mason Crest, 2004.

Ketcham, Ralph. *James Madison: A Biography.* New York: Macmillan, 1971.

Madison, James. *A Biography in His Own Words*. New York: Newsweek Books, 1974.

Moore, Virginia. *The Madisons: A Biography*. New York: McGraw-Hill, 1979.

Elizabeth Kortright and James Monroe

Ammon, Harry. *James Monroe: The Quest for National Identity*. Charlottesville: University of Virginia Press, 1990.

Foss, William O. *Childhood of the American Presidents*. Jefferson, NC: McFarland, 2005.

Gullan, Harold I. *First Fathers: The Men Who Inspired Our Presidents*. Hoboken: Wiley, 2004.

Israel, Fred L., ed. *Taught to Lead: The Education of the Presidents of the United States*. Philadelphia: Mason Crest, 2004.

Kane, Joseph Nathan. *Facts about the Presidents*. New York: H. W. Wilson Company, 1959.

Wead, Doug. *The Raising of a President: The Mothers and Fathers of Our Nation's Leaders*. New York: Atria Books, 2005.

Wright, Constance. *Daughter to Napoleon: A Biography of Hortense, Queen of Holland*. New York: Holt, Rinehart & Winston, 1961.

Louisa Johnson and John Quincy Adams

Adams, James Truslow. *Adams Family*. New York: Literary Guild, 1930.

Anthony, Carl Sferrazza. *First Ladies: The Saga of the Presidents' Wives and Their Power, 1789–1961*. New York: Morrow, 1990.

Anthony, Carl S., ed. *This Elevated Position: A Catalogue and Guide to the National First Ladies' Library and the Importance of First Lady History*. Canton: National First Ladies' Library, 2003.

Foss, William O. *First Ladies Quotation Book*. New York: Barricade Books, 1999.

McCullough, David. *John Adams*. New York: Simon & Schuster, 2001.

Melick, Arden Davis. *Wives of the Presidents*. Maplewood, NJ: Hammond, 1972.

Nagel, Paul C. *Adams Women: Abigail & Louisa Adams, Their Sisters and Daughters*. New York: Oxford University Press, 1987.

_____. *Descent from Glory: Four Generations of the John Adams Family*. New York: Oxford University Press, 1983.

Nevins, Allan, ed. *The Diary of John Quincy Adams, 1794–1845*. New York: Scribner, 1951.

Remini, Robert V. *John Quincy Adams*. New York: Henry Holt, 2002.

Schneider, Dorothy, and Carl Schneider, eds. *A Biographical Dictionary of First Ladies*. New York: Checkmark, 2001.

Truman, Margaret. *First Ladies: An Intimate Group Portrait of White House Wives*. New York: Random House, 1995.

Rachel Donelson Robards and Andrew Jackson

Brady, Cyrus Townsend. *The True Andrew Jackson*. Philadelphia: Lippincott, 1906.

Child, Marquis. *The Life of Andrew Jackson*. New York: Garden City Publishers, 1940.

Eisenhower, John S. D. *Agent of Destiny: The Life and Times of General Winfield Scott*. New York: Fine Press, 1997.

Harris, Bill. *The First Ladies Fact Book: The Stories of the Women of the White House from Martha Washington to Laura Bush*. New York: Black Dog & Leventhal, 2005.

Johnson, Gerald W. *Andrew Jackson: An Epic in Homespun*. New York: Minton Balch, 1927.

Mayo, Edith P., ed. *The Smithsonian Book of First Ladies*. New York: Henry Holt, 1996.

Meacham, Joe. *American Lion: Andrew Jackson in the White House*. New York: Random House, 2008.

Perdue, Theda. *Cherokee Women: Gender and Culture Change, 1700–1835*. Lincoln: University of Nebraska Press, 1998.

Richardson, James D. *A Compilation of the Messages and Papers of the Presidents, 1789–1897*. Vol. 2. Washington, DC: Bureau of National Literature and Art, 1910.

Hannah Hoes and Martin Van Buren

Biggs, Nick. "Tales from Merwin." *Columbia County History and Heritage Magazine* 1, no. 2 (Fall 2002).

Foss, William O. *Childhoods of the American Presidents*. Jefferson, NC: McFarland, 2005.

Israel, Fred, ed. *Taught to Lead: The Education of the Presidents of the United States*. Philadelphia: Mason Crest, 2004.

Kane, Joseph Nathan. *Facts about the Presidents.* New York: H. W. Wilson, 1959.

Lynch, Denis T. *An Epoch and a Man: Martin Van Buren and His Times.* New York: Horace Liveright, 1929.

Richardson, James D. *A Compilation of the Messages and Papers of the Presidents, 1789–1897.* Vol. 3. Washington, DC: Bureau of National Literature and Art, 1910.

Unger, Harlow Giles. *The Life and Times of an American Patriot, Noah Webster.* New York: Wiley, 1998.

Young, Jeff C. *The Fathers of America Presidents.* Jefferson, NC: McFarland, 1997.

Anna Symmes and William Henry Harrison

Foss, William O. *Childhoods of the American Presidents.* Jefferson, NC: McFarland, 2004.

Green, James A. *William Henry Harrison: His Life and Times.* Richmond, VA: Garrett & Massie, 1941.

Israel, Fred L., ed. *Taught to Lead: The Education of the Presidents of the United States.* Philadelphia: Mason Crest, 2004.

Kane, Joseph Nathan. *Facts about the Presidents.* New York: H. W. Wilson, 1959.

Lopresti, Rob. "William Henry Harrison on Slavery." In *Which U.S. Presidents Owned Slaves?* Web, 29 Nov 2008, http://home.nas.com/lopresti/ps.htm.

Melick, Arden Davis. *Wives of the Presidents.* Maplewood, NJ: Hammond, 1972.

Schneider, Dorothy, and Carl Schneider. *First Ladies: A Biographical Dictionary.* New York: Checkmark Books, 2001.

Sferrazza, Carl Anthony. *First Ladies: The Saga of the Presidents' Wives and Their Power, 1789–1961.* New York: Morrow, 1990.

Wead, Doug. *All the Presidents' Children: Triumph and Tragedy in the Lives of America's First Families.* New York: Atria Books, 2003.

Weeks, Philip, ed. *Buckeye Presidents: Ohioans in the White House.* Kent, OH: Kent State Press, 2003.

Letitia Christian, Julia Gardiner, and John Tyler

Bacon, Jacqueline. *The Humblest May Stand Forth: Rhetoric, Empowerment, and Aboli-tion.* Columbia: University of South Carolina Press, 2002.

Foss, William O. *Childhoods of the American Presidents.* Jefferson, NC: McFarland, 2004.

_____. *First Ladies Quotation Book.* New York: Barricade Books, 1999.

Israel, Fred L., ed. *Taught to Lead: The Education of the Presidents of the United States.* Philadelphia: Mason Crest, 2004.

Kane, Joseph Nathan. *Facts about the Presidents.* New York: H. W. Wilson, 1959.

Seagar, Robert, II. *And Tyler Too.* New York: McGraw-Hill, 1963.

"*Women at the College of William and Mary.*" Special Collections Research Center Wiki, College of William and Mary. Web, 29 Nov 2008, http://scrc.swem.wm.edu/wiki/index.php/Women_at_the_College_of_William_and_Mary.

Young, Jeff C. *The Fathers of American Presidents.* Jefferson, NC: McFarland, 1997.

Sarah Childress and James K. Polk

Baumgarner, John Reed. *Sarah Childress Polk: A Biography of the Remarkable Lady.* Jefferson, NC: McFarland, 1997.

Byrnes, Mark E. *James K. Polk: A Biographical Companion.* Santa Barbara: ABC-CLIO, 2001.

Dusinberre, William. *Slavemaster President: The Double Career of James Polk.* New York: Oxford University Press, 2003.

Foss, William O. *Childhoods of the American Presidents.* Jefferson, NC: McFarland, 2004.

Israel, Fred L., ed. *Taught to Lead: The Education of the Presidents of the United States.* Philadelphia: Mason Crest, 2004.

Kane, Joseph Nathan. *Facts about the Presidents.* New York: H. W. Wilson, 1959.

Harris, Bill. *The First Ladies Fact Book: The Stories of the Women of the White House from Martha Washington to Laura Bush.* New York: Black Dog & Leventhal, 2005.

Margaret Smith and Zachary Taylor

Bauer, Jack K. *Zachary Taylor: Soldier, Planter, Statesman of the Old Southwest.* Baton Rouge: Louisiana State University Press, 1985.

DeGregorio, William A. *The Complete Book of U.S. Presidents.* New York: Dembner Books, 1984.

Dyer, Brainerd. *Zachary Taylor.* Baton Rouge: Louisiana State University Press, 1946.

Foss, William O. *Childhoods of the American Presidents.* Jefferson, NC: McFarland, 2004.

Hamilton, Holman. *Zachary Taylor: Soldier in the White House.* Indianapolis: Bobbs-Merrill, 1951.

Harris, Bill. *The First Ladies Fact Book: The Stories of the Women of the White House from Martha Washington to Laura Bush.* New York: Black Dog & Leventhal, 2005.

Israel, Fred L., ed. *Taught to Lead: The Education of the Presidents of the United States.* Philadelphia: Mason Crest, 2004.

Kane, Joseph Nathan. *Facts about the Presidents.* New York: H. W. Wilson, 1959.

Nelson, Anson, and Fanny Nelson. *Sarah Childress Polk: Wife of the Eleventh President.* New Town: American Political Press, 1982.

Sferrazza, Carl Anthony. *America's First Families: An Inside View of Private Lives in the White House.* New York: Touchstone; Simon & Schuster, 2000.

_____. *First Ladies: The Saga of the Presidents' Wives and Their Power, 1789–1961.* New York: Morrow, 1990.

Abigail Powers and Millard Fillmore

Fillmore, Millard. "The Early History of Honorable Millard Fillmore — Written by Himself." *Publications of the Buffalo Historical Society,* vol. 2. New York: Bigelow Brothers, 1880.

Foss, William O. *Childhoods of the American Presidents.* Jefferson, NC: McFarland, 2005.

Horton, John T. *Millard Fillmore.* Vol. 11. Buffalo, NY: Buffalo and Erie County Historical Society, 1960.

Israel, Fred L., ed. *Taught to Lead: The Education of the Presidents of the United States.* Philadelphia: Mason Crest, 2004.

National First Ladies Library Exhibit. *Making the Grade: First Ladies and Education.* Canton: 3 October 2006–30 March 2007.

Snyder, Charles M. *The Lady and the President: The Letters of Dorothea Dix & Millard Fillmore.* Lexington: University of Kentucky Press, 1975.

Jane Appleton and Franklin Pierce

Israel, Fred L., ed. *Taught to Lead: The Education of the Presidents of the United States.* Philadelphia: Mason Crest, 2004.

Foss, William O. *Childhoods of the American Presidents.* Jefferson, NC: McFarland, 2005.

Venzke, Jane Walter, and Craig Paul Venzke. "The President's Wife, Jane Means Appleton Pierce: A Woman of Her Time." *Historical New Hampshire.* Concord: New Hampshire Historical Society, 2005.

Waller, Peter A. *Franklin Pierce: New Hampshire's Favorite Son.* Concord, NH: Plaidswede Publishing, 2004.

James Buchanan

Buchanan, James. *Mr. Buchanan's Administration on the Eve of the Rebellion.* North Stratford: Ayer, 2001.

Klein, Philip S. *Bachelor Father and Family Man.* Lancaster: James Buchanan Foundation, 1991.

_____. *President James Buchanan: A Biography.* University Park: Pennsylvania State University Press, 1962.

Sloan, Irving J., ed. *James Buchanan 1791–1868: Chronology-Document-Bibliographical Aids.* Dobbs Ferry, NY: Oceana Publications, 1968.

Mary Todd and Abraham Lincoln

Baker, Jean H. *Mary Todd Lincoln: A Biography.* New York: Norton, 1987.

Civil War Interactive. Web, 14 December 2008, http://www.civilwarinteractive.com/DocsLindolnLastSpeech.htm.

Donald, David Herbert. *Lincoln.* New York: Simon & Schuster, 1987.

Goodwin, Doris K. *Team of Rivals.* New York: Simon & Schuster, 2005.

Harnsberger, Caroline T., ed. *Treasury of Presidential Quotations.* Chicago: Follett, 1964.

Lightcap, Brad. "Morrell Act of 1862." University of Notre Dame. Web, 22 December 2008, http://www.nd.edu/~rbarger/www7/morrill.html.

Lubin, Martin, ed. *The Words of Abraham Lincoln.* New York: Black Dog & Leventhal, 2005.

Miller, William L. *Lincoln's Virtues*. New York: Knopf, 2003.

Turner, Justin G., and Linda Levitt Turner. *Mary Todd Lincoln: Her Life and Letters*. New York: Knopf, 1981.

USDA. Abraham Lincoln and Agriculture, "Morrill Land Grant College Act." National Agricultural Library. Web, 22 December 2008, http://www.nal.suda.gov/speccoll/exhibits/lincoln/lincoln_morrill.html.

Eliza McCardle and Andrew Johnson

Lawing, Hugh A. *Andrew Johnson National Historic Site*. Eastern National Edition, 2002.

Means, Howard. *The Avenger Takes His Place: Andrew Johnson and the 45 Days That Changed a Nation*. New York: Harcourt, 2006.

Orr, Robert. *President Andrew Johnson of Greenville*. Knoxville: Tennessee Valley Publishers, 2005.

Simpson, Brooks D. *The Reconstruction Presidents*. Lawrenceville, Kansas: University of Kansas Press, 1998.

Trefousse, Hans L. *Andrew Johnson: A Biography*. New York: Norton, 1989.

Williams, Frank B., Jr. *Tennessee's Presidents*. Knoxville: University of Tennessee Press, 1981.

Julia Dent and Ulysses S. Grant

Elliott, Mark. *Color-Blind Justice: Albert Tourgée and the Quest for Racial Equality from the Civil War to Plessy v. Ferguson*. Oxford: Oxford University Press, 2006.

Grant, Ulysses S. *Personal Memoirs*. New York: Barnes & Noble, 2003.

_____. *Ulysses S. Grant: Memoirs and Selected Letters; Personal Memoirs of U. S. Grant/Selected Letters, 1839–1865*. Edited by Mary D. McFeely and William S. McFeely. New York: Library Company of America, 1990, pp. 254, 867–1120.

Hoffman, Nancy. *Woman's "True" Profession: Voices from the History of Teaching*. Cambridge: Harvard Education Press, 2003.

Potter, Katerine, et al., eds. "President Grant Takes a Stand for Education." *News from White Haven* 111, no. 1 (Winter 2009).

Richardson, James D. A., ed. *Compilation of the Messages and Papers of the Presidents*. Vols. 6, 7, 8. New York: Library of Congress, 1910.

Simon, John Y., ed. *The Papers of Ulysses S. Grant*. Vol. 1, *1837–1861*. Carbondale & Edwardsville: Southern Illinois University Press, 1967.

_____. *The Personal Memoirs of Julia Dent Grant (Mrs. Ulysses S. Grant)*. New York: Putnam, 1975.

Simpson, Brooks D. *Ulysses S. Grant: Triumph over Adversity*. New York: Houghton, 2000.

Smith, Carter. *Presidents: Every Question Answered; Everything You Could Possibly Want to Know about the Nation's Chief Executives*. New York: Metro Books, 2004.

Smith, Jean Edward. *Grant*. New York: Simon & Schuster, 2001.

Thayer, William M. *From Tannery to White House*. New York: Albert Whitman, 1885.

U.S. Grant Homestead Association. *That Grant Boy*. Georgetown: C. J. Krehbiel, 1957.

Woodward, W. E. *Meet General Grant*. New York: Literary Guild, 1928.

Lucy Webb and Rutherford B. Hayes

Anthony, Carl Sferrazza. *First Ladies: The Saga of the Presidents' Wives and Their Power, 1789–1961*. New York: Morrow, 1990.

Caroli, Betty Boyd. *First Ladies from Martha Washington to Barbara Bush*. Garden City, NY: Doubleday, 1989.

Foss, William O. *Childhoods of the American Presidents*. Jefferson, NC: McFarland, 2005.

Harris, Bill. *The First Ladies Fact Book*. New York: Black Dog & Leventhal, 2005.

Hayes, Rutherford. *The Diary and Letters of Rutherford B. Hayes, Volume 4*. Author. Rutherford B. Hayes Presidential Center. Web, 7 July 2009, www.ohiohistory.org/onlinedoc/hayes.

Rubin, Louis D., ed. *Teach the Freeman: The Correspondence of Rutherford B. Hayes and the Slater Fund for Negro Education*. Vol. 1. Baton Rouge: Louisiana State University Press, 1959.

Simpson, Brooks D. *The Reconstruction Presidents*. Lawrenceville: University of Kansas Press, 1998.

Waldrup, Carole Chandler. *Presidents' Wives:*

The Lives of 44 American Women of Strength. Jefferson, NC: McFarland, 1989.

Lucretia Rudolph and James Garfield

Brisbin, James S. *From the Tow Path to the White House: Lives of Garfield & Arthur.* New York: Douglass Brothers, 1880.

Brown, Henry James, and Frederick D. Williams, eds. *The Diary of James A. Garfield.* East Lansing: Michigan State University Press, 1981.

Caldwell, Robert G. *James A. Garfield: Party Chieftain.* New York: Dodd Mead, 1931.

Elliott, Mark. *Color-Blind Justice: Albion Tourgée and the Quest for Racial Equality from the Civil War to Plessy v. Ferguson.* Oxford: Oxford University Press, 2006.

Foss, William O. *Childhoods of the American Presidents.* Jefferson, NC: McFarland, 2005.

Gawalt, Gerald W. *My Dear President: Letters between President's and Their Wives.* New York: Library of Congress, 2005.

Harnsberger, Caroline T., ed. *Treasury of Presidential Quotes.* Chicago: Follett, 1964.

Hinsdale, Burke A., ed. *The Works of James Abram Garfield.* Vol. 1. Boston: Osgood and Company, 1882.

Israel, Fred L., ed. *Taught to Lead: The Education of the Presidents of the United States.* Philadelphia: Mason Crest, 2004.

National First Ladies Library. Exhibit. "Making the Grade: First Ladies and Education." 3 October 2006–30 March 2007.

Olson, Otto H. *Carpetbaggers Crusade: The Life of Albion Winegar Tourgée.* Baltimore: Johns Hopkins Press, 1965.

Peskin, Allan. *Garfield: A Biography.* Kent: Kent State University Press, 1999.

Pitch, Anthony S. *Exclusively First Ladies Trivia.* Potomac: Mino Publications, 1993.

Simpson, Brooks D. *Ulysses S. Grant, Triumph over Adversity.* Boston: Houghton Mifflin, 2000.

Sky, Theodore. *To Provide for the General Welfare — A History of the Federal Spending Power.* Newark: University of Delaware Press, 2003.

Smith, Carter. *Presidents: Every Question Answered; Everything You Could Possibly Want to Know about the Nation's Chief Executives.* New York: Metro Books, 2004.

Smith, Don. *Peculiarities of the Presidents.* Van Wert: Wilkenson Press, 1938.

Waldrup, Carole C. *President's Wives: The Lives of 44 American Women of Strength.* Jefferson, NC: McFarland, 1989.

Chester A. Arthur

Brisbin, James S. *From the Tow Path to the White House: Lives of Garfield & Arthur.* New York: Douglass Brothers, 1880.

Foss, William O. *Childhoods of the American Presidents.* Jefferson, NC: McFarland, 2005.

"Kill the Indian and Save the Man." Digital History. Native American Voices, 2006. Web, 27 December 2008, http://www.digitalhistory.uh.edu/native_voices/nav4.html.

Reeves, Thomas C. *Gentleman Boss: The Life of Chester Alan Arthur.* New York: Knopf, 1975.

Richardson, James D. *A Compilation of the Messages and Papers of the Presidents, 1789–1897.* Vol. 3. Washington, DC: Bureau of National Literature and Art, 1910.

Frances Folsom and Grover Cleveland

Dole, Bob. *Great Presidential Wit.* New York: Scribner, 2001.

"Grover Cleveland Speaks at Princeton." *New York Times,* 4 October 1896.

Hamilton, Gail. *Biography of James G. Blaine.* New York: Bill Publishing, 1895.

Jeffers, Paul H. *An Honest President: The Life and Presidencies of Grover Cleveland.* New York: Morrow, 2000.

Kane, Joseph. *Facts about Presidents.* New York: H. W. Wilson, 1959.

McElroy, Robert. *Grover Cleveland: The Man and the Statesman.* New York: Harper Brothers, 1923.

Nevins, Allan. *Grover Cleveland.* New York: Dodd & Mead, 1932.

Parker, George F. *Recollections of Grover Cleveland.* New York: Century Press, 1909.

Caroline Scott and Benjamin Harrison

Capps, Jennifer E. The Benjamin Harrison Presidential Site. The President Benjamin Harrison Home, NellieBly/Caroline Scott Harrison, 8 September 1888. Web, 27 January 2011, www.pbhh.org.

Foss, William O. *Childhoods of the American Presidents*. Jefferson, NC: McFarland, 2005.
_____. *First Ladies Quotation Book*. New York: Barricade Books, 1999.

Gullan, Harold I. *Faith of Our Mothers: The Stories of Presidential Mothers from Martha Washington to Barbara Bush*. Grand Rapids, MI: Eerdmanns, 2001.

Hedges, Charles, ed. *Speeches of Benjamin Harrison*. New York: Lovell, 1892.

Mayo, Edith P., ed. *The Smithsonian Book of the First Ladies*. New York: Henry Holt, 1996.

McPherson, Edward. *A Handbook of Politics for 1884*. New York: Chapman, 1884.

National First Ladies Library Exhibit. *Making the Grade: First Ladies and Education*. Canton: 3 October 2006–30 March 2007.

Sievers, Harry J. *Benjamin Harrison: Hoosier Warrior—Through the Civil War Years 1833–1865*. New York: University Publishers, 1960.

Waldrup, Carole C. *President's Wives: The Lives of 44 Women of Strength*. Jefferson, NC: McFarland, 1989.

Young, Jeff C. *The Fathers of American Presidents*. Jefferson, NC: McFarland, 1997.

Ida Saxton and William McKinley

Belden, Henry S., III., ed. *Grand Tour of Ida Saxton McKinley and Sister Mary Saxton Barber*. Canton: Reserve Publishing, 1985.

Bryan, Mary B. *The Memoirs of William Jennings Bryan*. Chicago: Winston Company, 1925.

Everett, James. *The Complete Life of William McKinley*. New York: Coghale & Son, 1901.

Fallows, Samuel, Rt. Rev. *Life of William McKinley Our Martyred President*. Chicago: Regan Printing House, 1901.

Harnsberger, Caroline T., ed. *Treasury of Presidential Quotations*. Chicago: Follett, 1964.

Kane, Joseph. *Facts about the Presidents*. New York: H. W. Wilson, 1959.

McClure, Alexander, and Charles Morris. *The Authentic Life of William McKinley*. New York: W. E. Scull, 1901.

Pine, Joslyn, ed. *American President's Wit and Wisdom*. Mineola, NY: Dover, 2002.

Edith Carow and Teddy Roosevelt

Cutright, Paul R. *Theodore Roosevelt the Naturalist*. New York: Harper & Brothers, 1956.

McCullough, David. *Mornings on Horseback*. New York: Simon & Schuster, 1981.

Miller, Nathan. *Theodore Roosevelt: A Life*. New York: Morrow, 1992.

Morris, Edmund. *The Rise of Theodore Roosevelt*. New York: Coward, McCann & Geoghegan, 1979.

_____. *Theodore Rex*. New York: Random House, 2001.

Pine, Joslyn, ed. *American President's Wit and Wisdom — A Book of Quotations*. Mineola, NY: Dover, 2002.

Richardson, James D. *A Compilation of the Messages and Papers of the Presidents, 1789–1897*. Vol. 10. Washington, DC: Bureau of National Literature and Art, 1910.

Helen Herron and William Howard Taft

"100 Years Ago: William Howard Taft's Disgraceful Inaugural Address." History News Network. Web, 13 February 2009, http://hnn.us/roundup/entries/59984.html.

Anthony, Carl Sferrazza. *Nellie Taft: The Unconventional First Lady of the Ragtime Era*. New York: Morrow, 2005.

Harnsberger, Caroline T., ed. *Treasury of Presidential Quotations*. Chicago: Follett, 1964.

Hicks, Frederick. *William Howard Taft — Yale Professor of Law and New Haven Citizen*. New Haven: Yale University Press, 1945.

Kane, Joseph N. *Facts about the Presidents*. New York: H. W. Wilson, 1959.

Pringel, Henry F. *The Life and Times of William Howard Taft*. New York: Farrar & Rinehart, 1939.

Weeks, Philip, ed. *Buckeye Presidents: Ohioans in the White House*. Kent: Kent State Press, 2003.

Wertheimer, Molly Meijer, ed. *Inventing a Voice: The Rhetoric of American First Ladies of the Twentieth Century*. Lanham, MD: Rowman & Littlefield, 2000.

Ellen Axson, Edith Bolling Galt, and Woodrow Wilson

Auchincloss, Louis. *Woodrow Wilson*. New York: Viking, 2000.

Axson, Stockton. *Brother Woodrow — A Memoir of Woodrow Wilson*. Princeton, NJ: Princeton Press, 1993.

Baker, Ray S. *Woodrow Wilson, Life & Letters — Princeton, 1890–1910*. New York: Doubleday, 1927.

Bennicoff, Tad. "African Americans and Princeton University: A Brief History." 2 July 2009. Web, 27 January 2011, http://www.princeton.edu/mudd.news/faq/topics/African_Americans.shtml.

Bragdon, Henry Wilson. *Woodrow Wilson: The Academic Years*. Cambridge: Belknap Press, 1967.

Daniels, Josephus. *The Life of Wilson*. New York: Winston, 1924.

Day, Donald, ed. *Woodrow Wilson's Own Story*. New York: Little, Brown, 1952.

Lewis, McMillan. *Woodrow Wilson of Princeton*. Narberth: Livingston, 1952.

Mallon, Thomas. "Theodore Roosevelt's Daughter Alice Longworth Married One Politician and Had a Baby with Another." *Washingtonian New York Times*, 18 November 2007.

Osborne, George C. *Woodrow Wilson — The Early Years*. Baton Rouge: Louisiana University Press, 1968.

Pine, Joslyn, ed. *American Presidents' Wit and Wisdom — A Book of Quotations*. Mineola, NY: Dover, 2002.

Porty, Richard. "'The Education of John Dewey' — The Invisible Philosopher." *New York Times Book Review*, 9 March 2003.

Seely G. Mudd Manuscript Library, News and Information. Princeton University, 13 February 2009.

Wagoner, Kathy. *I Had a Great Teacher*. New York: Gramercy Books, 2001.

Walsworth, Arthur. *Woodrow Wilson: Noticeable Man*. Boston: Houghton Mifflin, 1958.

Wilson, Woodrow. *Selected Literary and Political Papers and Addresses of Woodrow Wilson*. Vol. 1. New York: Grosset & Dunlap, 1923.

Woodrow Wilson: Princeton in the Nation's Service. Web, 27 January 2011, www.Princetonol/com/patron/bios/Wilson.html.

Florence Kling and Warren G. Harding

Anthony, Carl Sferrazza. *Florence Harding: The First Lady, the Jazz Age, and the Death of America's Most Scandalous President*. New York: Morrow, 1998.

Chapple, Joe Mitchell. *Warren G. Harding — the Man*. Boston: Chapple Publishing, 1920.

Dean, John. *Warren G. Harding*. New York: Times Books, 2004.

"Harding Says Negros Must Have Equality in Political Life." *New York Times*, 27 October 1921.

Johnson, Willis Fletcher. *The Life of Warren G. Harding: From the Simple Life of the Farm to the Glamour and Power of the White House*. New York: Johnson Publishing, 1923.

Russell, Francis. *Shadow of Blooming Grove*. New York: McGraw-Hill, 1968.

Grace Goodhue and Calvin Coolidge

Anthony, Carl Sferrazza. *The Saga of the Presidents' Wives and Their Power, 1789–1961*. New York: Morrow, 1990.

Carolli, Betty Boyd. *America's First Ladies*. New York: Guild America Books, 1996.

Coolidge, Calvin. *The Autobiography of Calvin Coolidge*. New York: Cosmopolitan Book Corp., 1929.

_____. *Have Faith in Massachusetts: A Collection of Speeches and Messages*. Boston: Houghton Mifflin, 1919.

Faber, Doris. *The Mothers of the Presidents*. New York: New American Library, 1958.

Harnsberger, Caroline Thomas, ed. *Treasury of Presidential Quotations*. Chicago: Follett, 1964.

Kane, Joseph. *Facts about the Presidents*. New York: H. W. Wilson, 1959.

Kirk, Elsie K. *Music at the White House: A History of the American Spirit*. Urbana: University of Illinois Press, 1986.

Mayo, Edith P., ed. *The Smithsonian Book of Ladies: Their Lives, Times, and Issues*. New York: Henry Holt, 1996.

Meehan, Donna. "Words from Grace." Author telephone interview, 23 May 2006.

Morrissey, Charles. "The Many Myths of Calvin Coolidge." *Vermont Life Magazine*, Winter 1978.

Ross, Ishbel. *Grace Coolidge and Her Era.* New York: Dodd, Mead, 1962.

Schneider, Dorothy, and Carl Schneider. *First Ladies: A Biographical Dictionary.* New York: Checkmark Books, 2004.

Sobel, Robert. *Coolidge: An American Enigma.* New York: Regnery, 1998.

Lou Henry and Herbert Hoover

Ambrose, Stephen E. *Eisenhower Soldier and President.* New York: Simon & Schuster, 1991.

Colbert, Nancy A. *Lou Henry Hoover: The Duty to Serve.* Greensboro, NC: Morgan Reynolds, 1998.

Fesler, Ruth. *The President's Mountain School: A History.* West Branch, IA: Herbert Hoover Presidential Library and Museum Archives, 1931.

Foss, William O. *Childhoods of the American Presidents.* Jefferson, NC: McFarland, 2006.

_____. *First Ladies Quotation Book.* New York: Barricade Books, 1999.

Hoover, Herbert. *The Memoirs of Herbert Hoover: Years of Adventure, 1874–1920.* New York: Viking, 1951.

_____. On *Growing Up: His Letters to and from Children.* New York: Morrow, 1961.

_____. *Thank You, Miss Gray.* West Branch, IA: Herbert Hoover Presidential Library Association, 2010.

McLean, Hulda Hoover. *Uncle Bert: A Biographical Portrait of Herbert Hoover.* n.p.: McLean, 1974.

Telephone interview with docent. Herbert Hoover Presidential Library and Museum, 1 June 2009.

Veerman, Philip E. *The Rights of the Child and the Changing Image of Childhood.* The Hague: Martinus Nijhoff, 1992.

Vest, Christine. *The President's Mountain School: Crigslerville, Virginia.* West Branch, IA: Herbert Hoover Presidential Library and Museum Archives, 1960.

Eleanor and Franklin Roosevelt

Cook, Blanche Wiesen. *Eleanor Roosevelt: Volume One, 1884–1933.* New York: Viking, 1992.

Davis, Kenneth S. *FDR: The Beckoning of Destiny, 1882–1928.* New York: History Book Club, 2004.

Day, Donald, ed. *Franklin D. Roosevelt's Own Story: Told in His Own Words from His Private and Public Papers.* Boston: Little, Brown, 1951.

Gelderman, Carol. *All the Presidents' Words: The Bully Pulpit and the Creation of the Virtual Presidency.* New York: Walker & Company, 1997.

Gerber, Robin. *Leadership the Eleanor Roosevelt Way: Timeless Strategies from the First Lady of Courage.* New York: Penguin, 2003.

Hickok, Lorena. *The Story of Eleanor Roosevelt.* New York: Grosset & Dunlap, 1959.

Lash, Joseph. *Eleanor and Franklin: The Story of Their Relationship Based on Eleanor Roosevelt's Private Papers.* New York: Norton, 1971.

Longo, James McMurtry. *The Teacher behind the Teacher: The Influence of Teachers in the Teaching Career Choices of Their Students.* Cambridge: Harvard Graduate School of Education, 1994.

Potter, Jan. *Sara and Eleanor: The Story of Sara Delano Roosevelt and Her Daughter in Law, Eleanor Roosevelt.* New York: St. Martin's, 2004.

Roosevelt, Eleanor. *Eleanor Roosevelt: You Learn by Living — Eleven Keys for a More Fulfilling Life.* New York: Westminster Press, 1960.

_____. *If You Ask Me.* Philadelphia: Curtis Publishing, 1946.

_____. "On Teaching and Learning." *Harvard Education Review* 7, no. 4.

Roosevelt, Elliott. *FDR His Personal Letters: Early Years.* New York: Duell, Sloan & Pearce, 1947.

Roosevelt, Franklin. *The Public Papers and Addresses of Franklin D. Roosevelt, 1938.* New York: Macmillan, 1941.

Ward, Geoffrey C. *Before the Trumpet: Young Franklin Roosevelt, 1882–1905.* New York: Book of the Month Club, 1997.

Bess Wallace and Harry S Truman

Donavan, Robert J. *Conflict and Crisis: The Presidency of Harry S Truman, 1945–1948.* New York: Norton, 1977.

McCullough, David. *Truman.* New York: Simon & Schuster, 1992.

Miller, Merle. *Plain Speaking: An Oral History*

of Harry S. Truman. New York: Greenwich House, 1985.

Truman, Harry S. *The Autobiography of Harry S. Truman,* Robert H. Ferrell, ed. Boulder: Colorado Associated Press, 1980.

_____. *Off the Record: The Private Papers of Harry S. Truman,* Robert H. Ferrell, ed. New York: Harper & Row, 1980.

Mamie Doud and Dwight Eisenhower

Ambrose, Stephen E. *Eisenhower Soldier and President.* New York: Simon and Schuster, 1990.

Eisenhower, Dwight D. *At Ease: Stories I Tell My Friends.* New York: Doubleday, 1967.

_____. *Waging Peace: The White House Years, a Personal Account, 1956–1961.* New York: Doubleday, 1965.

Eisenhower, Susan. *Mrs. Ike: Memories and Reflections on the Life of Mamie Eisenhower.* New York: Farrar, Straus & Giroux, 1996.

Gollagher, Elsie, ed. *The Quotable Dwight D. Eisenhower.* New York: Droke House, 1967.

Harnsberger, Caroline Thomas, ed. *Treasury of Presidential Quotations.* Chicago: Follett, 1964.

Pipes, Kasey S. *Ike's Final Battle: The Road to Little Rock and the Challenge of Equality.* Los Angeles: World Ahead Publishing, 2007.

Russell, Don. *Invincible Ike: The Inspiring Story of Dwight D. Eisenhower.* Chicago: Successful Living, 1952.

Jacqueline Bouvier and John F. Kennedy

Davis, John H. *Jacqueline Bouvier: An Intimate Biography.* New York: Wiley, 1996.

Fields, Wayne. *Union of Words: A History of Presidential Eloquence.* New York: Free Press, 1996.

Filler, Louis, ed. *The Presidents Speak: From William McKinley to Lyndon B. Johnson.* New York: Putnam, 1964.

Goldman, Alex J., ed. *The Quotable Kennedy.* New York: Citadel Press, 1965.

Hamilton, Nigel. *JFK Reckless Youth.* New York: Random House, 1992.

Harnsberter, Caroline Thomas, ed. *Treasury of Presidential Quotations.* Chicago: Follett, 1964.

Kennedy, Edward M. *True Compass: A Memoir.* New York: Twelve Publishing, 2009.

Kennedy, John F. *Remarks of Senator John F. Kennedy at the 6th Annual Convention of United Cerebral Palsy.* Boston: JFK Library Archives, 1955.

_____. *Remarks of Senator John F. Kennedy at the Teacher's Association Convention.* Baltimore, MD, 10 October 1957. Boston: JFK Archives, 1957.

Kennedy–Rickover–White House Recordings. Boston: JFK Library Archives, 1963.

Life in the Shadows: John F. Kennedy's Pioneering Movement / The Emergence of Mental Retardation into Public Awareness. Guggenheim, Charles. DVD. Guggenheim Productions, 2006.

Oral History interview with Eunice Kennedy Shriver, 7 May 1968, for the JFK Library Archives, Boston, pp. 1–30.

Shorter, Edward. *The Kennedy Family and the Story of Mental Retardation.* Philadelphia: Temple University Press, 2000.

Simonelli, Susan Beale. *Rose Kennedy.* New York: Chelsea House, 1992.

Claudia Taylor and Lyndon Johnson

Anderson, Claudia Wilson. *Lyndon B. Johnson: The Teacher in the White House.* Letter from the LBJ Library, 13 July 1989.

Bronfenbrenner, Urie. "An Authority on Child Development Dies." *New York Times,* 27 September 2005, p. 88.

Burns, James MacGregor, ed. *To Heal and to Build: The Programs of President Lyndon B. Johnson.* New York: McGraw-Hill, 1968.

_____. *Lady Bird Johnson: A White House Diary.* New York: Holt, Rinehart & Winston, 1970.

Caro, Robert A. *The Years of Lyndon Johnson: The Path to Power.* New York: Knopf, 1982.

Dallek, Robert. *Lone Star Rising: Lyndon Johnson and His Times, 1908–1960.* New York: Oxford University Press, 1991.

Eskenazi, Stuart. "Poverty's Unrelenting Grip on Texas, Raw View of Poverty at Cotulla School Shaped LBJ." *Austin American Statesman,* 26 November 1995.

Foss, William O. *First Ladies Quotation Book.* New York: Barricade Books, 1999.

Hanna, Julia. "The Elementary and Secondary Education Act, 40 Years Later." *Harvard*

Graduate School of Education, Summer 2005.

Harnsberter, Caroline Thomas. *Treasury of Presidential Quotations*. Chicago: Follett, 1964.

Johnson, Lyndon, B. *Public Papers of the Presidents of the United States: Lyndon B. Johnson, 1965, Book I — January 1 to May 31, 1965*. Washington, DC: United States Printing Office, 1966.

_____. *Public Papers of the Presidents of the United States: Lyndon B. Johnson, 1967, Book I — January 1 to June 30, 1967*. Washington, DC: United States Printing Office, 1968, pp. 264.

_____. *The Vantage Point: Perspectives of the Presidency, 1963–1969*. New York: Holt, Rinehart & Winston, 1971.

Miller, Merle. *Lyndon: An Oral Biography*. New York: Putnam, 1980.

"The Root of the Great Society: Lyndon B. Johnson at Cotulla." *Southwestern Quarterly*. LBJ Library, June 1994.

Steinberg, Alfred. *Sam Johnson's Boy: A Close Up of the President from Texas*. New York: Macmillan, 1968.

Stossel, Scott. *Sarge: The Life and Times of Sargent Shriver*. Washington, DC: Smithsonian Books, 2004.

Pat Ryan and Richard Nixon

Angelo, Bonnie. *First Mothers: The Women Who Shaped the Presidents*. New York: HarperCollins, 2001.

David, Lester. *The Lonely Lady of San Clemente: The Story of Pat Nixon*. New York: Crowell, 1978.

Eisenhower, Julie Nixon. *Pat Nixon: The Untold Story*. New York: Simon & Schuster, 1986.

Foss, William O. *First Ladies Quotation Book*. New York: Barricade Books, 1999.

Lamb, Brian, and C-Span. *Who's Buried in Grant's Tomb? A Tour of Presidential Gravesites*. New York: BBS Public Affairs, 2000.

MacGregor, Jerry, and Marie Prys. *Faith of the First Ladies*. Grand Rapids, MI: Baker Books, 2006.

Nixon, Richard. *In the Arena: A Memoir of Defeat and Renewal*. New York: Simon & Schuster, 1990.

Schneider, Dorothy, and Carl Schneider. *First Ladies: A Biographical Dictionary*. New York: Checkmark Books, 2001.

Betty Bloomer and Jerry Ford

Ford, Betty, and Chris Chase. *The Times of My Life*. New York: Harper & Row, 1978.

Ford, Gerald R. *Public Papers of the Presidents of the United States: Gerald R. Ford, August 9 to December 31, 1974*. Washington, DC: United States Government Printing Office, 1975.

_____. *A Time to Heal: The Autobiography*. New York: Harper & Row, 1978.

Foss, William O. *First Ladies Quotation Book*. New York: Barricade Books, 1999.

Rosalynn Smith and Jimmy Carter

Ariail, Dan, and Cheryl Heckler-Feltz. *The Carpenter's Apprentice: The Spiritual Biography of Jimmy Carter*. Grand Rapids, MI: Zondervan, 1996.

Carter, Jimmy. *An Hour Before Daylight: Memories of a Rural Boyhood*. New York: Simon & Schuster, 2001.

_____. *Living Faith*. New York: Random House, 1996.

_____. *The Nobel Peace Prize Lecture*. New York: Simon & Schuster, 2002.

_____. "Simply the Best/Former U.S. President Jimmy Carter's Favorite Teacher." *Instructor Magazine*, October 1999.

Carter, Rosalyn. *First Lady from Plains*. Boston: Houghton Mifflin, 1984.

Israel, Fred L., ed. *Taught to Lead: The Education of the Presidents of the United States*. Philadelphia: Mason Crest, 2004.

Longo, James McMurtry. "The College Community as an Academic Village: Thinking Small, Global Society and the Changing Nature of Higher Education." Oxford Roundtable: Oxford University, 2004.

Michael, Deanna L. *Jimmy Carter as Educational Policy Maker: Equal Opportunity and Efficiency*. Albany: State University of New York Press, 2008.

Recording at Plains High School and Visitors Center, 20 April 2006.

School House to White House: The Education of the Presidents. National Archives Building, Washington, DC, 30 March 2007–1 January 2008.

Simon, Scott. Interview with Jimmy Carter. *Weekend Edition.* National Public Radio, 27 November 1999.

Nancy Davis and Ronald Reagan

Adler, Bill, and Bill Adler Jr., eds. *The Reagan Wit.* New York: Morrow, 1998.

Kengor, Paul. *God and Ronald Reagan: A Spiritual Life.* New York: Harper-Collins, 2004.

"Reagan at Eureka." *Journal Star,* 10 May 1982.

"Reagan's Dixon." *Official Dixon Press,* 1980.

Reagan, Nancy, and William Novak. *My Turn: The Memoirs of Nancy Reagan.* New York: Random House, 1989.

Reagan, Ronald. *An America Life: The Autobiography.* New York: Simon & Schuster, 1990.

_____. *Speaking My Mind.* New York: Simon & Schuster, 1989.

Skinner, Kiron S., ed. *Reagan: In His Own Hand; The Writings of Ronald Reagan That Reveal His Revolutionary Vision for America.* New York: Simon & Schuster, 2001.

"Things That Made Him President Were Begun Right Here in Dixon." *Chicago Tribune,* 4 June 2004.

Barbara Pierce and George H. W. Bush

Adler, Bill. *First Mom: The Wit and Wisdom of Barbara Bush.* New York: Rugged Land, 2004.

Bush, George H. W. *All the Best: My Life in Letters and Other Writings.* New York: Scribner, 1999.

_____, and Victor Gold. *Looking Forward: An Autobiography.* New York: Doubleday, 1987.

Foss, William O. *First Ladies Quotation Book.* New York: Barricade Books, 1999.

Israel, Fred L., ed. *Taught to Lead: The Education of the Presidents of the United States.* Philadelphia: Mason Crest, 2004.

Killian, Pamela. *Barbara Bush: Matriarch of a Dynasty.* New York: St. Martin's, 2002.

McGrath, Jim. *Heartbeat: George Bush in His Own Words.* New York: Scribner, 2001.

Phillips, Kevin. *American Dynasty.* New York: Viking, 2004.

Radcliffe, Donnie. *Simply Barbara Bush: A Portrait of America's Candid First Lady.* New York: Warner Books, 1989.

Hillary Rodham and Bill Clinton

Clinton, Bill. *My Life.* New York: Knopf, 2004.

Clinton, Hillary Rodham. *It Takes a Village.* 10th anniversary edition. New York: Simon & Schuster, 2006.

_____. *Living History.* New York: Simon & Schuster, 2003.

Cuomo, Matilda Raffa, ed. *The Person Who Changed My Life: Prominent People Recall Their Mentors.* New York: Book of the Month Club, 2002.

Dumas, Ernest, ed. *The Clintons of Arkansas: An Introduction by Those Who Know Them Best.* Fayetteville: University of Arkansas Press, 1993.

Hamilton, Nigel. *Bill Clinton: An American Journey — Great Expectations.* New York: Random House, 2003.

King, Norman. *Hillary: Her True Story.* New York: Carol Publishing, 1993.

Leopolis, Linda. E-mail to author. Clinton Presidential Library, 6 January 2006.

Maraniss, David. *First in His Class: A Biography of Bill Clinton.* New York: Simon & Schuster, 1995.

Moore, Jim. *Clinton: Young Man in a Hurry.* Fort Worth: Summit Group, 1992.

Rodham, Hillary. "Children Under the Law." *Harvard Education Review* 43, no. 4 (November 1973): p. 498.

Warner, Judith. *Hillary Clinton.* New York: Signet, 1993.

Laura Welch and George W. Bush

Bush, George W. "Anniversary of the Americans with Disabilities Act, 2008." White House, press release. http://www.whitehouse.gov/news/releases/2008/07/2008075.html.

_____. *A Charge to Keep.* New York: Morrow, 1990.

_____. "Remarks on the Anniversary of the American with Disabilities Act 2008." White House. Web, 25 January 2008, www.whitehouse.gov.

Bush, Laura. *Spoken from the Heart.* New York: Scribner, 2010.

Felix, Antonia. *Laura: America's First Lady, First*

Mother. Avon, MA: Adams Media, 2002.

Gerhart, Ann. *The Perfect Wife: The Life and Choices of Laura Bush.* New York: Simon & Schuster, 2004.

Green, Fitzhugh. *George Bush: An Intimate Portrait.* New York: Hippocrene Books, 1989.

Leo, Jacqueline. "A Second Look at the First Lady." *Readers Digest,* May 2005.

MacGregor, Jerry, and Marie Prys. *Faith of the First Ladies.* Grand Rapids, MI: Baker Books, 2006.

McQuillan, Laurence. "Laura Bush's Travel Agenda: Education." *USA Today,* 22 March 2001.

Minutaglio, Bill. *First Son: George W. Bush and the Bush Family Dynasty.* New York: Times Books, 1990.

White House Web Site. www.whitehouse. gov. Web, all retrieved 15 May 2003. Remarks of Laura Bush at Golden Apple Teachers Award; opening remarks by Mrs. Bush at the White House Conference on Preparing Tomorrow's Teachers; remarks by Mrs. Bush at the New Teacher Project — University of New Orleans; remarks by Mrs. Bush — New Leaders, New York (25 September 2001); Mrs. Bush's remarks at the White House Summit on Early Childhood Education; Mrs. Bush's remarks at Father Flanagan's Girls and Boys Town; Mrs. Bush's remarks at the Presentation of the Preserve America History Teacher of the Year Award; letter from Mrs. Bush; White House Conference on Preparing Tomorrow's Teachers; President Bush Celebrates First Anniversary of No Child Left Behind; President Joins Mrs. Bush at Teacher Quality Conference; President Launches Quality Teacher Initiative; remarks by Mrs. Bush to House Education and Workforce Committee; remarks by Mrs. Bush — Transition to Teaching New Teaches Project; remarks of Laura Bush at Troops to Teachers Event.

Michelle Robinson and Barack Obama

B., Adam. "Professor Obama and Me." *Daily Kos,* blog. Web, 27 January 2011, http://www.dailykos.com/story/2007/12/20 /12119/122.

"Comments on Barack Obama as a Law Professor." Free Republic, blog. 11 February 2008. Web, 22 June 2008, http://www.free republic.com/focus/f-news/1968734/posts.

Dougherty, Steve. *Hopes and Dreams: The Story of Barack Obama.* New York: Black Dog & Leventhal, 2008.

Grimes, Nikki. *Barack Obama: Son of Promise, Child of Hope.* New York: Simon & Schuster Book for Young Readers, 2008.

Lightfoot, Elizabeth. *Michelle Obama: First Lady of Hope.* Guilford, CT: Lyons Press, 2009.

Mundy, Liza. *Michelle: A Biography.* New York: Simon & Schuster, 2008.

Neer, Bob. *Barack Obama for Beginners: An Essential Guide.* Hanover: Steerforth Press, 2008.

Obama, Barack. *Dreams from My Father.* New York: Three Rivers Press, 1995.

"Remarks by First Lady Michelle Obama at UC Merced's 2009 Commencement." White House, press release. University of California, Merced, 16 May 2009. Web, 15 Mar 2009, http://www.ucmerced.edu/news_articles/05162009_remarks_by_first_lady.asp.

"Remarks by the President to the Hispanic Chamber of Commerce on a Complete and Competitive American Education." White House, Office of the Press Secretary, 10 March 2009. Web, 14 March 2009, http://www,whitehouse.gov/the_press_office/Remarks-of-the-President-to-the-Hispanic-Chamber-of-Commerce.

Swans, Rachel L. "First Lady Leads Famous Women to Schools." *New York Times,* 20 March 2009.

Sweet, Lynn. "Michelle Obama's First Outside White House Function: Visits Arne Duncan at the Education Department." 2 February 2009. Web, 27 January 2011, http://blogs.suntimes.com/sweet/2009/02/michelle_obamas_first_outside.html.

Index

211